English: One Language, Different Cultures

English: One Language, Different Cultures

Second Edition

Edited by
Eddie Ronowicz and Colin Yallop

continuum

Continuum

The Tower Building
11 York Road
London SE1 7NX

80 Maiden Lane
Suite 704
New York, NY 10038

British Library Cataloguing-in-Publication Data
A catalogue record for this book is available from the British Library.

ISBN − 10: HB: 0-8264-8175-2
            PB: 0-8264-9175-8
ISBN − 13: HB: 978-08264-1875-7
            PB: 978-08264-9175-6

Library of Congress Cataloguing-in-Publication Data
To come

Typeset by BookEns, Royston Herts.
Printed and bound in Great Britain by Cromwell Press

Contents

The Contributors

Sherry Ash is Associate Director of the Linguistics Laboratory at the University of Pennsylvania, Philadelphia.

Dianne Bardsley is a Lexicographer and the Manager of New Zealand Dictionary Centre, Victoria University of Wellington.

Vikki Cecchetto is Assistant Professor (Linguistics and Italian) in the Department of Modern Languages, McMaster University, Hamilton, Ontario.

Eddie Ronowicz is Associate Professor in the Department of Linguistics, Macquarie University, Sydney.

Michael Sharwood-Smith is Professor in the Department of Languages, Herriot Watt University, Edinburgh.

Magda Stroińska is Associate Professor (Linguistics and German) in the Department of Modern Languages, McMaster University, Hamilton, Ontario.

Colin Yallop is Adjunct Professor in the Department of English, Macquarie University, Sydney.

List of Maps

1 Introduction

Eddie Ronowicz

The history of foreign and second language teaching is also a history of consecutive changes in the stated objectives of teaching accompanied by sometimes dramatic changes in the form and content of teaching materials. During the twentieth century, these changes, which were initially based on the intuitions and experiences of eminent language teachers, came to be increasingly influenced by advances in linguistic research on language and language acquisition, and more recently also by the results of discourse analysis and findings in related humanities and social sciences. As a result, during the 1970s and 1980s the communicative approach to language teaching was widely accepted by the teaching profession and a new generation of textbooks appeared, which still followed a linguistic syllabus, but also introduced the learners to language functions and some non-linguistic elements of communication. It seems that now, thanks to a growing body of pragmatic and cross-cultural research, we are about to witness another addition to the list of objectives of language teaching: the achievement by the learners of cross-cultural competence, i.e. the ability to relate to differences between the learners' native and target cultures and thus enhance the effectiveness and quality of communication (cf. Crozet and Liddicoat, 1997, p. 3).

Robert Young is probably right when he says that in the case of untrained members of different cultures trying to communicate, only 'the kind of understanding two well-disposed strangers might have or develop were they to be thrown together on a long train journey' can be expected (Young, 1996, p. 13). The expected level of understanding between trained members of different cultures – for example, between students of English as a foreign or second language and native speakers of the language – should be much higher than that, however, provided cross-cultural aspects of communication are included in the teaching programme.

The main problem facing an English-language course designer wishing to introduce cross-cultural elements is when and how to do this. One has to agree with Crozet and Liddicoat (1997, p. 18) that 'culture has to be integrated into the language classroom from the very first day of language learning' and that 'culture must be taught in conjunction with language, not as an adjunct'. They are also right in suggesting that 'there is a need to develop new materials for language teaching ... which enable the learner to gain exposure to the target culture and to have opportunities to reflect on her/his own culture'. The text quoted above is, in fact, an introduction to an interesting collection of papers suggesting various ways of integrating cross-cultural elements in language teaching (Crozet and Liddicoat, 1997).

On the other hand, culturally determined aspects of communication not only constitute a huge body of knowledge, which is accumulated by native speakers throughout their lifetime, they also play a part in almost every instance of language use, which raises at least two practical problems. First, if all the necessary cultural comments were to be provided in each lesson or unit in the textbook, the books would probably grow to twice the present size. Second, while some of the cultural comments will be relevant to just one language item or communicative situation illustrated in the course, the majority of them refer to more than one item, to situations and communication strategies involving the use of a number of diversified vocabulary and grammatical structures in a single exchange.

It seems therefore that cross-cultural elements integrated into elementary and intermediate teaching materials will certainly ensure that language is taught in appropriate cultural context and they will sensitize learners to the fact of the existence of cultural differences. However, many important aspects of cross-cultural communication will not even get a mention in materials at this level. The reason is simple enough: elementary and intermediate learners do not have enough proficiency in the language either to notice all such nuances even if they are exposed to them or to apply such knowledge consistently while they are struggling with the language itself. Thus even if teaching texts and exercises include elements of the cultural context of their use, they cannot cover all or even most of the cultural information that may be relevant to the topic in question. Students will have to be told about those additional cross-cultural aspects briefly when the occasion arises and then constantly and consistently be reminded of their existence by their language teacher. It follows that language teachers should be the carriers and distributors of this additional information to students and that training practising and prospective teachers in cross-cultural communication is at least as important as the production of new materials.

The situation is different with advanced and tertiary students of English. They have sufficient communicative competence to read books, watch films or notice differences when travelling to countries where English is spoken as a native language. As a result, many of these learners will, like immigrants and other visitors at the same level of proficiency, develop what Larson and Smalley (1972) called 'culture stress' and a resulting motivation to find out more about those differences. Moreover, as our students' language competence and ability to participate in genuine communication grow, they are increasingly exposed to situations in which correct full comprehension and adequate responses depend as much on understanding cultural rules of communication as on understanding the words they hear. This phase of learning also corresponds to what Brown (1987, p. 135) calls the critical period for intensive, formal study of cross-cultural differences in foreign language learning, i.e. the period in which learners will be most receptive to this information and in which it will significantly enhance their overall proficiency in English.

This book, which is directed mainly at tertiary students of English as a foreign or second language, English language teachers, and translation and interpretation students and practitioners, assumes exactly that kind of willingness to spend some time exploring cultural differences between native speakers of English in various countries and provides the necessary tools to pursue further study of differences between English-speaking and other cultures and the effects these differences have on language communication.

This introductory chapter begins by looking at the relationships between language, culture and communication and their conse-quences. We then examine in some detail one of the most serious obstacles in cross-cultural communication – namely, stereotypes which most of us develop of other cultures. Finally we look at the incredible spread of English around the world and the resulting varieties of English and its speakers. This allows us to place American, Australian, British, Canadian and New Zealand English in the context of English as a global language. The introductory chapter ends with a brief overview of Chapters 2–7: 'About this book'.

Language and communication

Communication is one of the most important aspects of our everyday activity. In fact, most things we do are directly or indirectly connected with communication: we acquire (learn) or provide (teach) information, ideas, views, stories, give or follow instructions, requests or commands, express feelings, emotions, etc. There are a number of ways in which we can communicate, but natural languages, such as Chinese, English, French, Russian, Zulu, are certainly the most frequently used and most efficient carriers of messages between people.

A natural language is sometimes described as a communication tool consisting, in most simple terms, of a vocabulary, grammar and pronunciation and spelling rules, i.e. a list of words and a system of rules governing their use in speech and writing. If every item in the vocabulary had only one, unchangeable meaning, and if the grammar consisted of a finite number of fixed rules for every conceivable utterance, one might say that, in order to communicate effectively, the participants in a communicative act must both be competent in the use of the same vocabulary, grammar, pronunciation and spelling rules. This is indeed the case with artificial languages (e.g. computer languages), but not with natural languages, where both the vocabularies and the grammars offer practically unlimited possibilities for producing new, original messages. As Corder (1973, p. 201) rightly points out:

> No one knows 'the whole' of any language, or how to use it appropriately in all possible situations of language use. He acquires those parts of it which he needs in order to play his part in society. As he grows older, the roles that are ascribed to him or that he acquires change and develop, and as they change he learns more of his language (he may also forget some).

If even the majority of native speakers of a language are incapable of using fully the existing vast potential, what about learners of English as a foreign language in their native country? Are they automatically, as it were, in an inferior position at the outset, due to limited exposure (mainly in the language classroom and through books and short visits to English-speaking countries)? Not necessarily so: it must be said to the credit of English teachers around the world and the resolve of their students that quite a few tertiary learners achieve a remarkably high, near-native level of English after some years of intensive study. Compared to native speakers, they do have an additional problem to overcome, though, resulting from the fact that language is more than just a code or a symbolic system. As Anna Wierzbicka rightly points out, 'Languages differ from one another not just as linguistic systems but also as cultural universes, as vehicles of ethnic identities' (1985, p. 187). Every language functions in a community within the framework of its culture and, consequently, successful communication depends to a large extent on such things as what the content of the utterance actually refers to, which of the grammatically correct words, phrases or sentence patterns suit a given situation, and which do not, when to say things and how or, for that matter, whether to say anything at all. It follows that, to communicate effectively, the learner must be able to combine linguistic competence with the ability to operate within the accepted set of cultural rules of communication of a social group using it (cf. also Ronowicz, 1995).

Culture and communication

In its broadest sense, culture may be understood as a comprehensive view of history. It encompasses politics, economics, social history, philosophy, science and technology, education, the arts, religion and customs, which can be studied either as they have developed over a long period of time, or as they are or were at a given point in time. Culture includes the spiritual aspect of a society, embracing its ideological, artistic and religious trends. It may also be understood as a picture of everyday life, including everyday activities and entertainment, clothing, fashions, living conditions, family and social relations, customs, beliefs, morality, acceptable patterns of behaviour and rituals. Finally, social consciousness, which is expressed in the language of events and processes, institutions and organizations, social values and artistic creativity, are also part of culture expressed in the language. It is 'seemingly permanent, yet constantly changing' reality, which is ever present to all individuals belonging to the same cultural group (see Suchodolski, 1986, p. 5).

Suchodolski's definition gives us a general overview of the concept of culture. Larson and Smalley's explanation of the term 'culture' provides a rather good supplement to it in that they relate culture more directly to human behaviour, also linguistic behaviour. They define culture as a blueprint which:

> guides the behaviour of people in a community and is incubated in family life. It governs our behaviour in groups, makes us sensitive to matters of status, and helps us know what others expect of us and what will happen if we do not live up to their expectations. Culture helps us to know how far we can go as individuals and what our responsibility is to the group. Different cultures are the

underlying structures which make Round community round and Square community square. (Larson and Smalley, 1972, p. 39)

The political, social and economic history of a given cultural group, as well as its spiritual heritage, form an important source of background information that allows members of the language community to respond correctly to allegories, figures of speech, symbols and behavioural patterns which relate to its history. For example, if one knows the old story of King Arthur, one will comprehend better the idea of a 'Round Table'. While problems like those, which relate to the more distant and well described events in the life of a community or nation, can be solved by studying its history, the learner will find it much harder to comprehend fully the enormously complicated reality of everyday life and social consciousness of that language community. Not only do we have to deal with a multitude of culture specific patterns in communication, but also with the more recent social, cultural, political, economic and spiritual history of the group, especially that covering the lifespan of the people we communicate with. Having participated personally in a number of events, having had access to everyday local and national news, as well as personal communication with other people, adult members of a language community share a store of information built over a period of many years, and they use it actively in everyday communication.

The most obvious areas of culture-specific communication would be jokes, especially political jokes, but also sayings, metaphors, indeed most references to the not-so-distant past in the life of the language community. For instance, during the 1990s the then Australian treasurer, Mr Paul Keating, while defending his economic policies in parliament, described a recession the country was in as 'a recession we had to have'. At the time it caused not only outrage, but also a lot of jokes. It was a minor news item in other English-speaking countries, and it will have been forgotten by now, while in Australia it has become part of everyday language and will probably survive for quite some time: a variety of versions of this statement (such as 'the disappointment we had to have' or 'the power failure we had to have') have been used by Australians to add a touch of humour when announcing or discussing a bad piece of news. Unless they know the story behind it, neither people from non-English-speaking countries, nor most Americans, Britons or Canadians coming to Australia would probably be able to understand why most Australians laugh when they hear it, even if the phrase is used seriously.

There are a multitude of references like this present in everyday communication between members of any language community – some of them easier to follow, others completely inaccessible to non-members. Everyday life and social consciousness are shaped both by older traditions and current events, which influence directly and constantly the ever-changing vocabulary and idiom of the language, acceptable and unacceptable ways of linguistic behaviour in various situations, as well as the choice of those elements of the past which are considered relevant to the life of the language community and those which are not.

In terms of language communication, we are dealing here with second-level or specific meanings (i.e. additional meanings based on current and/or past cultural associations, specific contexts or situations) in contrast to first level meanings (i.e. conventional dictionary meanings of words, see Young, 1996, p. 72). First-level meanings may in fact be quite similar in two different languages, while second-level meanings may differ significantly. For instance, the colour 'white' means more or less the same at the first level in most languages, yet it may have quite different second-level meanings in different cultures. For example, in some Western European countries, white is the colour of purity or joy or life, while in many Asian cultures it is the colour of mourning and death. The numbers 4 and 13 have the same first-level meanings in English and in Chinese, yet 4 is an unlucky number for the Chinese, while 13 is for the English.

As Young observes, no meanings expressed in language are fixed or constant. They are:

> always moving and changing, but not necessarily in an arbitrary or senseless way. Meanings and rules of thumb for effective communication grow up in a culture and slip against each other like geological faults. The flow of first level meanings ... has a rate of change different from the flow of second level or specific meanings ... First order meanings are in movement, but their movement is much slower than the rate of change of second order meanings. (Young, 1996, p. 72)

It follows that it is second-level meanings, which depend so much on the knowledge of reality and culture of the community, that cause problems which are most difficult to overcome in cross-cultural communication.

People do not usually realize how much their daily life is influenced by unwritten rules automatically accepted and applied within their social class, their neighbourhood, their country. They not only tend to take them for granted, but also frequently make the wrong assumption that everyone operates within the same system of cultural rules. It is not until they come into contact with another culture, through the media or by travelling and especially by moving permanently from one region to another, from town to countryside or from one country to another, that they realize they have problems with interpreting other people's actions and reactions. They find out that the assumptions which have guided their behaviour at home are no longer valid in short, that the social environment encountered in this way follows a different set of rules, some of which may be quite difficult to comprehend. Such encounters with situations and behaviours which seem to be out of the ordinary will inevitably lead to comparisons and value judgements, or cultural stereotypes of members of other speech communities, many of which may be only partly true, and some of which may even be quite wrong. In the case of people who need to spend a longer period of time in a different cultural environment than their own, this may also be the cause of considerable stress, known as the phenomenon of 'culture shock'.

Cultural stereotyping and its consequences

In 1981 I was a research fellow at a large Midwestern university in the USA, which had a lively exchange programme with a number of countries, including my native Poland. For the majority of the Polish visitors, this was also their first visit to a Western country. Like J., a mathematician from my home university, they brought with them many misconceptions about the West and the USA in particular. On the one hand, the West was viewed as a sort of paradise, where people had plenty of money and life was easy and comfortable compared to Communist Poland. On the other hand, since early childhood, all people from countries behind the Iron Curtain were exposed to negative propaganda about social inequalities, the cult of the dollar, the high rate of crime and other darker sides of the capitalist society. This propaganda was partly successful in that J. brought with him some negative opinions about life in the USA and a fairly high level of anxiety at the outset. Additionally, quite by accident, J.'s scholarship was paid a week later than he expected and he had some problems with accommodation. Also other visitors had some minor problems during the first week, many of them caused by lack of knowledge of the ways administrative matters are dealt with at an American university.

Apart from the group of Poles, there were many young scholars from other countries visiting the university at the same time, all with a fairly good knowledge of English, who had similar little problems. Very soon after their arrival most of the newcomers got acquainted at a party organized by the Dean of Students and found they all shared rather negative attitudes towards various aspects of American culture and way of life. The result of this was, quite predictably, the creation of a sort of 'cultural ghetto' on campus: after they had done their time in the libraries or laboratories, the academics in question frequently spent time together. Towards the end of their six months in the USA they were a rather compact group of people who, outside their professional activities, managed to avoid any meaningful contacts with their American hosts. Having accomplished their research programmes and confirmed and enriched their negative stereotypes about Americans, they went back home where they, no doubt, contributed significantly to the maintenance of a distorted picture of this rich culture.

The behaviour of the above-mentioned group of academics can readily be explained. First, they were under the influence of cultural stereotypes about Americans which they brought with them from their home countries. A stereotype is 'a category that singles out an individual as sharing assumed characteristics on the basis of his or her group membership' (Brown, 1987, p. 125). Depending on the type of information available at the time of stereotyping, the result may be fairly accurate in describing a typical member of a given language community, or quite false. It is the false, negative stereotypes which are most destructive and were, in fact, at work in the group of scholars in question.

Second, stereotypes breed attitudes and, if the stereotype about a given second language culture is shared by a larger group, e.g. one's peers, these attitudes may be quite strong. In the case of the group of visiting scholars, we had a model situation of this type: they were all people in their late twenties or early thirties who had come to the university for the same purpose and they shared similar negative stereotypes about the locals. It was therefore inevitable that, as a group, they developed a strong negative attitude towards their environment.

Very soon after their arrival, when the novelty of the situation wore off, a third factor came into play: culture shock. The phenomenon and its causes are aptly described by Jean Brick:

> Culture shock is the result of the removal of the familiar. Suddenly the individual is faced with the necessity of working, commuting, studying, eating, shopping, relaxing, even sleeping, in an unfamiliar environment, organised according to unknown rules. In mild form, culture shock manifests itself in symptoms of fatigue, irritability and impatience ... Some people may respond by developing negative stereotypes of the host culture, by withdrawing as much as possible from contact with host-country nationals, by refusing to learn the language and by mixing exclusively with people of their own cultural background. (Brick, 1991, p. 9)

The scholars in question were a classic example of all three factors at work – negative stereotypes, negative attitudes and the resulting culture shock.

As a result, most members of the group, for whom English was a foreign language, failed to make any significant progress in learning either the language itself or culturally determined patterns of communication. It seems that the main reason for this was the integration strategy adopted by the group. As Schumann (1978) explains, in terms of cultural patterns involving lifestyle and values, there are three general integration strategies which the second language learning group might adopt: assimilation, acculturation or preservation. If the group decides to assimilate, then it gives up its own lifestyle and values and adopts those of the target language group (as very young or second-generation immigrants often do). If it chooses to acculturate, then its members adapt to the lifestyle and values of the target language group, but at the same time maintain their own cultural patterns for use in intragroup relations (as many first-generation immigrants do). Preservation, as defined here, is a strategy in which the second language group completely rejects the lifestyle and values of the target language group and attempts to maintain its own cultural patterns as much as possible (as some older first-generation migrants may do, especially those living in ghettos). Assimilation fosters minimal social distance, and preservation causes it to be maximal. Hence second language learning is enhanced by assimilation and hindered by preservation (Schumann, 1978, p. 78). Since the group in question adopted the strategy of preservation, the outcome was, predictably, minimal progress in the language and understanding of the host culture.

The situation described above might easily have been prevented if there had been a relevant cultural component in the intermediate or advanced English courses all members of the group had attended before they became eligible for their scholarships, or if they had undertaken an orientation programme dealing with these issues on arrival in the USA. The obvious failure of these academics (and of many other arrivals in English-speaking countries, especially older immigrants) to at least acculturate in the new environment would be a sufficient argument to include cultural information and practice in second language courses. There is also some empirical evidence available that positive attitudes to the target culture may increase second language proficiency (Oller, Baca and Vigil, 1978).

As the above discussion illustrates, all societies, groups and individuals have tendencies to create stories, interpretations and clichés about their own and other cultural groups, which are not necessarily true or only partly true. Under the influence of their own history and traditions, especially those which carry with them some strongly positive or negative content, people tend to build and maintain *myths* about themselves and others, such as, for example, the image of a typical Australian male as a tough, sun-tanned, resourceful adventurer, which may have been true some 150 years ago, but is quite false today.

Similarly, on the basis of understanding motivations and assumptions driving their own behaviour, people tend to make general statements about themselves and assumptions about the behaviour of others. These are known as *cultural stereotypes* and, like myths, are often only partly true, or even quite wrong for a number of reasons. For instance, in a questionnaire that we administered to a group of 40 people of different ethnic backgrounds, 61 per cent of people who were born and raised in Australia believed typical Australians to be hard-working, while only 6 per cent of first-generation immigrants and long-term foreign visitors believed this to be the case!

It cannot be emphasized too strongly that myths and cultural stereotypes are generalizations and, as such, they are never really true about the whole of a given community, about specific individuals, or about all individuals in a group. In this context it is interesting to note that since cultural stereotypes are highly dependent on the point of view and sources of people who uphold them, it often happens that members of different communities hold different, even quite opposite stereotypes about the same thing. For instance, in the same questionnaire, 50 per cent of Australians believed themselves to be patriotic, while 100 per cent of immigrants and foreigners (i.e. people who were born and raised in a variety of European or Asian countries) believed Australians to lack any form of patriotism whatsoever. Since there is no reason to disbelieve the answers of native Australians, one may speculate that the perceptions of European and Asian immigrants are not so much a reflection of the actual situation as a reflection of the fact that Australians understand and demonstrate their patriotism in a different way than the immigrants expect and therefore such behaviours are not recognized as patriotic. This is exactly how many false stereotypes are born.

English as a global language

Modern English, which began humbly as the native tongue of the inhabitants of England in the fourteenth century (see Chapter 3 for more information on the history of English), has now become the most popular lingua franca around the globe. According to Peter Strevens, the main reason for this incredible spread of English is that it has 'passed through several stages ..., which cumulatively yet inevitably led to the present state of affairs' (1992, p. 29).

The first stage, between 1350 and 1600, may be described as the development of modern English as a national language, 'when the influence of 300 years of Norman French occupation had been assimilated onto a basis of Germanic dialects, with some additions from the Norse of the Scandinavian invaders. For 250 years, until 1600, English was spoken only in England, probably not even by all the 7 million inhabitants' (Strevens, 1992, p. 29).

The second stage, between 1600 and 1750, may be described as the spread of English as a result of exploration and colonization. During this period the seeds of the global spread of English were sown by explorers, traders and settlers in overseas colonies. They still regarded themselves as native speakers (NS) of English from Britain living overseas, even though many of them were obviously more interested in local issues than in what was happening in Britain.

The third stage of the development of English as a global language, between 1750 and 1900, may be described as the development of English as a national language in the colonies. Three important changes took place during this period, which contributed significantly to the spread of English:

> First, the populations of the overseas NS English-speaking settlements greatly increased in size and became states with governments – albeit colonial governments – and with a growing sense of separate identity, which soon extended to the flavour of the English they used. Second, in the United States first of all but later in Australia and elsewhere, the colonies began to take their independence from Britain, which greatly reinforced the degree of linguistic difference: Noah Webster, for example, urged Americans to take pride in the fact of their English reflecting the dynamic new life of the United States. And third, as the possessions stabilized and prospered, so quite large numbers of people, being non-native speakers (NNS) of English, had to learn to use the language in order to survive, or to find employment with the governing class. These NNS learners were of two kinds: indigenous people and immigrants. Learning English (though not, generally speaking, being taught English) now became a major activity. (Strevens, 1992, pp. 29–30)

The fourth phase, between 1900 and about 1950, may be described as the spread of English through education. During this period the colonies began to offer education in English to indigenous populations, thus spreading the language to increasing numbers of local inhabitants. At the same time, the USA, Canada and Australia began to offer English language classes to migrants.

Until about the end of the Second World War, English was mainly spoken in existing or former colonies of Great Britain. It is the fifth stage, from about 1945 until the present, that may be described as the development of English as a global language. According to Strevens, this stage

> contains two distinct strands: first, nearly all the remaining colonies of Britain became independent states, and at once the role and function of English changed from being an instrument of subservience to other, quite different ends, such as a 'window on the world of science and technology,' or as the only language not rejected by one section of the population or another. (Strevens, 1992, p. 30)

This has led to a rapid growth in English language teaching to both adults and children all over the world.

The second strand of the current stage in the development of English mentioned by Strevens concerns the emergence of a number of activities, movements and subjects that are carried out predominantly (though not exclusively) in English across the world, mainly thanks to international agreements or to the fact that, for most people involved, English is the only shared language. Examples include the international agreement to adopt English for air traffic control and the use of English in the numerous bodies providing international aid and administration, in the international media such as radio, television, magazines and newspapers, in the international pop music industry, in space science and computing technology, and so on. As Strevens points out, 'the importance of this strand within the recent development of English has been not just the vast numbers of people who now need or want English for these activities, but the fact that using English suddenly has nothing to do with one's nationality or with the historical facts of the spread of English-speaking colonies' (Strevens, 1992, p. 31).

As a result, the total number of native and non-native speakers of English is now estimated at about two billion or more. There are more English speakers around the world today than there are speakers of Chinese or any other language. As Kachru (1986) says, English, which initially spread as a result of British imperialism, has largely lost its colonial and Western culture associations and is now:

> considered a symbol of modernisation, a key to expanded functional roles and an extra arm for success and mobility in culturally and linguistically complex and pluralistic societies. As if all this were not enough, it is also believed that English contributes to yet another type of transmutation: It internationalises one's outlook. In comparison with other languages of wider communication, knowing English is like possessing the fabled Aladdin's lamp, which permits one to open, as it were, the linguistic gates in international business, technology, science, and travel. (Kachru, 1986, p. 1)

One of the most amazing results of this almost uncontrollable spread of English is that there are now many times more non-native speakers of English than native speakers, as the following statistics illustrate. According to Strevens (1992, p. 28), the number of native speakers of English around the world is widely agreed to be around 350 million. This figure is based mainly on the population and school statistics of countries such as the USA, Canada, Britain, Australia and New Zealand, with allowances for the growing numbers of immigrants in these countries for whom English is not the mother tongue, and with some additions for 'expatriate' communities of native speakers of

English in various countries. Kachru (1986, p. 20) provides older but detailed figures totalling around 340 million, including 238.9 million Americans, 15.8 million Australians, 56.4 million Britons, 25.4 million Canadians and 3.3 million New Zealanders.

The total number of non-native speakers of English has, according to Strevens, been roughly estimated until recently at about 700 to 750 million.

> That figure has been arrived at by reference to such factors as the readership of English-language newspapers in countries where English is not a major mother tongue. Now David Crystal (1985) has called for a broader view of who should be counted as 'English users,' to include all those who do actually use it, even on a limited scale. Crystal's estimate is between 1 billion (1000 million) and 2 billion. His argument is persuasive: I shall take as a working figure the mid-point of 1.5 billion English users. (Strevens, 1992, p. 28)

It follows that, depending on which figure we choose, native speakers of English make up only a fifth to a quarter of the total number of speakers.

Kachru distinguishes two broad categories among the non-native speakers. First, there are those who consider English as a foreign language and use it in highly restricted domains – they can be found in rapidly increasing numbers in most non-English-speaking countries around the world. Second, there are those who use institutionalized second-language varieties of English. Kachru explains that 'the term "institutionalised" varieties generally refers to the varieties used by second language users to distinguish them from the "performance" varieties of English, used essentially as foreign languages' (Kachru, 1986, p. 19). Institutionalized use of English can be found on almost every continent – for example, in Nigeria, Kenya, the Republic of South Africa, Ghana, Bangladesh, India, Pakistan, Sri Lanka, the Philippines, Singapore, Malaysia, Thailand, American Samoa and Puerto Rico, among other countries.

Another important effect of the spread of English has been a dramatic increase in the number of its regional and functional varieties. What began as a limited number of dialects in England is now a conglomerate of national native and what we have called 'institutionalized' varieties of English, each of which can be subdivided into sometimes few, sometimes very numerous regional dialects. Moreover, some of these dialects or national varieties have become the basis for the development of pidgins in different parts of the world. Each of these varieties can be further studied for registers, styles, jargons and various other higher and lower order areas of use. If we consider that there is no English Language Academy to determine standards in England or in any other English-speaking country, whether English is of the native or institutionalized variety, we are dealing here with a researcher's delight and a student's nightmare. While the researchers deliberate on how many and what types of varieties of English exist in the world, what the relationships are among them, what their characteristic features are, who their users are, and so on, the language teacher and the student need to know what standard they should adhere to and why. The scholars, however, shy away from authoritative statements about standards.

Fortunately, there is some order to be found in this seemingly confusing picture. As Strevens says:

> there exists an unspoken mechanism, operated through the global industry of English teaching, which has the effect of preserving the unity of English in spite of its great diversity. For throughout the world, regardless of whether the norm is native-speaker or non-native-speaker variety, irrespective of whether English is a foreign or a second language, two components of English are taught and learned without variation: these are its *grammar* and its *core vocabulary*. There may be embellishments in the way of local vocabulary and expressions, and there will certainly be great differences of pronunciation, but the grammar and vocabulary of English are taught and learned virtually without variation around the world. (Strevens, 1992, p. 39)

In practical terms this means that most students are taught what we have called above first-level meanings and correct grammar and a limited amount of second-level or specific meanings, which is determined by the level of teaching (elementary, intermediate or advanced), the origin and knowledge of the teacher, the textbook used and where the actual teaching is taking place.

British and American English are undoubtedly the most popular varieties of English taught to students around the world. The choice of either of these usually depends on past influences of the two countries in a given region and/or the level of activities and assistance given to English as a Foreign Language (EFL) teachers by the British Council and American Cultural Centers. In more recent times, Australia and Canada have joined the English language training in a significant way and they now have large numbers of schools of English as a Second Language (ESL) catering for rapidly increasing numbers of overseas students. We hope that this book will be able to contribute to ESL students' awareness of the fact that they are learning the language spoken as native not only by the majority of Americans and Britons, but also by Australians, Canadians and New Zealanders.

Cross-cultural differences between native English-speaking communities

If we focus on the five countries of Australia, Canada, New Zealand, the USA and the UK, learners and native speakers of English have some justification for their common assumption that, except for noticeable differences of pronunciation and some orthographic, lexical and grammatical peculiarities, we are dealing with one and the same language. Many go even further and draw the seemingly logical conclusion that, since they are all speakers of the same language, speakers of English around the world use the language in the same way to communicate with one another. But this is clearly not the case with learners of English as a foreign or second language. The acquisition of English by non-native speakers does not usually lead to loss of cultural identity: for instance, a Thai student of English remains a full member of the Thai culture and, likewise, a French student of English does not lose his or her cultural identity, even if both have gained considerable knowledge of English and the culture associated with it. The same may be said of people living in countries where English is one of the institutionalized languages, a sort of lingua franca, as in India, Singapore or South Africa.

Contrary to common belief, it is also true that there are significant culturally determined differences in the way discourse is carried out by native speakers of English in countries like the UK, Australia or the USA, where English is the common language for most of the population. Unlike the habits and conventions of pronunciation, spelling and grammar, which are not changed frequently once a standard has been established, rules governing discourse in a given community are largely determined by historical, sociological and cultural factors, which develop differently in different societies. Moreover, these rules are continually being influenced by current developments and are changing. Consequently, while there are indeed a number of similarities in the way Britons, New Zealanders, Canadians, Australians or Americans conduct discourse, there are also differences which not only sometimes cause problems for native speakers from different countries, but are also known to have been responsible for culture-shock phenomena among immigrants moving from one English-speaking country to another.

Australia, Canada, New Zealand and the USA all began as British colonies and have had large numbers of immigrants from Britain and Ireland (and to some extent from each other). Indigenous people speaking languages other than English, who inhabited the lands before colonization, were rapidly dominated by an English-speaking majority and their languages and cultures have been partly or totally lost in subordination to English. This is, however, where the similarities in development end. Each of the four 'ex-colonial' countries gained independence at a different time and in a different way. The countries also differ in size, in the numbers and composition of their population and in their environment. Each of the countries has also developed its own national and social policies. As a result, from the initial common cultural core, four distinct cultures have emerged, each preserving different elements of the culture of origin and adding new elements determined by local conditions and development.

About this book

The present volume has been designed to assist advanced learners of English as a foreign/second language and native speakers with an interest in English-speaking cultures other than their own. It should also be an excellent source of information for people dealing with various Englishes as part of their profession, such as translators and interpreters. It aims to help them develop a better understanding of the ways in which social and cultural developments in Australia, Britain, Canada, New Zealand and the USA have influenced ways in which English is used to communicate. We also examine popular misconceptions and cultural stereotypes of native English speakers functioning around the world. Many of these views and attitudes are false, or partly false, and stem from ignorance of cross-cultural differences rather than fact.

Following this introductory chapter, Colin Yallop provides in Chapter 2 some linguistic background for the subsequent chapters in the form of a summary of differences among the five varieties of English. Pronunciation and spelling differences are the main focus of Chapter 2, with some references to differences in the vocabulary and idiom among the five varieties of English, most of which can be related to differences in the environment and in the historical development of each of the five nations, and to the input from indigenous languages.

The five chapters that follow, Chapters 3 to 7, deal with each of the five countries in turn. The chapters are similar to each other in their subject matter – they examine aspects of the history, culture, society and language use of the country – but they also differ, sometimes quite significantly, in length and structure. The first and most obvious reason for this is that each of the chapters was written by a different author or authors, familiar with the country, so that the book benefits from local knowledge and expertise. Second, every one of the societies covered in the selection has complex and constantly changing culturally determined communication strategies, and the editors judged that, since it would be impossible in any case to include every conceivably relevant detail, the authors should be allowed relative freedom to select and highlight what they considered to be of most interest and significance. The effects of this decision have surpassed our expectations: not only have we received chapters that give a picture of their countries and cultures, illustrating different approaches to cross-cultural studies, but also, more importantly, the texts themselves, their content and organization, as well as the authors' attitudes to the material they present, are to some extent a reflection of the very cultures they represent.

Chapter 3, written by Michael Sharwood-Smith, deals with Britain, the 'old world' source of the common language and of many cultural features shared by the four 'new world' nations. (See Chapter 3 itself for clarification of whether we should be talking about 'Britain', 'England' or 'the UK'.) Most visitors to Britain expect to see well-established old cities and institutions and buildings, like Oxford University and the Tower of London, or country areas like the Cotswolds or the Lake District, which look as if things have been much the same for hundreds of years – and the visitors are usually not disappointed. The British, who live with these reminders of the past constantly around them, tend to treat them as permanent features of the landscape, obvious and known to everyone. And, indeed, 10 Downing Street is probably the best known address in the world and many high-school leavers around the world might be able to associate Trafalgar Square with London or to identify Stratford-on-Avon as Shakespeare's birthplace. (By contrast, hardly anyone except Australians would know that 'the Lodge' in Canberra is the official residence of the Australian Prime Minister, and few outside New Zealand would know of the importance in that country of the Treaty of Waitangi.) Moreover, because British history, politics and culture have long been studied and noted (and sometimes imitated) in numerous countries old and new all around the world, they are fairly well known to many people. Sharwood-Smith therefore assumes some basic knowledge and hence, after a brief overview of English history and of how English came to be a world language, his main focus is on aspects of language and culture which are more likely to be unknown to the majority of people who were not brought up in the UK. It is this choice of content in particular that gives the chapter its very British flavour: it describes some details that may at first sight appear unimportant, and it seems to pass laconically over others, yet in the end it provides an amazing wealth of useful information about British culture and ways of conducting discourse in Britain.

All of the 'new world' chapters that follow share some features which seem to be generally true of many people living in Australia, Canada, New Zealand and the USA: these chapters acknowledge the darker aspects of their countries' beginnings, as revealed in the extermination of indigenous people or slavery, but they also demonstrate their authors' strong and positive attitude to the countries they live in, and they provide cultural and systematically ordered background information with some emphasis on things like multi-culturalism and equal opportunity for all. This is not surprising if we consider that all the non-indigenous people living in these countries are of immigrant stock, whether recent or not-so-recent, and in many cases they or their parents or ancestors came to the new country hoping to improve their lives and determined to achieve success. Moreover, all of these countries have had regular intakes of immigrants and not only know the problems connected with having multilingual and multicultural populations, but also have developed different policies attempting to deal with the problems. For example, the Australian and Canadian governments have initiated 'multi-cultural policies', while the USA is known for its historical 'melting pot' and for its current applications of human rights and equal-opportunity legislation. The chapters devoted to Australia, Canada, New Zealand and the USA are longer than the chapter on Britain, perhaps because so much inaccurate information about them circulates among non-English speakers.

Australia (Chapter 4 by Eddie Ronowicz and Colin Yallop) and New Zealand (Chapter 6 by Dianne Bardsley) are so far away from the rest of the world that there seems to be very little first-hand knowledge available to those seeking information. Australia is still often seen as 'the workers' paradise', a laid-back culture dominated by sporty Crocodile Dundee-type males who, when they are not chasing sheep in the paddock, spend the time in the bar or on the beach. The introductory parts of the text make it quite clear that Australia is in most important respects a modern economy, where many people have to work as hard as anywhere else in the world to earn a dollar. The main focus of the chapter is on what has remained from the older times – the relaxed and friendly attitudes in human relations which are reflected strongly in specifically Australian ways of using English and in the ways Australians socialize and spend their free time.

Canada (Chapter 5 by Magda Stroinska and Vikki Cecchetto) has the problem of being overshadowed, sometimes even confused with, its powerful southern neighbour. This is particularly true of Canadian English, which is often considered to be simply a variety or dialect of American English. The authors devote a considerable amount of space to demonstrate that this is not the case. The other issue given much attention in this chapter is the way Canadian multicultural and multilingual past has influenced its language and ways of commu-nicating, with a particularly interesting section on 'Canada through its vocabulary'.

Of all the countries dealt with in this book, New Zealand (Chapter 6 by Dianne Bardsley) is the smallest and probably the least known and studied by learners of English in other parts of the world. The chapter provides basic information about the history and geography of New Zealand and devotes some attention to the indigenous language Maori and its influence on language and culture in New Zealand. The Maori are a larger minority in New Zealand than any indigenous people in Australia, Canada or the USA, and their language and culture are of major current significance, even to the point of the country having an alternative Maori name, *Aotearoa*, 'the land of the long white cloud'. But, as the chapter makes clear, New Zealand also has perpetuated its own version of 'Englishness' and it is in its own way a major English-speaking country, offering English-medium education and training to students from abroad.

The United States of America (Chapter 7 by Sherry Ash) is an economic and military superpower, currently unmatched by any other country in the world on both counts. As a result, it is often looked at with some bias: many people have views about Americans which are often shaped more by the country's power and status and by media images of it than by the reality of everyday life as experienced by an insider in the country. As illustrated by the example quoted earlier in this chapter (pp. 8ff.), even visitors to the country seem to manage to see and remember what they want to see and, as a result, may leave with their preconceived ideas intact. For this reason alone, the chapter devoted to the USA deserves to be the longest. The author and the editors agreed that, while the focus of the text is comparable to that of the other chapters – cultural aspects of communicating in American English – the sections presenting background information needed to be extensive and to cover as much factual information as possible about life in the USA.

In addition to the text itself, each chapter ends with a number of cross-cultural tasks and exercises. These can be used for independent study, as topics of assignments, as mini research projects, for group discussions or for review purposes. As Michael Sharwood-Smith rightly points out, the way to uncover the cultural secrets of a nation is 'contrastively', i.e. by comparing similar situations in one's own culture and language use with those of the second or foreign language culture. (See the introduction to Chapter 3 for more on this topic.) The cross-cultural exercises have been included with the aim of assisting students in this undertaking. They should serve as a useful source of research techniques and topics for both teachers and students involved in the formal study of cross-cultural communication.

To conclude, it must be emphasized that the object of our study – culture and its influence on language and communication – is quite elusive. History, traditions, society and language never stand still. They develop and change constantly, sometimes in quite dramatic ways, as recently shown by political, economic and social changes in post-communist Eastern European countries, which in a matter of just a few years have also led to considerable changes in language and communication practices. It follows that readers of this book are strongly encouraged to engage in further individual inquiry. This is particularly true of students for whom English is a foreign language, who need to explore not only differences among the five varieties of English discussed here, but also differences between communication practices in their own native tongue and culture and those of native speakers of English.

As a demonstration of what we have been talking about and as a prelude to the tasks and exercises, consider the example of a recent lecture given in Australia to a group of people who were about to retire. The topic was in the general area of public health and medicine and the speaker used a great number of analogies, illustrations and jokes, most of which seemed to be appreciated by his audience and probably helped to make the talk clearer and more entertaining as well as informative. But many of these elements assumed a shared knowledge and experience. The speaker did not explain them, he simply assumed that his audience knew the relevance and connections. Instances in his lecture included simple analogies like 'this cell is shaped rather like a bluebottle you see on the beach' – drawing on his audience's familiarity with the appearance of the small bluish creatures with long tentacles that sometimes get washed up on Australian beaches. He also imagined a hypothetical husband and wife beginning a life of retirement and spoke of 'Jack and Jill' going to retire to the 'Costa Geriatrica'. His use of 'Jack and Jill' not only offers two simple alliterative names, but it also reminds the audience of the children's rhyme about the Jack and Jill who 'went up the hill to fetch a pail of water'. Since the rhyme ends with Jack and Jill tumbling back down the hill, and all of the audience can be assumed to know this, the use of these names is a neat and subtle way of anticipating that there is trouble ahead for this hypothetical couple. The imaginary name 'Costa Geriatrica' also draws on the audience's knowledge that many people in Australia retire to coastal areas away from the cities. The name will also remind the audience of famous holiday areas in Spain like the Costa Brava and the Costa del Sol. But combined with 'Geriatrica' (based of course on the medical term 'geriatric', referring to aged people and their care) the effect is a slightly cynical and humorous comment on coastal areas of Australia which have disproportionate numbers of retired people. In yet another example from this talk, the speaker had taken a couple of questions and realized that he couldn't explain everything immediately and that he would have to mention a couple of points and come back to them later. As he reassured the audience that he would return to these points, he quickly remarked 'I'm not Irish, I will come back to that' – drawing on the (unwarranted) stereotype among many English-speaking peoples that the Irish are disorganized or muddled.

Many other examples could be taken from this and other lectures.

This particular speaker, for example, assumed that his audience knew who Don Bradman and Bob Simpson were (famous Australian cricketers), and he said 'we've all heard of "mind over matter"' (a familiar but cryptic saying meaning that the human mind or spirit can overcome material circumstances). Discourse will often include such elements. Those who know what is meant may be grateful for the simple clarification, they may enjoy the humour or the allusion, they may even enjoy the sense of drawing on shared knowledge and experience. It will of course be different for those who are mystified by these elements from a foreign culture. Worse still, the native speakers may not even realize why the newcomer has a problem. After all, the speaker was so clear and entertaining, we understood the lecture and enjoyed it. Surely you did too?

Tasks and exercises

1. Have you ever spent a period of time in a country other than your own? Use your knowledge and experiences from that country to answer the questions below.
a) Were you surprised about anything the natives of that country did or said? What were those things?
b) Was there anything about the natives of that country that you found annoying, frustrating, unpleasant or unacceptable? What were those things? Why do you think you noticed them? How are those things done in your country?
c) Did you experience any of the symptoms of culture shock?

2. Take some time to consider your feelings and experiences regarding your own native culture. Share your answers to the following questions with fellow students and your teacher in class.
a) What are, according to commentators, the most typical features of your culture? Do you agree that this is, indeed, the case? Are there any other features you would like to name?
b) What are, according to commentators, the most typical features of the target culture? Do you agree that this is the case? Are there any other important features of the target culture you would like to name?
c) What criticisms do foreigners most often make about your country?
d) To what extent do you think these criticisms are justified?
e) How do you feel when you hear such criticisms?
f) Do you ever make negative statements about members of other cultures? How do you think they feel about the correctness of your statements?

References

Brick, J., (1991) *China: A Handbook in Intercultural Communication.* Sydney: National Centre for English Language Teaching and Research, Macquarie University.

Brown, H.D. (1987) *Principles of Language Learning and Teaching.* Englewood Cliffs: Prentice Hall.

Corder, S.P. (1973) *Introducing Applied Linguistics.* Harmondsworth: Penguin Books.

Crozet, C. and Liddicoat, A.J. (1997) 'Teaching culture as an integrated part of language teaching: an introduction', in Liddicoat and Crozet (eds) (1997).

Crystal, D. (1985) 'How many millions? The statistics of English today', *English Today* 1:1.

Kachru, B.B. (1986) *The Alchemy of English.* Oxford, New York, Sydney: Pergamon Institute of English.

Kachru, B.B. (ed.) (1992) *The Other Tongue. English across Cultures* (2nd edn). Urbana and Chicago: University of Illinois Press.

Larson D.A. and Smalley, W.A. (1972) *Becoming Bilingual: a Guide to Language Learning.* New Canaan, CN: Practical Anthropology.

Liddicoat, A.J. and Crozet, C. (eds) (1997) *Teaching Languages, Teaching Culture.* Australian National University, Canberra: Australian Review of Applied Linguistics Series S, No. 14.

Oller J., Baca, L.L. and Vigil, A. (1978) 'Attitudes and attained proficiency in ESL: a sociolinguistic study of Mexican-Americans in the Southwest', *TESOL Quarterly* 11: 173–83.

Ronowicz, E. (1995) *Poland. A Handbook in Intercultural Communication,* Macquarie University, Sydney: National Centre for English Language Teaching and Research.

Schumann, J.H. (1978) *The Pidginization Process. A Model for Second Language Acquisition.* Rowley, Mass: Newbury House Publishers.

Strevens, P. (1992) 'English as an international language. Directions in the 1990s', in Kachru (ed.) 1992, pp. 27–47.

Suchodolski, B. (1987) *Dzieje kultury polskiej* (2nd edn). Warszawa: Polska Agencja Wydawnicza Interpress.

Sussex, R. and Zubrzycki, J. (eds) (1985) *Polish People and Culture in Australia.* The Australian National University, Canberra: Department of Demography, Institute of Advanced Studies.

Wierzbicka, A. (1985) 'The double life of a bilingual', in Sussex and Zubrzycki (eds) 1985, pp. 187–223.

Young, R. (1996) *Intercultural Communication. Pragmatics, Genealogy, Deconstruction.* Clevedon, Philadelphia, Adelaide: Multilingual Matters.

2 English around the world

Colin Yallop

This chapter gives a basic introduction to differences in the English language, with particular attention to Britain, the United States, Canada, Australia and New Zealand. It begins with an overview of differences in spelling conventions among these five countries and moves on to pronunciation, providing in turn a regional survey and comments on the pronunciation of consonants and vowels. There are then remarks on variations in grammar, vocabulary and idiom.

In general, this chapter will take the view that written English, especially in its most formal versions, does not vary radically. Among the five countries that are the focus of this book, spelling practices and grammatical usage are relatively uniform, and there is a large common vocabulary. Spoken English does show more variability, both in pronunciation itself and in the kind of vocabulary and idiom that is more likely to be used in speech.

Spelling

In its written form, English is a remarkably uniform language. This was not always so. The notion that there is one correct way to spell English words is a consequence of various developments over the past 500 years, including the invention of printing, the publication of dictionaries such as Dr Samuel Johnson's of 1755, the institution of universal compulsory education, and the gradual development of a strong public commitment to the importance of having a standardized written form of language.

In the eighteenth century, when Dr Johnson published his dictionary, it was still possible to write 'fabrick' rather than 'fabric'; 'recal' rather than 'recall'; 'authour' rather than 'author'; and 'croud' rather than 'crowd'. Dr Johnson himself, in his correspondence, seems to have used three different spellings for the word we now write as 'governor'. (His other spellings were 'governer' and 'governour'.) A quick glance at these alternative spellings is enough to show that there is no compelling reason to accept one rather than the other. After all, if we can now write 'appal' and 'enrol' with a single l, why not also 'recal'? If we write 'loud' and 'cloud', why not also 'croud'? And so on. But public acceptance of a standardized spelling is now such that these eighteenth-century alternatives would simply be judged incorrect.

There are still a few English words that do remain open to alternative spellings: you can write 'aging' or 'ageing', 'judgment' or 'judgement', 'queuing' or 'queueing', 'annex' or 'annexe', 'drier' or 'dryer', 'instal' or 'install', 'gibe' or 'jibe', 'whir' or 'whirr'. Publishers and editors usually have their own preference for one or the other of these spellings and will regularize for consistency, but they are unlikely to claim that the alternative is incorrect. Needless to say, words such as these are a very small fraction of English vocabulary.

There are rather more instances of words which are usually written differently in Britain and the USA. Several kinds of words are involved.

There are about 30 words that end in '-our' in British spelling but '-or' in American. Examples, in the American spelling, are:

behavior	harbor	neighbor
color	honor	odor
favor	humor	rumor
flavor	labor	vapor

The British spellings of these words are:

behaviour	harbour	neighbour
colour	honour	odour
favour	humour	rumour
flavour	labour	vapour

But '-our' spellings can be found in American publications ('glamour' occurs, as well as 'glamor', for example) and there are also plenty of '-or' spellings in British usage ('author, error, squalor').

Some words ending in '-re' in British spelling have '-er' in American usage. Some American examples are:

center	liter	somber
fiber	scepter	theater

The British versions of these words are:

centre	litre	sombre
fibre	sceptre	theatre

Again, the distinction is not quite as straightforward as it may seem. American usage has many words ending in '-re' (for example, 'genre, mediocre, ogre').

In American usage, the letter 'l' is usually not doubled in words such as:

counseling	labeled	traveling
jeweler	traveled	woolen

But British usage normally does double the consonant:

counselling	labelled	travelling
jeweller	travelled	woollen

The '-ize' spelling is normal in the USA, in words like:

apologize	civilize	recognize
authorize	organize	specialize

The alternative spellings are of course:

apologise	civilise	recognise
authorise	organise	specialise

This '-ize' spelling is often claimed to be a feature of American writing, but in fact '-ize' is also common in Britain, and preferred by some British publishers in many words. A strong preference for '-ise' is probably more characteristic of Australia and Canada than of Britain (see Chapter 5 for some comments on the tension between American and British spellings in Canada). But it should also be noted that there are words ending is '-ise' or '-ize' in which the ending is not a suffix. Some of these are always written with '-ise', throughout the English-speaking world (e.g. 'advise, surprise') and some always have '-ize' (e.g. 'prize, seize, capsize'). There is no regional variation in the spelling of these words.

Where the two-letter combinations 'ae' and 'oe' occur in words based on Latin or Greek, they are often maintained in British usage but simplified to 'e' in American. Examples in the simplified spelling are:

esthetic	hemorrhage	gynecology
anesthetist	leukemia	pediatrics
diarrhea	esophagus	estrogen

Those who retain the 'ae' or 'oe' spell these words as:

aesthetic	haemorrhage	gynaecology
anaesthetist	leukaemia	paediatrics
diarrhoea	oesophagus	oestrogen

But again we have to be careful not to overgeneralize. Even in America, 'aerobic' retains an 'ae' and 'phoenix' an 'oe'; while spellings like 'encyclopedia' (for 'encyclopaedia') and 'medieval' (for 'mediaeval') are increasingly common, even outside the USA.

American usage generally has the shorter form of some words:

analog	catalog	program
ax	dialog	

whereas Britain tends to prefer the longer forms:

analogue	catalogue	programme
axe	dialogue	

American usage has the letters' in these words:

defense	pretense	vise

where British usage has the letter 'c':

defence	pretence	vice

(In America, the Vice Squad deals with vice, but the clamping device on a workbench is a vise.)

There are a few other variants, such as the following, with American variants on the left and British on the right:

disk	disc
draft	draught
gray	grey
plow	plough
skeptical	sceptical

And in Britain, you 'check' up on something but cash a 'cheque', and you 'tire' of something but have 'tyres' on a car. American usage has 'check' and 'tire' without distinction.

Many of the spellings that are now considered American were once alternatives in Britain. (Spellings like 'favor' and 'honor' were common in Britain until Johnson's dictionary began to be taken as an authority, and 'ax' was a frequent British spelling until the latter part of the nineteenth century). And some of them are now (re)gaining acceptance in Britain. The spellings 'disk' and 'program', for instance, are common in the context of computing (and note also the earlier remark about the international spread of the spellings like 'encyclopedia' and 'medieval').

Many of the American spellings can be traced to Noah Webster (1774–1843) who, as Samuel Johnson was in England, was influential in America as a lexicographer and man of letters. He proposed considerable reform of English spelling, including simplifying 'head' to 'hed', 'give' to 'giv', 'friend' to 'frend', 'mean' to 'meen', and 'grieve' to 'greev', among many others. Webster's interests and enthusiasm were not peculiar to the USA. A movement to promote spelling simplification in Canada in the late nineteenth century produced a publication called the *Fonetic Herald* (see Chapter 5). Among famous advocates of spelling reform in Britain were Isaac Pitman (inventor of Pitman's shorthand) and the author George Bernard Shaw.

Obviously most of Webster's (and other reformers') proposals were not taken up, and English spelling is now highly conservative. Most readers of this book will be well aware that English spelling does not correspond closely to pronunciation and that many details of spelling represent obsolete features of pronunciation, such as the 'silent' initial consonant letters in words like 'gnaw, knife, write' and the 'gh' in words like 'bough, dough, through'. Even those who grow up with English as a first language often make spelling mistakes: it is not uncommon to find even well-educated native speakers of English writing 'accommodate' with one 'm' instead of two, or 'minuscule' with an 'i' instead of the first 'u'.

Australia and New Zealand have inherited the same conservative spelling system, with very little local innovation. Where British and American practices diverge, Australia and New Zealand have tended to follow British practice in most respects. This is hardly surprising, given the extent of immigration from Britain and continuing political and cultural connections with the United Kingdom. But Australia has been relatively open to '-or' spellings, which were normal in the state of Victoria for most of the twentieth century and are still used in some contexts such as the 'Australian Labor Party'. As mentioned earlier, current usage in Australia also strongly favours the '-ise' spelling of words like 'apologise, authorise, characterise, emphasise, organise, polarise, specialise'.

Canada also has a history of links to Britain, of course, but is geographically much closer to the USA than to any other English-speaking country, and spelling practices reflect both British and American influences. In general, the education system tends to favour British conventions, but the influence of American spellings through publications and films and television programmes is extremely strong. (See Chapter 5 for some further remarks on Canada between 'two big brothers'.)

Pronunciation

A regional survey

English is not at all uniform in pronunciation, but one advantage of English spelling is that it is more or less the same across the English-speaking world. Indeed, if we followed the principle that spelling should closely reflect pronunciation, we would have to start coping with alarmingly divergent spelling practices.

Britain itself reveals considerable diversity of pronunciation, of course. What many people think of as traditional and correct pronunciation – and what is sometimes referred to as BBC English or Oxford English – is the accent of a very small minority. Known to phoneticians as Received Pronunciation, or RP for short, this way of pronouncing English was spread through the prestigious private schools in England and has thus become a pronunciation with high social status. Although it derives originally from south-eastern England, its adoption by speakers from various parts of Britain (and even elsewhere) means that many people have come to think of it as a non-regional standard. It continues to be important, not only because the minority who speak it includes highly influential people, but also because descriptions of English pronunciation and the pronunciations given in British dictionaries are often based on RP. Many learners of English around the world, especially in areas where Britain is still regarded as the home of the English language, are introduced to RP as the 'best' or 'normal' pronunciation of English.

RP was first described by the British phonetician Daniel Jones in his *English Pronouncing Dictionary* of 1917, when it was already well established as a prestigious pronunciation. Jones was actually more interested in describing RP than in promoting it, and in the introduction to his dictionary he wrote that 'RP means merely "widely understood pronunciation"', going on to say that 'I do not hold it up as a standard which everyone is recommended to adopt'. His dictionary, and appeals to it as an authority, nevertheless became extremely popular, and it reached its twelfth edition in the 1960s. Since Jones's death in 1967, the dictionary has appeared in later versions edited by other phoneticians, the most recent being the sixteenth edition of 2003, edited by Roach, Hartman and Setter. Other recent dictionaries of English pronunciation are Wells (2000) and Upton, Kretschmar and Konopka (2003).

What most people in Britain actually speak is not RP but various styles of pronunciation that can be identified with regional districts and urban centres, such as East Anglia, South Wales, Tyneside, Glasgow or London. Many of the older regional pronunciations have been heavily modified over the last hundred years or so, partly because mobility and urbanization have broken down the older closer-knit communities that sustained marked regional diversity, and partly because schoolteachers have often encouraged children to eliminate some of the most obvious regional features of their speech. But there are still identifiable regional pronunciations across Britain, even if their precise characteristics and the boundaries among them are not as clear cut as they once were. Because of the high status of RP, regional pronunciations have sometimes been regarded as 'lower class' accents; but this in turn has meant that many citizens of Britain have reacted against RP as 'posh'. Many Britons probably now want (consciously or not) to speak something like 'standard English' but without abandoning all the features of their local speech. An important illustration of this newer kind of regionalism is Estuary English, spoken in much of south-eastern England and named after the Thames Estuary (Rosewarne, 1984; Graddol *et al.,* 1996, p. 299). Viewed phonetically, this is a compromise between RP and London speech. Many people in south-eastern England would consider it an 'ordinary' way to talk, neither affected (as RP might seem to be) nor uneducated (as a strongly regional accent might be thought to imply).

Scotland, Ireland and, to a lesser extent, Wales have traditions and regional or national identities that make them more independent of RP than areas of England. In Scotland, for example, while there is a very small minority of RP speakers, most of the population has an identifiably Scottish pronunciation (phonetically quite different from RP or Estuary). Within Scotland, there is substantial regional differentiation, but the factors already noted above – mobility, urbanization, and so on – have tended to reduce the extent of variation.

In both Australia and New Zealand, English-speaking settlers seem to have developed a local pronunciation quite early, but the precise mechanism of this development is not known. Both countries have lived under the shadow of RP in much the same way as many parts of Britain. Both countries have had an educational and cultural tradition of decrying local speech and admiring an (often highly idealized) English model. The tradition is far weaker than it was – but it does still happen that an Australian or a New Zealander speaks admiringly of RP, even though they are unlikely to have any real aspiration to speak RP themselves. In both countries it is possible to identify a range of accents along a continuum from the most local kind of speech to forms of pronunciation that are much closer (but not of course identical) to RP. In Australia in particular, the most distinctively local end is known as Broad Australian, while the other end is sometimes referred to as Cultivated Australian. Between Broad and Cultivated is a range of pronunciations that can be labelled General Australian. In both Australia and New Zealand it is probably fair to say that most speakers have forms of speech of the General kind, which are distinctively local but which lack or constrain the traditionally stigmatized features of Broad.

The pronunciation of English in the USA is noticeably different from RP (and in some respects shows more similarities with Irish, Scottish and regional British forms of speech than with RP). Regional diversity is not as marked in the USA as in Britain, but is certainly evident. As a very rough generalization, two areas stand out as divergent from most of the USA. One is the north-east USA (loosely New England, but sometimes including New York), the other is the south-east, sometimes referred to simply as 'the South'. These two regions stand apart from what some linguists call 'General American'. One interpretation of the term General American would see it as a somewhat idealized standard form of American accent, spoken widely through the USA; a more negative but probably more realistic interpretation would see General American as the kind of pronunciation that most Americans would consider neither markedly New England (or New York) nor markedly southern. (See Chapter 7 for more details.)

Canadian English is similar to that of the USA, partly for the historical reason that many North Americans moved into Canada after the USA won its independence from Britain in the late eighteenth century (see Chapter 5). Canadian English thus shares many phonetic features with General American, and many people from outside North America find it hard to distinguish between a Canadian and an American accent. But, like the USA, Canada also shows some regional variation from an otherwise rather negatively defined standard. It is in eastern Canada, in the Maritime Provinces and Newfoundland, that the most obvious regional variation is found, while the rest of the country is more uniform.

Consonants

Turning to some details of pronunciation, we will focus on RP, General American (GenAm), and the 'general' accents of Canada (Can), Australia (Aus) and New Zealand (NZ). Inevitably, we can look at only some of the wealth of phonetic detail that is relevant to variety of pronunciation.

In general, consonants vary less than vowels, but there is a major division between those who pronounce the so-called 'post-vocalic r' and those who don't. In RP, Aus and NZ, there is no 'r'-sound in words such as 'car, card, four, fort, spur, spurt, beer, beard, stare, stairs'. The 'r' standing after a vowel (post-vocalic) and either at the end of a word or before a consonant is simply not pronounced. Thus in RP, Aus and NZ, sometimes called non-rhotic pronunciations, each of the following pairs of words is pronounced identically: 'spat/spar, ma/mar, tuba/ tuber, fought/fort'. By contrast, GenAm and Can are rhotic. (Note that Scotland, Ireland and a large area of western and south-western England are also rhotic, while one of the features that makes New England and the South distinctive within the USA is that those regions are typically non-rhotic.)

In non-rhotic accents, the post-vocalic 'r' is pronounced if immediately followed by a vowel. Thus while RP, Aus and NZ have no 'r' in 'car, star, fur, stare, four', there is a so-called linking 'r' not only in words like 'starry, furry, staring' but also in connected speech where a vowel follows, as in 'a car engine', 'a star is born', 'don't stare at me', 'four and a half', 'four o'clock'.

By analogy, most non-rhotic speakers also pronounce a linking 'r', even when this is not justified by history or spelling, as in 'ma(r)and pa', 'a tuba(r) is a brass wind instrument'. This kind of linking 'r', technically an intrusive 'r', is sometimes criticized as bad pronunciation, but many speakers of RP, Aus and NZ use it.

One other noticeable feature of consonant pronunciation which is often commented on concerns the pronunciation of 't' in words such as 'metal, writer, plenty, Santa'. In GenAm and Can, this 't' is normally pronounced more or less as 'd', and, after 'n', may be deleted altogether. Hence those who call attention to this pronunciation may jokingly respell Ottawa as Oddawa, or Santa Fe as Sanna Fe. In fact, pairs of words like 'metal/medal, writer/rider, winter/winner' often remain distinct because of the timing: for example, the first vowel of 'medal' may be distinctively longer than that of 'metal'.

This feature of pronunciation is also found in other parts of the English-speaking world: it is noticeable in the speech of many Australians, for example, and it is found in some regional speech in England. But a quite different feature is found in some areas of Britain, namely the pronunciation of word-medial or word-final 't' either with an accompanying glottal stop or as a glottal stop (a momentary closure of the glottis, interrupting the flow of air). This pronunciation is particularly associated with cities like London and Glasgow and is sometimes represented with spellings like 'be'er' for 'better' or 'be'' for 'bet'. In conservative RP, the medial 't' is neither voiced to 'd' nor replaced by a glottal stop, but the use of the glottal stop is one of the features that is found in Estuary English, illustrating the way in which London features have been taken up in Estuary.

Vowels

English has a relatively large number of different vowel sounds, including several diphthongs (vowels which move quickly from one vowel quality to another). The four diphthongs in words like the following vary considerably across the English-speaking world. It would be a valuable exercise to have these words read by speakers from different parts of the English-speaking world and to listen carefully to the pronunciation.

say, bay, bait, made, main
so, toe, boat, mode, moan
sigh, buy, bite, side, sign
sow (female pig), bough, bout, loud, crown

In RP the diphthong illustrated by 'so' is quite distinctive, and is sometimes mimicked as if it began with a vowel like the short 'e' of 'bet' and then moved towards the vowel of 'boot'. In Aus and NZ (especially Broad varieties) the diphthongs in 'say' and 'so' begin with the tongue relatively low in the mouth, so much so that others sometimes claim that 'say' sounds like 'sigh' and 'so' sounds like 'sow'. In fact, 'say' and 'sigh' are not identical, even in the Broadest Australian speech, because the beginning of 'sigh' is even further back and lower, making it closer to (though again not identical with) the diphthong of 'toy'. And 'sow', in Aus and NZ (as well as in some regional British and North American speech), tends to begin with a relatively low front vowel similar to that of 'sat' before moving towards a vowel like that of 'boot'.

Canadians are often identified by their pronunciation of the 'sigh' and 'sow' diphthongs before voiceless consonants (thus in words like 'bite, right, rice, bout, lout, mouse' but not before voiced consonants as in 'side, rise, tribe, loud, blouse'). Before a voiceless consonant, the beginning of the diphthong is higher than in most other varieties, so that non-Canadians may hear a Canadian's 'right about' as if it were 'rate a boat'. As with many of these misperceptions, the distinction is quite clear to Canadians themselves, of course. (And this feature is actually not confined strictly to Canada, as it can also be heard in some parts of the USA; see also Chapter 5.)

The three vowels illustrated by 'bit, bet, bat' have the tongue positioned relatively forward in the mouth in most varieties of English, but in NZ all three vowels are shifted relative to RP, with 'bit' more central and 'bet' and 'bat' noticeably higher. This leads to mimicry by outsiders (again, as in many popular perceptions of speech variation, not entirely accurately) of NZ 'bit, bet, bat' as if they had been shifted to 'but, bit, bet'. Aus shows a similar tendency to raise the vowels of 'bet' and 'bat' but not to the same extent as NZ. In fact Australians often joke about NZ pronunciation, accusing New Zealanders (quite unfairly) of saying 'fush and chups' or 'thenk hivvens', instead of 'fish and chips' and 'thank heavens'.

There are many other features of vowel pronunciation which distinguish our varieties of English speech – for example, the vowel of words like 'tune, student, dune, duke', which is typically a diphthong (more or less 'you') in RP, Aus and NZ but simplified to a simple vowel in GenAm (as in 'toon, stoodent', etc.); and the vowel of words like 'after, laugh, path, bath, pass, fast' which is typically a long vowel in RP, Aus and NZ (the same as in 'spa, start, sparse'), but in GenAm is either the same as or similar to the vowel of 'bat, bad'.

The tendency of most varieties of spoken English is to make a major difference between stressed and unstressed syllables and to show vowel reduction in unstressed syllables. In the word 'banana', for example, the middle vowel (which is stressed) is very different from the first and last (unstressed) vowels. In RP, the combined effect of non-rhotic pronunciation and of vowel reduction is such that the words 'China, diner, minor' all end in the same indeterminate vowel (sometimes called 'schwa'). But the details of vowel reduction do vary across the English-speaking world. GenAm tends not to reduce the penultimate vowel of words like 'secretary, February' (so that these words are pronounced as if ending in 'erry' or 'arry') whereas RP usually does show reduction and may even omit the vowel altogether (yielding something like 'secretry' and 'februry' or even 'febyuri' – in all cases with prominent stress on the first syllable of the word). RP does maintain a distinction between 'schwa' and a short 'i' vowel in unstressed syllables. For example, the words 'carrot, chattered, fishers' have 'schwa' in the second (unstressed) syllable, while 'rabbit, carpet, chatted' commonly have a short vowel like that of 'kit' in the second syllable. But Aus and NZ do not make this distinction, so that a pair of words like 'chatted/chattered' is pronounced identically, with 'schwa' in the second syllable. (Remember that there is no 'r'-consonant in the pronunciation of words like 'chattered' and 'fishers' in RP, Aus or NZ.)

Given the characteristic rhythm of spoken English, in which stressed syllables are much more prominent than unstressed, it is surprising that vowel reduction (and omission of unstressed vowels and even syllables) has not progressed further than it has. Indeed, highly reduced versions of what you might expect from the spelling are quite common in English place names (for example, 'Gloucester' pronounced as 'Gloster', 'Worcester' as 'Wooster', and 'Norwich' as 'Norritch' or 'Norridge') and in some areas of vocabulary (such as nautical terms like 'boatswain' pronounced as 'bosun', and 'forecastle' as 'focsle'). It is probable that reduced pronunciations of this kind were once more common in English, and that increasing knowledge of, and respect for, the written form of the language in the last 200 years has led to the adoption of many 'spelling pronunciations', that is pronunciations motivated by the written form rather than by the traditional pronunciation. A simple example is the word 'author', which used to be pronounced 'autor' (compare the French *auteur*). Because of the 'th' spelling, it is now normal to pronounce the word with the same fricative sound that occurs in words like 'north' and 'fourth'. (But obviously not all 'spelling pronunciations' are acceptable. Pronouncing the name of the river in London as 'Thames', as it is written, rather than as 'Temms', might sometimes be done jokingly but will usually count as a plain error; while pronouncing 'parliament' as if it had an 'i'-vowel in it, rather than just as 'parlament', will be judged wrong or substandard by most speakers.)

In some instances, the choice between reduced and unreduced vowels in unstressed syllables reveals regional preferences. Thus where RP has 'hostel' with a reduced second syllable, Aus commonly has a full vowel, more or less as if 'hos-tell' (but still with the stress on the first syllable). Speakers of GenAm usually have a reduced second syllable in 'a record', but RP generally has a full vowel, more or less as if 'reck-awd'.

Most of these very general statements could be qualified and refined but they offer a brief overview, particularly of those features that are often commented on and mimicked by other speakers who find the features noticeable and characteristic.

It is important to note here the general point that the spoken Englishes of the world have quite different systems of pronunciation, especially in their vowel distinctions. The number of distinct vowel sounds ('phonemes') and the way in which the distinctions are phonetically realized are not constant across the world. But the varieties we are focusing on here – Aus, Can, GenAm, NZ, RP – are usually not highly problematic. Of course newcomers may have to go through a period of adjustment, and even experienced users of English may be confused by a variety of speech that they are not familiar with. But, in general, adjusting to the English pronunciation of, for example, teachers or businesspeople speaking relatively formally will not present major difficulties to those who have some fluency in the language and are aware of the sort of details we have mentioned in this section. This is of course no guarantee that newcomers to a country will find it easy to cope immediately with casual and colloquial conversation at a bus stop, in a pub or at a sports stadium – but even newcomers from English-speaking countries (say Americans in Australia, or Australians in Scotland) may find that difficult!

Grammar

The grammar of English varies much less obviously than pronunciation, and varies very little among the written varieties of Aus, Can,

GenAm, NZ and RP. A few minor variations in grammatical patterns are evident in both speech and writing. For example, Americans use 'gotten' rather than 'got' as the past participle of 'get', as, for instance, in 'he had gotten the wrong key from the janitor'. There are also some variations in past forms of verbs, such as 'dived' or 'dove'. Some British and Australian people are surprised or amused by the title of an American film 'Honey, I Shrunk the Kids', which they think should be 'I shrank'. In fact there is considerable variation of this kind, but in most cases one of the variants is widely considered non-standard. Thus some people, in various parts of the English-speaking world, may say 'I rung him up' (standard: 'I rang him up'), 'I seen her yesterday' (standard: 'I saw her yesterday') or 'he come round for a chat' (standard: 'he came round for a chat'), but these non-standard forms are not likely to be heard in formal educated discourse nor to appear in print.

There are also some differences in the use of prepositions (including whether a preposition is used at all): Americans typically say 'on the weekend' compared with British 'at the weekend', Americans may 'protest a decision' where the British are more likely to 'protest at a decision' or 'protest against a decision', and Americans may either 'write to someone' or simply 'write someone' whereas British usage rarely omits the 'to'.

Differences such as these are noticeable and may even irritate some users of the language. In Australia, for example, traditional usage tends to follow British patterns, but many younger speakers adopt some of the American patterns (such as 'on the weekend') and may be criticized by some older speakers for picking up 'Americanisms'.

Spoken English of a very informal kind reveals far more grammatical diversity, not only in the past tenses of verbs already mentioned, like 'he rung me up', but also in the use of forms like 'ain't' (as a contraction for several possibilities including 'am not, is not, are not, have not') and various non-standard negative constructions, like 'I never seen it' (standard: either 'I've never seen it' or 'I didn't see it') or 'I ain't done nothing' (standard: 'I haven't done anything'). The effects of general education are such that the grammar of formal written English is quite conformist (even though many of the now non-standard forms were once widely used and tolerated) and non-standard variants are likely to be edited out, if not by authors themselves then by careful editors and proofreaders.

Thus the impact of grammatical variation should not be exaggerated. Formal written English of the kind found in scientific journals, academic textbooks and 'serious' newspapers and magazines does not vary radically in its grammar. Formal written English, in its restricted contexts, functions remarkably well as a relatively consistent vehicle of international communication.

Vocabulary and idiom

English reveals a rich variety of vocabulary and idiom, ranging from local discourse about landscape, political and social institutions, buildings, cultural events, sports, and so on, to colloquial expressions and slang. Australians talk of being 'on the electoral roll' (registered to vote), usually refer to an owner-occupied flat or apartment as 'a unit', and, in colloquial mode, describe workers' compensation as 'compo' and a day's sick leave as 'a sickie' (especially if the sickness is not genuine). Canadians talk of 'ridings' (political constituencies) and of 'anglophone' and 'francophone' citizens. New Zealanders may talk of 'a bach' (a holiday house) and of 'a section' (a plot or block of land). And so on.

Some of the variation is of course related to – although rarely fully explained by – differences in situation and culture. Australians distinguish between the 'Prime Minister' (the leader of the government in the federal parliament) and the 'Premier' (the leader of the government in one of the state parliaments). Thus Australia has one Prime Minister, but each of the states of Australia – New South Wales, Victoria, Queensland, and so on – has its own Premier. The United Kingdom has a Prime Minister but the country is not politically organized as a federation. Hence in Britain 'Premier' is virtually a synonym of 'Prime Minister' and is often used in the newspapers to refer to the 'prime ministers' of countries other than Britain. The United States of America has neither Prime Minister nor Premiers (although of course the words are used to refer to the leaders of other countries) but has its own institutional roles, including 'President' (of the USA) and 'Governor' (of a state).

Similarly, physical differences among the English-speaking countries, and differences in the way that land has been settled and used, may be reflected in different vocabulary and different ways of using that vocabulary. The word 'prairie', for example, refers to the large, relatively flat expanses of grassy land found in parts of North America. Britain simply does not have such terrain. Australia does have some large plains, but they are mostly dry and not thickly covered in grass, and they are not referred to as 'prairies'. On the other hand, a 'moor' is an area of higher ground, with poor soil covered with grass or heather or other low vegetation, which is a feature of some parts of Britain. Comparable terrain in other countries is usually not defined or identified in the same way. The word 'stream' is relatively common in Britain to describe a small river, but rare in this sense outside Britain. In Australia and North America, small rivers are often called 'creeks', a word which in Britain refers to relatively long and narrow inlets from the sea. The reason why 'creek' is used in this different way may be that when English-speakers first began to map Australia and North America they approached from the sea. What at first seemed an inlet of the ocean might be called a 'creek'; when the inlet later proved to be the mouth of a small river, the term 'creek' was easily extended to the river itself.

The word 'bush' has come to be used in Australia and New Zealand (as well as in parts of Africa) to mean the more sparsely settled parts of the country, away from the large cities, somewhat as British people speak of the 'country' or 'countryside'. But of course the Australian bush is far larger, less cultivated and less populated than the British countryside and a number of expressions (some of which are now known and used around the world, even in countries like Britain where there is no 'bush' in the Australian sense) reflect a sharp distinction between the bush and the city. A contrast between two radical alternatives, or a choice between everything and nothing, may be referred to as 'Sydney or the bush'; or 'bush' is used as a verb, in passive structures, as in 'we were bushed', meaning initially 'we were totally lost (in the bush)' but now more commonly 'we were totally exhausted'. (See Chapter 4 for more about 'the bush'.)

In some cases there is no longer any obvious reason why words and idioms are localized. The word 'fortnight' meaning 'two weeks', is common in Britain and Australia, but rare in the USA. The word 'highway' was once common in Britain, but is no longer the usual term for a main road, although it survives in common usage outside Britain – and indeed the word is likely to strike the British as an 'Americanism', even though the word is common in other countries as well, such as Australia. (The subsequent chapters will give more details of the spread of – and resistance to – 'Americanisms'.)

Many of the colloquial expressions used to refer to people, to describe people's moods, to greet friends, and so on, are local: some are quite short-lived; some survive long periods; some remain local in flavour; some spread to other countries. The word 'bloke', for example, is a colloquialism for a man (as in 'I saw this bloke in the car park'). It is widely used in informal speech, in Australia, Britain and New Zealand in particular, and there is evidence that the word has been around for at least 150 years. By contrast, the word 'sheila' is an equally colloquial term for a woman or girl (as in 'there were a couple of sheilas coming out of the cafe') but the word has a peculiarly Australian flavour. It is actually not very common in modern Australian speech and, when it is used, may be humorous or self-conscious, but the word is nevertheless known outside Australia as an Australianism and tends to be quoted as an example rather more than its usage deserves.

Illustrating colloquialisms further from words to do with anger and stupidity, Australians have used the word 'ropable' to mean 'angry' or 'bad-tempered' (as of a bull needing to be roped) but the word is unlikely to be heard nowadays except from older Australians. The word 'crook' meaning 'angry' in expressions like 'he went crook at me' (he got very angry with me) is also a typical Australian usage, but again probably becoming rarer among younger speakers. The word 'mad', in a similar sense of 'angry' rather than 'crazy', was once regarded as American usage, but has now become quite common around the English-speaking world. The word 'daft', meaning 'silly' or 'stupid', remains typically British, although it is not unknown outside Britain.

Among greetings, the informal 'hello' and 'hi' are common around the world, as are the more formal 'good morning' and 'good afternoon'. 'Good day' is old-fashioned in most of the English-speaking world, but does have a colloquial use in Australia, often abbreviated to 'g'day', although it is probably becoming rare in city speech (see Chapter 4 for warnings about its use). In Britain the question 'how are you?', following an initial greeting, is an enquiry about someone's health or condition, but it is conventional to reply positively ('Very well, thanks!' or 'I'm fine, how are you?', for example) rather than to take the question too seriously and to give details of one's backache or incipient influenza. In Australia, however, the question may be used as a greeting, even to strangers, often without real expectation of any reply at all. (Details of greetings and styles of interacting will be found in the various chapters that follow this one.)

Of course not all local expressions are mysterious to other speakers of English. Some words have been shared by some countries for many years, like 'lollies' (sweets, candy) and 'wharfie' (docker, waterside worker), which are in use in both Australia and New Zealand. Moreover, the international circulation of films, television programmes, magazines and books means that English speakers are increasingly exposed to a variety of expression. Most of the English-speaking world sees American films and television programmes; many British television programmes are shown in Australia and New Zealand; in recent years Australian television programmes have become popular in Britain; and so on. Of course the forces are not equally balanced: Australians living in Sydney have relatively little knowledge of Canada and Canadian English, are more familiar with New Zealand English but scarcely influenced by it, and are much more aware of British and American English. Canadians are very aware of the USA as their powerful southern neighbour, whereas Canada looms nowhere near as large in the consciousness of the USA. But being aware of other usage does not necessarily mean imitating it. Australians who regularly watch American films may gain a good knowledge of American idiom and may mimic it from time to time without regularly using all the expressions they come to understand. For some Canadians, familiarity with American usage may be a strong motive to resist the American model and to assert their Canadianness (see Chapter 5).

We must also recognize that some of the vocabulary of English which seems to have local colour is in fact international. The words 'boomerang' and 'kangaroo' may have come into English from indigenous languages of Australia, but they are not really Australianisms. A boomerang in a museum in New York or Edinburgh is still a boomerang; an argument can 'boomerang' in London or Auckland as well as in Melbourne or Alice Springs; and a Canadian or New Zealander who describes something as 'shaped like a boomerang' is not thereby talking Australian English. The same applies to most of the words for flora, fauna and artefacts which have come into English from indigenous languages in Canada, New Zealand and the USA. Words like 'moose, toboggan, kiwi (the bird and the fruit), hickory, skunk, moccasin, totem', for example, can all be considered international English, despite their origin in one particular country.

As we noted above at the end of the section on grammar, formal written English of the kind found in scientific journals and academic textbooks does not vary radically, whether in its grammar or vocabulary. Much of the regional variation in vocabulary and idiom is colloquial and some of it rarely finds its way into writing or print. There are other differences, such as the political and geographic terms illustrated at the beginning of this chapter, but these remain a relatively small proportion of the total resources of English.

Overview

In summary, while the pronunciation of English differs radically among the English-speaking countries, the written form of the language is relatively uniform. This is in part the consequence of a conservative spelling system, now remarkably standardized across the English-using world in such a way that the vast majority of words have a single approved spelling – despite the fact that these correct spellings often do not match pronunciation in any sensible way and that even well-educated and experienced users of English are known to make spelling mistakes. The standard spellings of Britain and America do diverge in some respects, but the words affected are a very small proportion of English vocabulary.

There are also substantial regional differences in English vocabulary and idiom, far more noticeably in speech and informal writing than in formal texts published for a wide audience. When reading journals, textbooks or international magazines, those who are interested in what they are reading are not likely to find regional variation a serious obstacle to understanding. But learners who want to enter into conversation and informal discourse in an English-speaking country are likely to find it necessary to learn local words and expressions. The following chapters will take the reader into further detail about English in each of our five countries. This chapter has been no more than a quick tour of the landscape to be explored and enjoyed. More detailed discussion of how English varies across the world can be found in Bauer (2002), Crystal (2003) and McArthur (2002).

Tasks and exercises

1. Choose a page from a printed text. (You could take a page from this chapter.) Identify as many words as you can that have a different spelling in British and American usage. Roughly what percentage of words on the page had alternative spellings?

2. Take a paragraph from the same page and read it aloud to listen to the pronunciation. If possible, get other readers from different parts of the English-speaking world to read the same paragraph and take note of particular points of variation in pronunciation.

3. What do the following words mean and what different meanings do they have in different parts of the English-speaking world?
- biscuit
- chips
- creek
- crook
- station

4. If you had difficulty with exercise 3, why was this? What English language dictionaries are available to you and what information do they give about regional variation? If you are not satisfied that you can answer exercise 3, find out whatever you can about sources of information on vocabulary.

5. What, if anything, is regionally distinctive about the following phrases?
- Monday through Friday
- a fortnight ago
- a quarter after six
- a storm in a teacup
- good on you!

References

Bauer, L. (2002) *An Introduction to International Varieties of English*. Edinburgh: Edinburgh University Press.

Crystal, D. (2003) *English as a Global Language* (2nd edn). Cambridge: Cambridge University Press. [First edition 1997]

Graddol, D., Leith, D. and Swann, J. (eds) (1996) *English: History, Diversity and Change*. London: Routledge.

Jones, D. (1963) *English Pronouncing Dictionary* (12th edn). London: J.M. Dent. [First edition 1917]

Jones, D., Roach, P., Hartman, J. and Setter, J. (2003) *English Pronouncing Dictionary* (16th edn). Cambridge: Cambridge University Press.

McArthur, T. (1992) *The Oxford Companion to the English Language*. Oxford: Oxford University Press.

McArthur, T. (2002) *Oxford Guide to World English*. Oxford: Oxford University Press.

Payne, J. (1995) *Spelling*, COBUILD English Guide 8. London: HarperCollins.

Rosewarne, D. (1984) Estuary English, *The Times Educational Supplement*, 19 October.

Upton, C., Kretschmar, W.A. Jr and Konopka, R. (2003) *The Oxford Dictionary of Pronunciation for Current English*. Oxford: Oxford University Press.

Wells, J.C. (1982) *Accents of English* (3 vols). Cambridge: Cambridge University Press.

Wells, J.C. (2000) *Longman Pronunciation Dictionary* (2nd edn). Harlow: Pearson Education. [First edition 1997]

3 British shibboleths

Michael Sharwood-Smith

Introduction

Some cultures have the reputation of being impenetrable. That of Japan, for example, is sometimes claimed to be incomprehensible to foreigners. George Mikes (a British humorist of Hungarian origin) tells the story of an American journalist who amazed her Japanese male audience by hugely enjoying a joke one of them had just told. When asked if she had really understood the joke, the American confirmed that she had, whereupon the Japanese joke-teller exclaimed: 'Oh dear, I must have told it the wrong way!' The need to be inscrutable to outsiders is presumably a strategy of self-protection, a way of protecting your identity as a member of a particular culture. We all need to belong somewhere and to feel we belong. To know something that needs no special explanation for others in your own culture helps to foster that sense of belonging.

To be special, to have a separate identity, means being rather mysterious to outsiders. Some cultures appear to be more mysterious to outsiders than others. One might suspect the British, another island people but at the opposite end of the Eurasian land mass from the Japanese, of being one of the more mysterious ones. But every nation seems to feel the need to create its own cultural 'shibboleths' – test words, things which detect outsiders, especially when the outsiders are trying to be insiders. The name is derived from a story reported in the Bible (in the book of Judges, ch. 12, vv. 5 and 6). After a battle in which Gileadites had defeated Ephraimites, some of the Ephraimites were trying to slip away across a river, but the Gileadites were stopping strangers and making them say 'shibboleth'. Ephraimites pronounced the word as 'sibboleth' and thus betrayed their identity. Much more recently, the Dutch are supposed to have had a shibboleth of their own when their country was occupied by German forces during the Second World War. If someone claimed to be Dutch but was suspected of being a German, the conversation might turn to the town of Scheveningen. The Dutch pronounce the initial 'sch' as [s] followed by the velar fricative [x]. (This [x] sound is like the Scottish 'ch' in 'loch' or Spanish 'j' in 'Juan'.) But Germans pronounce initial 'sch' more or less as an English 'sh' as in 'ship', and they find the Dutch [sx] a difficult combination of sounds.

Knowing the cultural shibboleths may not always save you from trouble but, for people who wish to perform easily and appropriately in a second language, it is an important way to get inside the culture and at least reduce their chances of getting into trouble. Shared knowledge is an important factor in everyday communication and native speakers do not need to explain this shared knowledge to each other. Without this shared knowledge, non-native speakers will miss a lot.

It is not always a good thing to behave like an insider, especially when you only know a little. Being an obvious outsider can elicit sympathy from insiders: they recognize you as being deficient and in need of help. But, despite the risks attached to appearing to be 'too good' in a foreign language and culture, knowing about the more subtle or less explicitly mentioned aspects of the target culture brings tremendous benefits in terms of insights and feeling at home in a language.

It is impossible to cover all the relevant aspects of British culture within this chapter, but becoming aware of some of them should remind students that knowing the vocabulary and grammar of English is often not enough to understand the linguistic behaviours of British people in different situations. That is, it ought to sensitize students of the language to misunderstandings that can happen without them ever really noticing that anything is wrong. What is dealt with in this chapter, then, is a broad selection of phenomena, including ways of reacting to specific situations, knowledge of customs, holidays and nicknames, and humorous ways of viewing different places and the people that inhabit them. Customs, cultural shibboleths, stereotypes and the like should become part of any student's educational experience in a language.

Finally, a warning is in order about what are sometimes gross generalizations about people's behaviour. People love their stereotypes since they give structure to life and are reassuring. At the same time, these generalizations are like rules which are often broken in real life. Many generalizations represent wrong or partly wrong perceptions. Not everyone in England has cornflakes for breakfast and turkey at Christmas, nor do all English people automatically say sorry when bumped into, even if it was not their fault. Not all Scots wear a kilt and are careful with their money. And there are also differences in speech and custom between generations: the culture never stops changing. Nevertheless, what I have called shibboleths do represent important tendencies in the culture and they have consequences for the use of the language.

The way to uncover the cultural secrets of a nation, in this case Britain, is 'contrastively'. That is, students should ask themselves what they would do and say in various situations both in their own country and in Britain. By doing this, you will be more aware of things you have taken for granted and more sensitive to potential differences in the culture you are learning about.

When students contrast their own culture, which they may not have thought about much previously, with a target culture, they often go through three phases: a phase of denial (there can be no serious differences, we all act in the same ways), a phase of criticism (my way is right and the other way is bizarre or ridiculous) and then a phase of relativism (both ways can be silly or reasonable depending on your point of view).

First, when confronted with differences, a student may exhibit blank disbelief that there can be any other way of behaving in a given situation. We are all products of a complex cultural process but we do not normally have a sense of being culturally programmed in any way. What we do is simply 'right'. By implication, anything else is 'wrong'. In the phase of criticism, students accept that there is a cultural difference but, maintaining their cultural beliefs, they perceive the target variant as 'silly', 'exaggerated', 'unnecessarily polite', 'needlessly impolite', 'hypocritical' or 'just plain rude'. It often takes some effort to move on to the next phase and to see the target variant as a different way of solving or dealing with a problem that is common to both cultures. If students do not move to this third phase, they can of course learn the sociocultural rules of the new culture but are not likely to practise them with conviction.

Before we explore British culture as it is today, we turn to a British perspective on how English came to be a world language. The next section is a historical outline, and the section after that will sketch the geography and current political organization of the British Isles.

Historical background

Around 2,000 years ago, the British Isles were the home of Celtic peoples, speaking languages related to modern Irish and Welsh. There were no such people as the English, and no English language.

From AD 43, the Romans began to occupy Britain and made much of the island part of their empire, but never conquered Scotland or Ireland. The Romans built towns, with baths and amphitheatres, and established estates, but Britain was far from Rome and troublesome to keep subdued. At one time, a tenth of the Roman army was stationed in Britain. Soon after AD 400, the Romans withdrew from Britain. Traces of their occupation remain in the ruins of buildings, in the routes of some old straight roads and in place names ending in '-caster', '-cester' or '-chester' (all from the Latin *castra*, a military camp). The countryside remained Celtic – as much of it had even during the Roman occupation.

The history of England and the English language begins from around AD 450, when Germanic peoples from the mainland of Europe (related to those we now call Frisians, Dutch and Germans) began to settle in Britain. These peoples are usually referred to as the Anglo-Saxons or Angles, although they were probably not all Angles or Saxons. They established kingdoms over most of what is now England (from 'Angle-land') and, while there is evidence that Celts may have continued to live in pockets of territory in England, Celtic Britain was henceforth reduced to western and northern parts of the island.

Anglo-Saxon England was initially quite turbulent, with kingdoms at war with one another, but as one or another kingdom became dominant, its ruler might be recognized as the ruler of England. From around AD 600 onwards, the Anglo-Saxons became Christians and the introduction of writing (previously unknown to the Anglo-Saxons) as well as the adoption of a common new religion were important early factors in unifying England and its language.

After the adoption of Christianity, Ireland (still Celtic) and England became possibly the most civilized countries of Europe. The period from around 650 to 900 saw the translation of many Latin works into Old English and the writing of poetry and chronicles in Old English. Incursions by Danes (or Vikings) from around AD 800 were a threat to Anglo-Saxon civilization, but the processes of resisting and then compromising with the invaders were further significant factors in the development of England as a nation: not only did England form something like a modern navy and militia, but it also developed what was probably Europe's most well-organized government, with a system of shires and shire courts, military duties and tax obligations.

But Britain was not yet free of invasions, and in 1066 William of Normandy (William the Conqueror) led what is probably the most famous invasion in British history. The Normans were actually of Viking descent (Northmen) but they had settled in northern France and spoke a kind of French. England was rapidly brought under Norman control and the land was divided among the conquerors. The country remained Christian, but William controlled the Church. The people were English, but they were now ruled by a French aristocracy who owned the land.

For at least 150 years after the Norman Conquest, a form of French and an early form of English co-existed in England, and English still shows enormous influences from French. A comparison of English with related Germanic languages like Dutch and German reveals that English has hundreds of common words of French origin, words like arrive, boil, carry, certain, chase, doubt, face, join, level, move, quarter, reply, sort, stomach, turn, value, and voice, many of them displacing earlier Old English words.

In this period of Norman rule, England began a long orientation to France, such that, even in times of hostility or war between France and England, France generally remained the model of high culture for the English. Even today, English people who otherwise use little or no French accept French terms in cooking (*haute cuisine*) and fashion (*haute couture*), while products associated with elegance and affluence, like champagne and perfume, are often advertised in the English-speaking world with an overt appeal to their Frenchness.

But the French language, despite its influence and prestige, never seriously threatened to replace English as the language of England. By 1300, England had lost Normandy – although England continued to claim and sometimes control parts of France until the sixteenth century – and French had become a foreign language, even for the nobility. In fourteenth-century England, the English language, in a form called Middle English by today's language historians, was well established as the national language, despite considerable dialect variation across the country. In this century, Geoffrey Chaucer was writing his *Canterbury Tales* in English and John Wycliffe, an Oxford professor, was advocating the translation of the Bible into English (even though Wycliffe and his followers were judged heretical at the time).

By 1300, England had also begun to extend its territory. The English were often at war with the Celtic territory of Wales, and in 1301, after the death of the last Welsh prince, the invading English king, Edward I, named his son the Prince of Wales and commenced the process of amalgamating Wales with England. Since then the title of Prince of Wales has been regularly carried by the eldest son of the king or queen of England, and Wales is now, technically, a principality within the United Kingdom.

By 1600, England was a powerful country, nationalistic and expansive. Wales had been incorporated into the kingdom and English had become the language of administration, education and trade, thus making Wales the first of many countries to undergo a take-over by England and the English language. Under King Henry VIII, the English church had been detached from Roman papal authority and the Prayer Book and liturgy of what was now the Church of England were in English. English literature was flourishing and Shakespeare was only the most famous of many popular poets and playwrights. Many English-speaking people today still look back to Shakespeare's works, the Authorized Version of the Bible in English (first published 1611) and the Book of Common Prayer, as some of the finest examples of written English, even though the language is now old-fashioned by twenty-first-century standards and at times quite obscure to modern readers. (For example, when Shakespeare's Juliet asks 'wherefore art thou Romeo?', she asks 'why are you Romeo?', a meaning that is lost on many modern readers, who assume that 'wherefore' has something to do with asking 'where', rather than understanding that 'wherefore' was simply an earlier form for 'why'. When the Prayer Book speaks of rulers administering justice 'indifferently', it means 'impartially' rather than the modern sense of 'indifferently'.)

Under Henry VIII's daughter, Elizabeth I, the English navy (assisted by storms, it must be said) defeated the Spanish Armada in 1588, and English sailors had begun to roam the high seas in search of wealth and glory. Ireland was attacked and, in 1603, completely conquered. In the same year, England and Scotland were united by the more peaceful strategy of 'a union of the crowns': the two countries remained separate kingdoms, each with their own parliament, but were now ruled by one monarch. James VI, King of Scotland, now became also James I, King of England. But the partnership was not to endure as an equal one. In 1707, an Act of Union dissolved the Scottish Parliament and expanded the English Parliament as a British Parliament. Under that Act, Scotland has nevertheless kept its own legal and educational systems and its own Protestant Church of Scotland. Many Scottish people have had misgivings about the union, but it was only in the late 1990s that the reinstitution of a Scottish Parliament, under some kind of genuinely federal relationship with England, became a serious possibility.

It was from around 1600 that English began to expand into territories outside the British Isles. The East India Company was founded in 1600, to promote trade with and settlement in India, and the first permanent English settlement on the mainland of North America dates from 1607. Ultimately, the status of English today, and its use as an international language of commerce, science and scholarship, reflects not just the history of the British Isles and the United Kingdom but the remarkable spread of English to other countries, both to countries where it was introduced as a language of administration and education, such as Bangladesh, Ghana, India, Nigeria, Pakistan, Sri Lanka, Malaysia, Nigeria and Singapore, and to countries where an English-speaking settler population became the dominant group, as in Australia, Canada, New Zealand and the United States of America. In particular it is the USA who, after declaring their independence from Britain in 1776, not only acquired further territory in North America and expanded their population to become one of the largest and most populous countries in the world, but also developed industrially and economically to become the world's great superpower. Other chapters in this book will deal with the divergent development of an English-speaking culture in each of these countries.

At home, Britain became a rich country in the seventeenth century, partly because of its colonial trade and military successes. The creation of a permanent national debt from 1693 was a sign of wealth, not poverty – the country could afford a national debt! – and the Bank of England (chartered in 1694) and the stock exchange in London were to become institutions with far-reaching financial power. By the early nineteenth century, relative political stability, economic prosperity, increasing control of infectious diseases such as smallpox, and the development and application of steam power and other technical innovations which revolutionized mining and manufacturing provided a basis for enormous growth in power and influence. In about 50 years, from around 1780 to 1830, the amount of coal mined in Britain multiplied by four, while the production of cotton textiles increased twelvefold. Truly this was an 'industrial revolution', making Britain 'the workshop of the world'.

The United Kingdom today

The homeland of the English language – the area in which the language first developed as English and the area from which it has spread through colonization and commerce – is in the island of Britain, off the coast of north-western Europe. Britain is actually part of a group of islands known as the British Isles: the two main islands are Britain (some 230,000 sq. km.) and Ireland (some 85,000 sq. km.) and the others are much smaller in size, including the Isle of Man, which lies between Britain and Ireland, as well as many offshore islands close to Britain and Ireland.

The island of Britain is sometimes referred to as Great Britain. This name was originally not motivated by any sense of imperial grandeur but to distinguish the island of Great Britain from an area in western France known as Less Britain (compare modern Brittany, French *Bretagne*). The people known to the Romans as *Britanni* were Celts who at one time occupied both Britain and Brittany, hence the need to distinguish the two Celtic territories.

The political organization of the British Isles is complex and causes some confusion in terminology. The island of Britain consists of three countries: the largest is England (over 130,000 sq. km., covering most of the southern two-thirds of the island), the next largest is Scotland (nearly 79,000 sq. km., covering roughly the northern third of the island) and the smallest is Wales (about 20,750 sq. km., to the west of England). Ireland consists of two countries, the Republic of Ireland, with jurisdiction over more than 80 per cent of the island's area, and Northern Ireland. The Republic is sometimes referred to by its Irish name of Eire, and is sometimes simply called Ireland. Northern Ireland is sometimes referred to as Ulster, but this is not strictly accurate. The whole of Ireland was at one time divided into four provinces, and the northern province was called Ulster; but present day Northern Ireland is actually not the whole area of the old province of Ulster, some of which is within the Republic.

England, Scotland, Wales and Northern Ireland form together a nation whose correct title is the United Kingdom of Great Britain and Northern Ireland. This title is often abbreviated as the United Kingdom or the UK. It is common to refer to the country as Britain or Great Britain, but in some contexts it may not be clear whether this means the full UK or just the island of Britain. Many people also say England when they mean to refer to the entire UK, but this is particularly unfortunate. The people of Scotland, Wales and Northern Ireland have every reason to object to the practice: they are citizens of the UK and are in some sense British, but they are not English.

The four states making up the UK have important traditions and distinctive features that set them apart from each other. Scotland, for example, was a separate kingdom until 1603 and retained its own parliament until 1707. To this day there are differences between the Scottish and English legal systems, Scotland prints its own banknotes (although they have values in UK pounds sterling) and there is a distinct tradition of Scottish pronunciation of English, which most Scottish people feel to be a legitimate part of their heritage. It is nevertheless fair to say that England is the dominant country within the UK and that London, the capital of both England and the UK, is dominant as its largest city. The population of England, at over 48 million, is far larger than that of Scotland (just over 5 million), Wales (just under 3 million) and Northern Ireland (about 1.5 million). London,

The British Isles

with a population of around 7 million people (not including the millions more who live close to London and either work in London or are in other ways economically tied to the city) is itself larger than any of the non-English countries of the UK. As such figures may suggest, it is England, governed from London, that has, at various stages of history, conquered, incorporated and absorbed the other areas of the British Isles. Indeed, the whole of Ireland was at one time brought into the UK, and it is only since 1921 that the southern part of Ireland has been once more independent from the UK, and only in 1949 that this territory became the Republic of Ireland. From the long-term perspective of many residents of the British Isles, England has been as much a colonizing power within the British Isles as it has across the oceans.

The UK is now widely regarded by its own citizens as well as others as a country of long tradition and stability, and the very contrast between the old 'homeland' of English and the newer English-speaking countries invites people to think of the UK as old (perhaps negatively as staid and old-fashioned, perhaps positively as solid and stable) in opposition to, say, Australia or the USA as young (perhaps negatively as brash and naive, perhaps positively as fresh and dynamic).

Reality is not that simple of course. It is true that the UK has known no real invasion of its soil for a thousand years, since 1066. But there was considerable warfare within the British Isles for much of these thousand years, including a major civil war in the 1640s, followed by more than ten years in which Britain abolished the monarchy and was ruled as a commonwealth; and the country has faced serious threats of invasion, from the Spanish Armada in the late sixteenth century, from Napoleon's forces in the early nineteenth century and from Hitler in the 1940s. Though the British Isles were not invaded during the Second World War, bombing caused massive damage and the cost of waging war was a heavy burden. It is true also that since its experiment with a commonwealth government in the mid-seventeenth century, Britain has been far more politically stable than most countries, with a unique compromise of a hereditary monarchy (with increasingly restricted powers), a democratically elected house of parliament (the House of Commons) and a house of parliament largely constituted by the hereditary aristocracy (the House of Lords). But it is also true that Britain has known many periods of intense reform and innovation, not only in commerce and industry, as during the Industrial Revolution, but also, for example, in administration in the latter part of the nineteenth century, when the British army and Civil Service were radically reformed and various kinds of privilege and patronage were removed, and in health and education in the years following the Second World War, when the National Health

Service was introduced and private schools were opened up to competitive state-funded entrants.

It would be quite wrong to assume that any of these changes in industry, public administration, health and education were accomplished as a smooth, universally accepted transition, and Britain today is not as smugly self-confident as this little sketch might suggest. Europe increasingly dominates the thinking of modern 'Brits' (as they are sometimes called by other English-speaking people). They have become more inclined to learn languages than their American cousins across the Atlantic, and the different regions of the UK, outside England, have begun to assert themselves. Now, as a result of devolution, Scotland has its own parliament again, elected by a system of proportional representation and with the power to raise taxes. The Welsh have an assembly which cannot raise taxes but nonetheless gives the Welsh considerable power to run their internal affairs. In both systems, the title 'Prime Minister' is not used, but rather 'First Minister', and, in the case of Scotland, perhaps reflecting unease in Westminster about Scottish nationalism, the word 'government' is avoided and instead the Scots have a 'Scottish Executive'. For the first time, some of the English are asking themselves whether they should have their own English parliament and a special identity like that of the Scots and the Welsh. Perhaps the truth of the matter is that Britain is in transition and the behaviour of the British contains elements of both their former self-confidence and their current insecurity. Since the 1960s, they have shown an ability to produce startling innovations in music, fashion, science and technology while at the same time holding on to many of the old traditions. To everyone's surprise, for example, and despite the wave of criticism of the royal family's treatment of Diana, Princess of Wales, there is no sign that the monarchy is genuinely under threat. While Australians debate the possibility of becoming a republic, an apparently archaic institution like the British monarchy, with all its quaint trappings, has survived in its country of origin into the twenty-first century.

English in the UK and around the world

It is a fascinating fact that a dialect born in the south-eastern corner of a multilingual offshore island, together with an accent spoken by a small minority in that island, has had such a successful worldwide career and has, indeed, come to be the current lingua franca, that is, the language of international communication. From a modern perspective, the most salient reason for this is the economic power of the United States. From a historical point of view, it began with the economic and military might of an island off the coast of mainland Europe.

In the time of Queen Elizabeth I, there were roughly five million speakers of English, mostly in England. When James VI of Scotland ascended the English throne, as James I, in 1603, he brought to the English court speakers of a strange tongue, Scots. Some people might have considered Scots a dialect of English but others might have called it a closely related language. Even then, looking beyond the frontiers of England, you could find other people speaking something like English. Still, as is the case nowadays, the population of the British Isles was concentrated in the part we still call England in fact – in south-eastern England, and with it the population of speakers of English. By the middle of the twentieth century, however, these restless native speakers had travelled far and wide, trading with, and frequently coming into possession of, parts of the world thousands and thousands of miles away.

British 'ownership' of other parts of the world often happened in a haphazard way, not so much because of any long-standing national dream of world domination. The guiding forces were economic, to maintain trade routes. Strictly imperial ambitions appear to have been more of an afterthought or the personal obsessions of individuals. Historians may disagree, but, however it happened, by the mid-twentieth century, the figure of five million had become more like five hundred million. And these speakers were spread over all the world.

One might imagine that the decline of Britain as a world power – even granting that Britain is still an influential country – might have led to the swift adoption of American English as the world standard, to the exclusion of British English. But Britain is still the closest source of English for European countries, and its standard is still strongly established in the educational systems of its former colonial territories outside North America. For some countries, especially for those who are less enamoured of the USA, British English provides a more acceptable variety of the lingua franca. It is also accepted by most users of other standard varieties as an alternative standard. At the same time, British English itself is exposed to the influence of American English and the distance between the two varieties, already not so great, is diminishing with each successive decade. To take two small recent examples, British schools now talk of 'grades' as well as 'marks', and school 'pupils' may also be referred to as 'students'; not so very long ago British speakers would have used the word 'student' only of people who had completed school and were undergoing post-secondary education at a college or university.

In sum, as the British, and more specifically the English, look out from their particular part of a small island across to Australia and Canada and the USA and many other countries in between, they see 'their' language spoken far and wide in various forms and with various accents. These accents amuse and occasionally horrify them but nonetheless this variety of English has provided the British with the reassurance that it is not really necessary for them to learn a foreign language. More than that, the British can cling to the irrational but unsurprising notion that the 'true' form of English is the one spoken in the island where it originated.

The idea of a correct way of speaking English suggests that there is a single standard for all to follow. From afar, it might indeed seem that educated people in Britain all speak one kind of English. Watching British films might lead you to add a few non-standard options, perhaps Cockney, Liverpudlian, Scottish or Irish (depending on the films you watch). In reality, the majority of the inhabitants of the British Isles speak what might be called non-standard English. This is particularly true when it comes to accent. The standard British accent taught all over the world is RP (Received Pronunciation, see Chapter 2) but speakers of RP are a small minority in their own country. Nevertheless, RP is a widely understood accent, free of any regional association within England itself and spoken throughout the UK. It is the most exhaustively described accent in the English language and is still held up as the accent to aim at in many non-English-speaking countries. Within the UK, it is popularly associated with the royal family, the BBC and those who were educated at private schools.

The success of RP is that it is an accent that everyone understands – even though they might not speak it. When the BBC World Service first tried to make its English more representative of the country at large and introduced different accents into its news broadcasts, there was a chorus of complaints from listeners in other countries, and the BBC went back to RP.

If we take 'standard' to refer to grammar and vocabulary, and particularly to written English, not to pronunciation or accent, then the number of users of standard British English is quite large and may be said to include the majority of educated native speakers, whatever accent they happen to speak. As has been mentioned before, standard British English (but not including pronunciation) is really very close to educated English in North America and indeed to educated English around the world.

In spoken English, the various regions of the British Isles not only have local accents but also local vocabulary and idiom. It is therefore not surprising that people from, say, Fife in Scotland or Cardiff in south Wales or Cornwall in south-western England, may sound very different from each other. Not only foreigners but also people from other parts of Britain may have difficulty in understanding some local speech. The reality of Britain is far from the stereotype of a country bursting with RP speakers. And even RP speakers may betray regional traces. (See Chapter 2 for mention of Estuary English, a compromise between RP and local south-eastern accents.) Many people blend in to their accent enough of RP to sound educated and worthy of employment but not enough to be associated with the upper social class that RP traditionally represents.

Attitudes to accents change. The national accents – educated Welsh, Scots and Irish – have always been more socially acceptable in Britain, but since the 1960s the respectability of regional accents has grown considerably. As suggested above, many people even avoid a pure RP for fear of sounding snobbish or, if they are from outside England, 'too English'. Many non-native speakers of English are more conservative in this regard, and as learners are unlikely to be judged 'posh' for speaking RP. When actually visiting the UK, they still need to be prepared for constant exposure to accents that are not RP.

Immigration has made modern Britain a multilingual, multi-ethnic society, but it has always been so since English was first spoken there. Celtic languages, spoken in the British Isles before the arrival of the Germanic peoples who brought what was to become English, have continued to be spoken and survive in several areas. Welsh is enjoying a strong revival and there are even attempts being made to bring Cornish back to life. Moreover, Irish Gaelic (now known simply as Irish) is an official language of the Republic of Ireland. A small percentage of the population of Scotland speaks Scottish Gaelic (not to be confused with Scots, the Germanic language of the old Scottish court referred to earlier) and another closely related Gaelic language, Manx, is spoken on the Isle of Man. But English is of course the main language of the British Isles and is spoken as first language by the vast majority of the population.

Social encounters

Introduction

As a British citizen, albeit expatriate, I have no illusions that any culture in the world is totally superior to any other. You can only really compare particular aspects of cultures. Taking individual aspects, it may be fair to make value judgements, to say, for example, that in this respect the culture seems more efficient or more pleasant (or whatever) than some other cultures. But even if you can make such value judgements, it seems to turn out that all cultures have weaknesses as well as strengths. It seems to be a matter of 'swings and roundabouts' – as the saying goes, 'what you gain on the swings you lose on the roundabouts'.

The paragraphs that follow present a selection from what could be a much larger list of culturally determined ways of verbal interacting characteristic of the British, as well as some elements of British culture that seem to be part of the assumed knowledge of most adult inhabitants of the British Isles and, as such, may frequently be used or referred to in everyday conversation. The starting point is always the question: 'What would a proficient speaker of English as a second language miss out on by not being brought up from birth in the English-speaking community, i.e. the target culture?' More specifically, I asked myself what linguistic behaviour would be expected by native speakers. What assumptions would be made that would lead to misunderstanding because they would not be shared by foreign learners, however good their accent, grammar and vocabulary? The examples are not exhaustive but should be enough to begin the sensitizing process which will hopefully go on throughout language learning.

Here, then, are some examples that illustrate ways of exploring alien cultures and learning to understand the subtle cultural signals effectively. Students are also encouraged to notice facts about their own culture which have not been mentioned in the paragraphs below, write them down and compare them with what happens in Britain.

Students should also be aware of what we might call 'international youth culture', which may obscure some real differences among cultures. If students travel to other countries and interact mainly informally with students of their own age, they may encounter only a few of the cultural differences mentioned in these examples. This is because they are mixing with like-minded people of the same generation in casual situations and not necessarily meeting the full range of cultural habits of the students they are interacting with. It is precisely because it is possible to go to another country and fail to notice differences, to behave inappropriately and never to get corrected, that a course in cross-cultural habits is so important.

Close encounters

An underlying principle of cultural behaviour which is clearly reflected in the language is the need to avoid face-to-face conflict. Even though the British may appear unpleasantly blunt when compared with some Asian cultures, they are on the whole concerned to offer a way out whenever a potential conflict between individuals occurs. This may be compared with public confrontations in large committees or in parliament where much more confrontation goes on. Some cultures are, by way of contrast to the British, much less concerned to avoid conflict in private or personal encounters. Perhaps there is a principle of 'aggression management' here: every culture has developed some way of letting off steam, has some areas in which people are allowed to express their true feelings.

The immediate linguistic consequence of open-conflict-avoidance is that you need to know what to do and what to say – for example, when someone takes a position in a queue in front of you, accidentally stands on your toe in a bus or disagrees with you in a public gathering. In the public gathering, depending upon the nature of the meeting, the British reaction may be to confront disagreement openly and to respond vigorously. In the other more personal situations, the same individual may work hard at taking a middle route between doing nothing and engaging in open conflict. In doing so, he or she will expect a similar co-operative response from the other person, such as an apology like 'Oh, sorry, I didn't realize …'. In other cultures, behaviour might well be the opposite – a great effort to reduce conflict in a public meeting and robust response in the private situations. Within our own cultures, we understand the conventions and know when people are being normally polite or normally outspoken. The difficulties come when we make errors in an unfamiliar environment.

The right approach in a British situation is to treat exchanges between individuals with caution. Avoid conflict. Be slow to take offence and – it is very important to keep this in mind – assume a similar willingness in the people you are dealing with. Even pretend to be in the wrong where this is manifestly not true. Two British people bumping into each other will often both assume they are in the wrong and apologize. In a different culture, both people might assume the other was wrong and there might be an immediate exchange of insults. In both cultures, both participants may really know that one person was to blame, but they handle the situation differently. The people who insult each other may benefit from releasing their emotions, while those who make peace with each other may see the benefit in minimizing the incident and getting on with their lives. In the British style of interaction, the real culprit, relieved that no insult has been forthcoming, will redouble the apologizing and no offence will be caused. This may seem like a crazy attempt to create an illusion of general and consistent goodwill. Less cynically, it can be seen as an extremely efficient way of promoting optimal social harmony so that people can get things done without the disruption that conflict causes. The general principle is to make it easy for the other person, the interlocutor. If this does not work, the situation can then escalate and more open conflict develop.

We should note here that in Britain the phrase 'excuse me' is usually not an apology. The phrase is often used, but to draw someone's attention to something. The general sense is 'Excuse me for interrupting or disturbing you but …'. With a greater degree of urgency, 'excuse me' can be pronounced more loudly or, if niceties are set aside, a simple shout 'Hey' or 'Hoy' or 'Oi' can be used, but these express straightforward annoyance or amusement ('Hey, get off the grass, you!'). When you are trying unsuccessfully to catch the barman's eye in a pub, you might call out loudly with a complaining intonation and ironic politeness 'Excuse me please, can I order now? I've been waiting for ten minutes.' In Britain, if some offence is caused, the words 'Sorry' or 'I apologize' are used, not 'Excuse me'.

If you have caused obvious pain or discomfort, you can emphasize the apology with 'do', 'so' or 'really', as in 'I do apologise', 'I'm so sorry', 'I'm really sorry'. And while we are on the subject of pain, let us also note that the sound you make provides an easy shibboleth. Drop a heavy object on someone's foot. If he or she shouts something like 'Ai-ee!' or 'A-yee!', they are definitely not British – you would expect 'Ow!' or 'Ouch'! Something as basic as a cry of pain is still culturally constrained.

It is usual not to include Sir or Madam in encounters of this type (in contrast to similar terms of address often used in other languages). This reflects a characteristic British preference to avoid formality when possible. This sometimes surprises people, since it goes against the traditional stereotype of the 'polite English'. The point is that formality is not necessarily a marker of politeness. It is quite easy to be formal and rude. Sir and Madam are typically used in British English where there is a predefined relationship like hotel receptionist and guest, or shop assistant and customer, or boss and employee. And even in those relationships the terms may not occur. A shop assistant who met you later outside the shop would no longer call you Sir or Madam.

Even important people are not always addressed as Sir or Madam. It is quite normal for British radio and television journalists to leave out such forms of address in situations where this would be unthinkable rudeness in other countries. Hence the Foreign Secretary of the UK is not addressed as 'Mr Secretary' and often not even as 'Sir'. There is an assumption of equality between speakers that normally excludes this.

Sometimes you may want to be rude or at least to understand the rudeness of others. Swearing and insults are an important part of life. Even if you yourself avoid them on principle, you will certainly encounter them. The British do not spend their whole time being polite. Here there are some interesting things to say about cultural differences. For example, in British English at least, expressions with a religious origin are generally weaker than words referring to bodily functions like 'shit' and the even stronger 'fuck'. (Both of these words are considered quite offensive and 'fuck' in particular is usually edited out of newspaper reports and films intended for a general audience.) In other countries other values may apply. In Scandinavian languages, words connected with the devil are still quite taboo, whereas in English they are quaint, mild and amusing: to say that something is 'devilish difficult', for example, sounds old-fashioned and quite harmless. Again 'damn(ed)' is somewhat old-fashioned and quite mild in English, whereas its equivalent in Dutch is not. Be aware that when English swear words are borrowed into another language, their value may alter. An exclamation of the word 'shit!' is quite strong in English and not to be used freely in public situations; whereas young Dutch or German people who have picked this word up from English-language films and television programmes may use the word as a borrowing in their own language without the same strength or force.

Friendly encounters

We have already noted that the use of Sir and Madam to address people is generally not a sign of friendliness in Britain. A shop assistant or a waiter may call you Sir or Madam, but even they may avoid doing so if they want to appear friendly rather than formal. This is different from the United States where Sir and Madam (or Ma'm) are used more liberally, perhaps following the pattern of some European languages. An interesting principle emerges from this: the British avoid signs of formality wherever there is no established relationship. In this light, some Americans, by using forms of address, strike the British as unnecessarily polite. Excessive politeness creates distance and may be embarrassing or ridiculous. Politeness can even be used sarcastically, as in 'would it be too much trouble to ask you to remove your foot?'

The ideal British approach when dealing with strangers is to be friendly and to keep the situation open, not too distant and not too close. You should assess whether someone wants to be left alone or wants to engage in conversation and react accordingly. You should apologize if you have to interrupt, use 'Excuse me' when trying to attract someone's attention and say 'Sorry' when you have accidentally done something which might cause offence or pain.

British people are not always as quick as other English-speaking people to use first names. In Australia or the USA, for example, neighbours may assume they can use each other's first names from their first meeting, and even someone performing a service like mending your washing machine or fixing your telephone may expect to call you by your first name (although a difference in gender and a large difference in age may limit this easiness). In Britain this may seem too intrusive. While many British people do use each other's first names, it is generally unwise to assume that you can. Allow people, especially senior people, the opportunity to decline formality and to invite you on to first name terms. Often people will then say something like 'Please call me Mary' or 'Please don't call me Mr Jones, the name is Andrew.'

In introductions, some cultures value a certain amount of independence and self-promotion, You want to talk to someone, so you introduce yourself. The norm in British culture is to wait until a friend or host has had a chance to introduce you to a newcomer. That is his or her responsibility to make life easy for you. If that does not happen, you can then say 'I don't think we've met' and then 'My name is ...'. (Offer your own name and the other person should offer theirs; asking someone's name before giving your own is not considered friendly.) If your friend or host hears you introducing yourself, they may well apologize: 'I'm sorry, I thought you knew each other' or 'I'm sorry, I should have introduced you.' Since introductions sound a bit formal they may be accomplished hurriedly, to get them over quickly and resume a relaxed style of interaction.

By way of contrast, if you answer your own telephone, you are not obliged to say who you are. Some British people may do so ('Hello, Mike Sharwood speaking') but many do not, answering the phone with either just their number ('seven one nine, double three seven nine') or simply 'Hello'. It is the responsibility of the caller to say who they are and why they are ringing you. At work, of course, you answer more informatively, with your name or the name of your office or company (e.g. 'Brown and Ledbury, can I help you?' or 'Good morning, Brown and Ledbury'). The more guarded response is appropriate at home – after all, 'an Englishman's home is his castle'.

Friendliness and politeness in English interactions are often supported by the use of modals, especially 'could' and 'would', and sometimes by extra expressions of tentativeness like 'possibly' and 'perhaps', as in 'Could you take a seat and I'll see if Mr Brown is available', 'Would you like to leave your name perhaps?' or 'Could you possibly give me your name, please?' When asking someone the way, you should also be tentative, as if you are almost sure that the person you are asking has better things to do than help you. So, instead of saying 'Where is the exit?' or, worse still, 'Tell me where the exit is', you normally begin with 'Excuse me' (meaning 'excuse me for interrupting you') followed by something like 'could you tell me where the exit is please?' or 'I wonder if you could tell me where the exit is?'

Sometimes the right response to a situation is very difficult to predict. To take one example, if you are with someone in their room or office and you hear a knock at the door but the other person evidently has not heard the knock, what might you say? A British person might say 'I think there's someone at the door' rather than just 'Someone is knocking at the door'. The use of 'think' is not to be taken literally of course. It is just a (very common) mark of tentativeness or deference: it is not your room after all.

If you want to arrange to see someone for professional or business reasons, such as a doctor or a dentist or a university teacher, you make an appointment, usually by telephone. Again, polite wording is called for – for example, 'I wonder if I could make an appointment to see Dr Enderby, please' or 'Could I arrange a time when Professor O'Reilly would be free to see me, please?' The words 'making a date' or 'arranging a date' should be used cautiously, as the term 'dating' (once American but now widespread in the English-speaking world) is particularly used of friendships between members of the opposite sex. To say 'I have a date with Sophie' implies an intimate outing to dinner or a film. If you want to start 'dating' someone, then you would probably avoid the term 'date', for the very reason that it may imply that the other person is already committed to a relationship with you. Better simply to ask the other person whether they would like to go out with you some time (for a meal or some other such simple occasion).

Whether you are 'dating' or simply going out with friends or work colleagues, you will want to go to cafes and restaurants sometimes. But a word like 'cafe' means different things in different countries. A British cafe is typically a place where you go to have coffee or tea, and light meals or snacks, but not alcoholic drinks. It is also assumed that you will sit down at a table and be served. If you are after alcoholic drinks, the right place to go is a pub (short for public house).

In a pub, you do not order your drinks from a waiter – you go to the counter (the bar) and order drinks directly. It is also quite acceptable to stand near the bar, especially when the pub is busy. You can also buy soft drinks in a pub (like lemonade and orange juice) and in recent years many pubs have started to advertise morning coffee or afternoon tea as well.

An important feature of pub culture in Britain is that drinks are ordered in 'rounds', that is, each person will pay for a round of drinks for the group. If the group is so large that it would take too many rounds for everyone to have a turn to pay, the suggestion is usually made to split the group into sub-groups. The other possibility, that everyone pays for themselves, is considered quite unsociable, and is avoided if at all possible. (The term for each person paying for their own food or drinks is 'going Dutch'. Like a few other phrases that come from the days of hostility between the Dutch and English, such as 'Dutch courage', this reflects some distaste for the practice.) Tables and chairs or benches are provided in pubs, but it is also quite normal to stand near the bar or sit on a barstool and there is always a reasonable amount of space for standing in groups. Rounds require a special form of linguistic behaviour. Traditionally the first to enter a pub is the first to approach the bar and order the round, although this is not obligatory. People are expected to take their turn cheerfully, with expressions such as 'What are you having?', 'What are you drinking?', 'What's yours?', 'This one's on me' or 'My round!' (or, using an Australianism, 'My shout!').

When drinking alcohol together, it is common to begin by raising glasses to each other and wishing each other 'Good health!' or 'Your health!' or, more informally, 'Cheers!' But there is no equivalent routine at the beginning of a meal in Britain. Some British people use the French *Bon appetit* and some British waiters have begun copying the American habit of saying 'Enjoy your meal'. But there is actually no set phrase in English corresponding to *Bon appetit,* which is frustrating for people who are used to such a phrase in their own language. In a private house, the host or hostess will simply continue talking while serving food, perhaps saying things like 'I hope you like this' or 'Careful, the plates are hot' or, in very British style, offering apologies like 'Sorry, I think this is a bit overdone' or 'Sorry it's taken so long'. Good British guests of course respond to such apologies with assurances that the food looks wonderful, that it is a very enjoyable evening, and so on. Again frustratingly for many visitors to Britain, there is no simple English word to use as you hand someone a plate or a drink or something else they are waiting for. Many learners translate something from their own language and say 'please' as they offer or give something, but this is quite un-English (another shibboleth!). English speakers sometimes say 'Here you are' but only when some emphasis is required – for example, if the intended recipient isn't aware that something is being offered. Learners sometimes seize on this expression as the phrase to use, but should realize that it is emphatic and not obligatory. Most of the time, English speakers say nothing at all as they hand things to others.

Some eating and drinking habits vary around Britain – and we should make the general point that Britain is not a culturally uniform society in every respect. In the UK, the evening meal can be at any time between about 5 pm (when it is often called tea) and 8 pm. Eating later rather than early seems to be considered more sophisticated, hence the name of a popular brand of mint chocolates *(After Eight)* designed to go with coffee after the meal. But many families eat earlier, especially in northern areas of Britain. There is something of a class distinction here too, perhaps because factory workers have tended to work an earlier day (finishing perhaps at 4.30 p.m.) and eat earlier than office workers and business people (finishing work at perhaps 5.30 or 6.00 p.m.). It may also have to do with the climate, with northern Europeans tending to eat the evening meal earlier than southern Europeans.

Traditionally breakfast in England is a large meal, with cooked food like bacon and scrambled or fried eggs. Few people still seem to eat like this at home but hotels and restaurants keep the tradition alive when they offer a 'full English breakfast', usually as an alternative to a 'Continental breakfast' of toast or croissants with tea or coffee. The custom of eating porridge for breakfast is traditionally associated with Scotland but by no means limited to Scotland nowadays. The meal in the middle of the day is most commonly called 'lunch' but the upper classes used to insist on calling it 'luncheon' and that term is still used for special formal occasions such as a 'literary luncheon'. If you eat your main hot meal at lunchtime you probably call it 'dinner'. If your main hot meal is late in the evening, then you may have 'tea' (with tea to drink and biscuits or cakes to eat) in the afternoon, although the tempo of modern life and work make this something of a luxury, like the English breakfast. In areas like northern England, where the evening meal is likely to be eaten earlier, it may be called 'tea' or 'teameal'. Southern English people may refer to this as 'high tea'. 'Supper' is also a term for an evening meal, but this can also mean a snack late at night before going to bed.

When a new neighbour moves in, tradition dictates, as with introductions, that newcomers should be looked after and should not need to take the initiative. Hence the neighbours make the first move to welcome new arrivals. In large blocks of flats it is increasingly unlikely that people will socialize much with their neighbours and there may be little in the way of welcome at all, but in smaller communities neighbours may still try to be neighbourly.

The British are by no means unfriendly but it is unfortunate that some of their behaviour, particularly in southern and south-eastern parts of England, does strike outsiders as reserved, sometimes even as cold. Often, as with some of the features we have mentioned above, such as a certain reluctance to introduce yourself to strangers and a hesitation over using first names, the motive is not at all hostile but a concern not to impose on other people, a concern not to demand attention and friendship from other people who may prefer to be left alone. Even the rather elaborate English wording of requests like 'Could I perhaps have a timetable, please?' or 'I wonder if you could possibly change a ten-pound note for me, please?', which is motivated, from the English perspective, by a desire not to be blunt and demanding, may seem to outsiders to be fussy and distant. Here once more we have to remind ourselves that it is dangerous to judge one culture from the perspective of another. The most generous view of English politeness is that it is highly considerate of others, respecting privacy and personal space. But that will not always be obvious to newcomers.

Feasts and holidays

Although modern Britain is a secular, multi-ethnic society, the predominant model for holidays and celebrations (and for many other language-related things) is a Christian one, whether or not people actually are practitioners of that faith. Many cultures celebrate Christmas of course, but they may celebrate it in different and sometimes surprising ways. For example, Christmas Eve is less of a family celebration in England than elsewhere and the big day is 25

December, Christmas Day, when children get their presents. Presents are supposedly delivered by the imaginary man who comes down the chimney, Santa Claus or Father Christmas. Some children may leave out a sock or stocking for small presents, while larger presents will be placed under the Christmas Tree. But many families have their own variations on this theme.

A typical feature of the Christmas meal, which could be at any time after midday, is roast turkey (or in an even older tradition, roast goose) served with various vegetables, followed by a rich plum pudding or 'Christmas pudding'. At the meal, there may be Christmas crackers on the table, tubes of shiny, coloured paper about 25 cm long, twisted at both ends and containing a paper hat, a little present and a strip of paper with a joke. When pulled from both ends, the cracker makes a small explosion and the contents fall out on the table, and people then put on the paper hats, read out the jokes and generally compare and contrast the contents of the crackers. At Christmas time people also eat small mince pies, which are sweet, the mince being a sticky concoction of dried fruits, not minced meat.

Families often play traditional games together at Christmas and television provides seasonal programmes. Outside the home, there may be public performances of Christmas concerts and pantomimes. Despite its name, a pantomime ('panto' for short) is not mimed but spoken (part in rhyme) and sung. Pantomimes are musical comedies designed for families, based on children's fairy tales like *Cinderella*, *Aladdin* and *Puss in Boots*. They usually contain slapstick (physical) comedy and some jokes designed to be obscure to young children but entertaining to adults. There is always a pantomime 'dame', a leading older female role played by a man, and a young male 'hero' or 'prince' role, played by a woman. A special attraction is that famous characters from British television often go to regional cities and towns to play one of the main roles in the local pantomime.

The time for fireworks in the UK is 5 November, Bonfire Night, which commemorates the capture of conspirators (in the Gunpowder Plot) who were planning to blow up the king and parliament in 1605 (or so it is alleged). Effigies of the chief conspirator, Guy Fawkes, are burned on large bonfires. Before Bonfire Night, children may wheel these effigies around collecting 'money for the guy'.

The New Year is one of the occasions when the British show that they are not always reserved. On New Year's Eve, 31 December, people gather in central places, such as Trafalgar Square in London, where the police try to restrict the numbers of people for safety reasons and board over the fountains to stop people dancing in the freezing water. Similar noisy public merrymaking takes place in other cities, especially in Scotland which has traditionally celebrated New Year's Eve (known there as Hogmanay) more than Christmas. The scene in George Square in Glasgow rivals that in Trafalgar Square, while Edinburgh is now promoting its public Hogmanay festivities as the biggest party in Europe. Scotland also has the custom of 'first-footing', entering a house after midnight as the first visitor of the new year. Tradition has it that if the first person to set foot in your house is black-haired or has something black, it will bring you good luck for the rest of the year.

A more recent tradition is the Last Night of the Proms (the final night of the Henry Wood Promenade Concerts, held in the summer in London's Albert Hall and designed to bring classical music to a wider audience). Here the audience look and behave like a friendly and mildly disrespectful football crowd. The musical programme is treated as fun and in some items the audience join in or even compete with the orchestra. The concert is usually televised within and beyond the UK.

The Bank Holidays (May Day and the August Bank Holiday) have no religious significance and simply take their name from the closure of banks (but they are now holidays for everyone, not just bank employees). The August Bank Holiday in particular is marked by enormous traffic congestion as families rush in their thousands to seaside resorts and then return in the evening. England does not have the sensible Scottish custom of staggering holidays and having different times for different cities.

British regional and national shibboleths

There are countless events associated with the particular regions of the UK. Some of them are quite well known to the majority of inhabitants of the British Isles, even if only from television, radio or reading about them in the papers and, as such, they may be said to be an important part of British culture. There are events in a variety of areas, ranging from the Grand National, an annual steeplechase (a horse race with ditches and obstacles which the horses must jump) held at Aintree, Liverpool, and the Oxford and Cambridge Boat Race (a rowing race between the two universities on the Thames in London), to the National and International Eisteddfods in Wales, which feature poetry, music and dancing. In Scotland, there are Highland Games, featuring such contests as 'tossing the caber' (throwing a huge log as far as you can) and Highland dancing. On such occasions, Scotsmen may wear the kilt, a garment like a heavy skirt, now part of the popular image of Scotland, but actually a nineteenth-century romantic stylization of (the bottom half of) traditional dress once worn by Scottish Highlanders, in which a tartan cloth is flung around the waist and shoulders like a short toga. Similar to a Welsh eisteddfod is an Irish or Scottish ceilidh (pronounced as if written like the name Caley), a social gathering devoted to folk music, singing, dancing and story-telling.

Also, some British views and attitudes are connected with regional diversity within the UK. For instance, there are many nicknames for people from various parts of the British Isles. The English may call a Scotsman 'Jock', a Welshman 'Taffy' and an Irishman 'Paddy' or 'Mick'. These terms may be used both to address someone ('Where are you going, Jock?') and to refer to the whole group ('Jocks make good soldiers') but they are often used in jokes and insults and not always welcomed. Outsiders are not advised to use them. The Scots and the Welsh have words for the English based on the word 'Saxon', Scottish 'Sassenach' and Welsh 'Sais' (pronounced to rhyme with 'nice' but not always used nicely). There are also many slang terms for people from smaller regions, for example 'Scouse' (rhyming with 'house') for Liverpool and 'Geordie' for the Tyneside area of north-eastern England. Some of these terms are quite local or vary in meaning locally: for example, while some Scots use 'Sassenach' to mean an English person, some Scottish Highlanders may use the term to refer to Lowland Scots (who are mostly of Anglo-Saxon and Norman descent rather than Celtic). When southern English people speak of 'the North' or 'the North Country' or 'northerners' they are referring to northern England, not to Scotland, and as southerners they may even include some areas of 'the Midlands' (around Birmingham and Coventry) in their loose conception of 'the North'.

Since there is still considerable regional diversity in the pronunciation of English in the British Isles, many people are aware of some of the distinctive features, and these are often linked with characterizations and stereotypes. In the Midlands and north of England, many people pronounce words like 'bus, cup, mug' with a vowel that sounds to southerners more like the 'oo' of (RP) 'book, good, look', rather than their lower back vowel. In return, northerners say that the southern or RP pronunciation of 'cup, mug' makes these words sound like 'cap, mag'. Neither perception is based on accurate phonetic analysis of course, but awareness of such differences in pronunciation is often linked to sweeping generalizations about 'plummy southerners' (who talk as if they have a plum in their mouth) or 'blunt northerners'. Continuing these rash stereotypes, northerners generally pride themselves on being 'straightforward' and 'down-to-earth': their view of southerners is sometimes similar to a common foreign view of the English in general, that they are amazingly polite and perhaps artificially so. The 'West Country', referring particularly to south-western England, is an area of mild climate and relatively little heavy industry, which conjures up images of apple orchards, strong cider and cream teas. This area is one part of England in which the local pronunciation retains the post-vocalic 'r'-sound (in words like 'car, purr, sort, beard') and this means that many English people think that the utterance of a thoughtful 'arrr', sounding the final 'r'-sound, is enough to imitate a rustic peasant.

Looking to other parts of the English-speaking world, the English sometimes call Australians 'Aussies' (sometimes mispronounced with [s] but correctly pronounced 'Ozzies') and the Americans 'Yanks'. There are no common special terms for Canadians, New Zealanders or South Africans. (The term 'Boer', from the Dutch for a farmer or peasant, was once used of Afrikaans-speaking South Africans, but no longer.)

Religious divisions are not prominent in Britain today: the traditional church in England, with the Queen as its head, is the Church of England or Anglican Church, and many English people belong to it, nominally if not very seriously, although there are substantial numbers in other Protestant churches, sometimes called non-conformists. In Scotland, the Church of Scotland, which is a Presbyterian, not Anglican, church, has the same kind of traditional standing as the Church of England in England. In Wales there is a strong tradition of non-Anglican Protestant churches, usually referred to as chapels, in which the preaching and singing have a reputation for vigour and liveliness. The population of the Republic of Ireland is strongly Roman Catholic and there are areas of Britain, such as the cities of Liverpool and Glasgow, where Irish immigration has resulted in substantial Catholic minorities. In Northern Ireland, the conflict between Protestants and Catholics has been tragically violent and widely reported in the media. The rest of Britain has relatively little religious tension of that kind, although there are pockets of it − for example, in the rivalry between the two Glasgow football teams of Rangers and Celtic. Without official endorsement or encouragement, Rangers is identified as the Protestant team and Celtic as the (Irish) Catholic team, and violence among supporters has been notorious.

Regional stereotypes often feature in jokes. A common type of joke begins 'There was an Englishman, an Irishman and a Scotsman' and then goes on to tell how they each behaved or reacted differently in a situation. The assumption is that the Englishman will be superior, the Irishman silly and the Scotsman mean. Although these jokes may be objected to as racist or at least shockingly overgeneralizing, they are not always considered offensive and Scottish people may tell jokes about mean Scotsmen, just as Jewish people tell Jewish jokes and Australians tell jokes about stupid Australians. But the characters in these jokes do vary. When someone from southern Scotland tells one of these jokes, the mean character may be a 'man from Aberdeen' rather than just a Scotsman. In fact everyone has their prejudices. In Holland, the stupid character is a Belgian, in Belgium the mean character is a Dutchman. In Poland the stupid character is a Russian, in North America he is a Pole. Learners should be careful. If you tell one of these jokes without the necessary fluency, listeners may be more aware of the unintended offence than of the intended humour.

Sport is a strong ingredient of British culture and it is unthinkable that anyone would not know that the Grand National is a horse race, that Lords is one of the London cricket grounds, that Wembley is where the football cup final is played, that Wimbledon is where lawn tennis is played, and so on. In Britain, the word 'football', without qualification, means what some other countries call 'soccer'. Rugby football is usually called 'rugby' and American football is either 'American football' or 'gridiron'. Similarly, 'hockey' refers to land hockey, and ice hockey is 'ice hockey', never just 'hockey'. Sport also provides metaphors for daily discourse, like 'sticky wicket', a difficult situation in cricket, and hence a difficult situation more generally.

There are many associations with particular places that need no explanation within Britain, such as Harley Street (in London, a street associated with medical specialists), the City (the old city of London, now particularly the financial district), the West End (of London, associated with theatres), Scotland Yard (in London, the headquarters of the Metropolitan Police) and Oxford and Cambridge (the cities housing the two oldest universities). Newspapers and advertisers can draw on such associations with phrases like 'panic in the City' or 'a West End success'.

Newspapers themselves have particular well-known associations. Page 3 of the *Sun* refers to pictures of scantily clad or nude young women, a *News of the World* story suggests something scandalous, and a *Guardian* reader conjures up images of a left-of-centre intellectual, perhaps an earnest social worker or an academic in a tweed jacket.

Public signs are also part of the linguistic landscape, and sometimes intriguingly different around the world. The British are used to seeing 'Give Way' at intersections and find the American 'Yield' amusing. (To most British people, 'yield!' sounds like a medieval knight demanding surrender.) But Americans no doubt find 'Give Way' equally strange. Where traffic is diverted, the British sign says 'Diversion', the American 'Detour'. Some signs show traces of British tentativeness: 'Please Do Not Disturb' alongside the more direct 'Do Not Disturb'. Compare the straightforwardness of signs like 'No Smoking' with a sign on an Edinburgh bus which read 'These Seats are Particularly Appreciated by the Elderly and Infirm'.

Finally, we should note that even though we have mentioned various parts of the British Isles, England, and particularly London and south-eastern England, remain prominent. This is the most densely populated part of the British Isles and the region which continues to be dominant in power and wealth. Many of the images which outsiders have of the British – from businessmen in bowler hats to guardsmen in red tunics outside Buckingham Palace, from elegant department stores to red double-decker buses – are really images of London. This is not surprising, and if you learn to speak English as a foreigner, you are far more likely to follow the model of RP or the pronunciation of south-eastern England than you are to learn northern English or Scottish or Irish pronunciation, and you are likely, at least to some extent, to start acquiring the perceptions (and the prejudices) of south-eastern England. The aim of this section is not to deny the influence and importance of south-eastern England, but at least to remind people that there is more to the British Isles than its south-eastern corner.

Some of the exercises that follow will require – if you don't already know the answer – diligent work with dictionaries or encyclopaedias or perhaps some conversation with friendly native-born English people who will be able to supply answers. However you go about it, and however difficult the tasks, you should learn much that will help you. When non-English-speaking students study or train in English, it may not always be the academic or professional language and the technical terms that constitute the major problem. Sometimes it is the teacher's jokes, the little stories, the allusions, that are far more bewildering. Precisely because such language draws on what is assumed to be common knowledge, it may be very helpful to native speakers, for it anchors the discourse in familiar territory and helps to assimilate the unfamiliar. But the teacher may not realize how far those who have not had the same cultural experiences may be being left behind.

Tasks and exercises

Below can be found some tasks and exercises related to well-established British institutions, including commercial institutions, traditional titles, abbreviations denoting honours, etc. which have not been discussed in any detail above but are part and parcel of British life and known to most people living in the UK. We hope that by researching the topics (and information can be found readily in any good encyclopaedia or in more specialized publications) students will learn more than by studying a general text designed just to provide answers to the questions below. Students are also encouraged to compare the traditional political and other institutions, titles and honours of their native cultures with the British ones.

1. There are many traditional ways of honouring people. Although there is often talk of radically changing the system, many of the old titles are still used, e.g. people are knighted every year for

their services. Answer the following questions connected with people being honoured in Britain:

a) When, in the year, do people look in the papers to see if they/ their friends have been honoured for public service with a life peerage, knighthood or some lesser order?

b) What is a Life Peer?

c) Mary Jones was knighted for her services to the Trade Union movement. What is she called?

d) Sheila Maclean's husband, Angus, was knighted for his services to industry. What is he called? And what is she called?

e) How do you generally know, from the way they are addressed in writing, that someone had been given some honour or got some professional qualification?

2. Who are the following people?
   - The Chancellor of the Exchequer
   - The Home Secretary
   - The Foreign Secretary

3. Identify the profession or professional institution associated with the following:
   - QC
   - MB
   - MSc
   - PhD
   - FRCS

4. Which of the military services train their officers here?
   - Sandhurst
   - Dartmouth
   - Cranwell

5. What do the following abbreviations mean?
   - NHS
   - TUC
   - HMS
   - RAF
   - RN
   - GP

6. What do you associate with the following long-standing brand names?
   - Bell's
   - Marmite

- Horlicks
- Cadbury
- Wall's
- McVitie's
- Callard and Bowser
- Lea and Perrin's
- Bass
- Worthington
- Coleman

7. What do you associate with the following long-standing shop names?
- Boots
- Harrods
- Selfridges
- W.H. Smith
- John Menzies

8. What would you say, if anything, in the following situations? What would you normally say in your own language (up to three versions if you like, but always ones which you think most native speakers like yourself would give) and what would a British person normally say?

a) You are in a room with a number of people. Someone who is very near you but is not looking in your direction accidentally drops some money on the ground. You want to catch their attention in order to tell them they have dropped it.

b) The same happens as in a), except that the person is further away and is just on the point of leaving. Give a warning shout, preferably in one word.

c) You are in a crowded bus and, by accident, bump into someone, slightly upsetting their balance, in a way that can easily happen on a crowded bus.

d) The same happens as in c) but you have clearly caused the person some pain.

e) What does the person in d) say as they experience the pain? What is the exclamation expressing pain?

f) Your watch has stopped and so you stop a stranger in the street to ask the obvious question. What do you say?

g) Someone you do not know very well is talking to you but you are desperate to leave. The other person doesn't know it but you have a train to catch. The person is talking very quickly. What do you say when you cut short the conversation by interrupting?

h) Someone is very angry and utters a very offensive swear word. What is it likely to be? In British English, which of the following pairs of words and phrases is likely to count as the stronger?

Damn!	Shit!
God!	Fuck!
Bloody awful!	Fucking awful!
Get the hell out of here!	Bugger off!

9. You answer the phone in your flat. What do you say in your own country? What do you say in Britain?

10. You want to ring Peter Walker at work. He is a sales manager at Harvest Industries. How does the telephone receptionist answer your call and how do you ask for Peter Walker?

11. You again want to ring Peter Walker at work, but he is not in the office. What does the receptionist say and what are your options?

12. You walk into a shoe shop in your home town and look for a shop assistant. The assistant sees you, smiles and says what? What would the assistant say in a British shop?

13. You are in your home country, talking to a friend at a party. This friend is there for the first time and doesn't know anybody. Someone comes up to you and interrupts your conversation by greeting you. As she does so, she looks at your friend, a new face, expectantly. What happens next? What might happen in Britain?

14. Someone junior to you at work addresses you very formally and respectfully. You would like them to be more informal. Would you say anything to them in your own country? What could you say in the same situation in Britain?

15. You are in the office of someone who doesn't hear a knock at the door. What do you do in your country? What would you do Britain?

16. You ring a dentist because you need to have a tooth filled. What do you say?

17. You are writing to the following people. How would you address them? Begin 'Dear ...' and replace the Mr or Ms with the proper title, as appropriate.

- Mr Raj Singh (medical doctor/physician)
- Mr William Bond (dentist)
- Ms Jennifer Simmons (medical doctor, surgeon)

18. What do you say in your country when:
   - you have just served food to someone?
   - you ask someone if they want more coffee?
   - someone offers you more coffee but you don't want any more?
   - when you hand something to someone?

What would you say in these situations in Britain?

19. You go out for a drink with two friends, to a place called 'The Bull and Bush' which doesn't look too crowded. You are the first to enter. What typically happens next?

20. You decide to go and visit a friend and her family who live in a cottage in Kent. They have said they won't mind at all if you drop in when they are having their evening meal. What time might that be?

21. You move into a new neighbourhood. What is the first contact that you would expect with your new neighbours in your country? What would you expect to happen in Britain?

22. What are the following dishes made of, what are their origins and when are they eaten?
   - Cream or Devonshire tea
   - Haggis

23. Britain follows a Christian tradition when it comes to many holidays, Christmas and Easter in particular. Do you follow a similar tradition in your home country? If it is not Christian, is it based on another religion or is it secular in nature?

24. What would you expect to eat at an English Christmas dinner?

25. Give two names for the man who brings presents.

26. How does he traditionally enter the house?

27. On what date do children get their Christmas presents?

28. Name two places where children might find their presents.

29. What would a pantomime typically be based on?

30. Name one unusual feature of the roles in a pantomime.

31. When do you expect to see fireworks in Britain? What else happens around that date?

32. When might you find people dancing under the fountains in a very crowded Trafalgar Square?

33. What is Hogmanay? Where and when is it celebrated?

34. Where might you find people waving flags and singing 'Land of Hope and Glory'?

35. On what day in August might you expect to find British motorways clogged with traffic?

36. Do you have a traditional holiday similar to the British Christmas, New Year's Eve or Easter in your home country? What time of year does it happen and what are the foods and events associated with this occasion?

37. What would you expect at an eisteddfod?

38. What is a 'caber' and what do people do with it? Where?

39. What sports are associated with the following places?
- Epsom and Ascot
- Wembley Stadium
- Wimbledon
- Edgbaston, Lords and Old Trafford
- Brands Hatch and Silverstone
- Murrayfield
- Henley
- Braemar, Scotland
- Cowes, Isle of Wight
- Bisley

40. What cities do you associate with the following football teams?
- Rangers
- Celtic
- Arsenal

What distinguishes Rangers and Celtic?

41. Someone from Manchester may be called a 'Mancunian', What are the nicknames for someone from:
   - Glasgow
   - Liverpool
   - Newcastle?

42. To which cities or areas of the UK do these adjectives refer?
   - Brummie
   - Geordie

43. Who is:
   - a Paddy
   - a Sassenach
   - a Taffy?

44. What does 'O' mean in O'Connell, or 'Mac' in MacDonald? Do you have any idea how the Welsh surname 'Pritchard' relates to this question?

45. What person, profession, type of profession or institution is traditionally associated with:
   - Fleet Street
   - Harley Street
   - Savile Row
   - Sandringham
   - Whitehall
   - Westminster
   - West End
   - Scotland Yard
   - The City
   - 11 Downing St
   - Windsor
   - Bond St
   - Balmoral?

46. What are the addresses of the Prime Minister's official residences in and outside London?

47. Name five national daily newspapers in Great Britain.

48. Who would be the usual reader of the *Guardian* newspaper?

49. What wording would you expect on a notice:
   - to stop people knocking at your door?
   - to warn people that a vending machine is not working?
   - to tell people not to smoke?

50. Why might you offend people by saying that Cardiff is one of the nicest cities in England?

51. Who are the following fictional characters and who created them?
- Alice in Wonderland
- Christopher Robin
- Jeeves
- Miss Marple
- Mrs Tiggiewinkle
- Lord Peter Wimsey
- Rinceweed
- Bilbo
- Sherlock Holmes

52. Nursery rhymes are part and parcel of growing up in the UK. Find a book of English nursery rhymes and try to determine what animals are associated with the following:
- Hickory Dickory and 'running after the farmer's wife'
- 'Incy wincy', and Little Miss Muffet
- '... jumped over the moon'
- Banbury Cross
- Going to London to see the Queen.

53. National legends are an important part of growing up in Britain. Try to find the texts of the relevant legends and explain the following:
a) Why did King Alfred burn the cakes?
b) What did the Danish King of England, Canute, try to prove by getting wet in tidal waters?
c) What did a spider teach Robert Bruce of Scotland?

54. Each of the component nations of the United Kingdom has its own saint and symbolic national emblem. Match the saint with the nation and the national emblem:
- Patrick, David, George, Andrew
- Scotland, Wales, Ireland, England
- thistle, leek, rose, shamrock (four-leafed clover).

55. Can you pronounce the following?
- The Taylor of Gloucester
- Worcester Sauce
- Leicester Square
- Chiswick
- Harwich
- Norwich

References

Black, J. (1996) *A History of the British Isles*. Basingstoke: Macmillan.

Bryson, B. (1995) *Notes from a Small Island*. London: Black Swan.

Cannon, J.A. (1988) *The Oxford Illustrated History of the British Monarchy*. Oxford: Oxford University Press.

Davies, C. (1997) *Divided by a Common Language*. Sarasota, Florida: Mayflower Press.

Davies, N. (1997) *Europe, a History*. London: Pimlico.

Fowler, H.W., Fowler, F.G. and Thompson, D.F. (1995) *The Concise Oxford Dictionary of Current English*. Toronto: Oxford University Press.

Hole, C. (1975) *English Traditional Customs*. London: Batsford.

Johnson, P. (1985) *A History of the English People*. London: Weidenfeld and Nicolson.

O'Driscoll, J. (1994) *Britain: the Country and its People*. Oxford: Oxford University Press.

Pounds, N.J.G. (1994) *The Culture of the English People: Iron Age to the Industrial Revolution*. Cambridge: Cambridge University Press.

Randle, J. (1981) (reprint 1988), *Understanding Britain*. Kingston-upon-Thames: Filmscan/Lingual House.

Royale, E. (1987) *Modern Britain: a Social History, 1750–1985*. London: E. Arnold.

4 Australia – the Great South Land

Eddie Ronowicz and Colin Yallop

When one remembers that less than two hundred years have elapsed since that first handful of convicts landed at Botany Bay, one cannot help admiring the sheer tenacity that in such a short time has given Australia the place she occupies in the world today and the great future she is bound to have. (Lacour-Gayet, 1976, p. xii)

The Great South Land – its discovery and colonization

When Europeans were beginning to make their long sea journeys of exploration around the world, map-makers believed there must be a great Terra Australis Incognita, an 'unknown southern land' to balance the land masses of the northern hemisphere. In English, this land was sometimes known simply as 'the Great South Land'.

What we now call Australia did not live up to these expectations; it was initially a source of disappointment rather than excitement. Even when they found its shores, the early European explorers – including Captain Cook (1728–89), who found that Australia was indeed a continent – failed to identify it as the Great South Land. As Jose says: 'Cook had no idea of the importance of his discovery; indeed, he was rather apologetic for having done so little. Both he and those who sent him out were much more interested in the Great South Land, whose whereabouts was still a puzzle...' (Jose, 1914, p. 15).

In the end, Australia proved to be the only Great South Land there was. It was not particularly fertile and the few large rivers that were found often failed to run their full course from the source to the sea. In fact, most of Australia, whose total area is roughly equivalent to that of the United States, strikes Europeans as a dry inhospitable country which, from the point of view of its usefulness, may be divided into three zones (Lacour-Gayet, 1976, pp. 1–3).

Along the East Coast there is a rather narrow belt (between 10 and 100 kilometres wide) of coastal plains and hills suitable in some parts for intensive agriculture. This is where the largest Australian cities of Brisbane, Melbourne and Sydney are situated. The Great Dividing Range, extending from Cape York in the north to Tasmania in the south, a very old mountain range, interrupted by Bass Strait between the continent proper and Tasmania, is the western boundary of this zone.

Beyond the ranges there is a belt of vast plains, in some places over 1000 kilometres wide, suitable for cattle and sheep raising and agriculture. Even though there is a temperate climate zone in the south, a subtropical zone in the centre and a tropical zone in the north, there is an almost permanent shortage of rainwater throughout the area. Fairly frequent droughts are partly to blame for this, but the main problem is the thin layer of top soil. Even in periods when rains are

plentiful, the top soil gets saturated very quickly and the rest of the water is wasted: it fills creeks, causing flash floods, and then it evaporates quickly in the harsh Australian sun. It follows that farmers in the area have to depend heavily on collecting rainwater in tanks and dams and on pumping water from deep artesian wells. In Australia, a 'dam' is not just a large wall of earth or concrete, forming an artificial lake, but also the lake itself, especially a relatively small one on a farm, often constructed by bulldozing earth to retain the water in a natural slope or depression. Dams like these, and large tanks of concrete or iron, are characteristic features of the landscape in this part of Australia.

With important exceptions, notably areas of fertile land around Adelaide in South Australia and Perth in south-west Western Australia, most of the rest of the country is barely habitable desert.

When the British began to settle Australia in 1788, the continent had already been inhabited for many thousands of years by people now known in English as Aboriginal people. Their numbers were relatively small – most estimates range from around 300,000 to 500,000 over the whole continent. They gathered and hunted their food rather than farmed the land or grazed flocks or herds of animals; their social organization was complex, but oriented to small communities, unlike European-style states or nations; and they had developed a culture that was rich in local meaning but which did not need the innovations that most Europeans considered essential to civilization, such as writing, the use of metals or the construction of large buildings. These very features of Aboriginal society helped them to survive in a country whose fauna and flora did not lend themselves to pasturing and agriculture and whose terrain and climate did not encourage European- or Asian-style intensive occupation and exploitation. But these features also meant that the British newcomers found it difficult to deal with the indigenous people and, indeed, imperialist and racist sentiments among British settlers through the nineteenth century made it all too easy to treat the Aborigines as an obstacle to progress. The newcomers soon began to drive Aborigines off their land and to confine them to restricted areas. Resistance was usually dealt with harshly, whether officially or unofficially. By the end of the nineteenth century, the Aboriginal population had fallen to about 70,000 or fewer. Only in the twentieth century did the population climbed back to 170,000 or so (Borrie, 1989, p. 119)

The British decided to establish a penal colony in Australia and sent a small fleet carrying convicts, marines and supplies. After a long voyage the fleet arrived in Botany Bay on 18 January 1788. The bay proved to be disappointing as a place for settlement and Port Jackson (where today's Sydney Harbour is) was chosen. In the evening of 26 January 1788 the party that arrived on the ship *Supply* 'were assembled at the point where they had first landed in the morning, and on which a flag staff had been purposely erected and a Union Jack displayed, when marines fired several volleys, between which the Governor and the officers that accompanied him drank the healths of His Majesty and the Royal Family, and success to the new colony' (Jose, 1914, p. 20). This colony was known as New South Wales.

Immediately to the west of Sydney are the Blue Mountains, not very high but with some deep valleys lined by sheer rock faces, which proved to be a serious obstacle to early inland exploration. For some three decades after 1788 most of the newcomers were either convicts or those assigned to administer and guard the colony. The number of white people living in Australia remained relatively small and most of the effort went into exploring and describing coastal areas. The island of Tasmania (then still known as Van Diemen's Land, after the Dutch explorer of that name) was settled and also became a destination for convicts, and various settlements were established on the coast of the mainland, including one north of Sydney at Moreton Bay (at the mouth of the Brisbane river, on which the city of Brisbane developed into the capital of the separate colony of Queensland) and places nearer

Sydney where coal was discovered (near the present-day industrial cities of Newcastle and Wollongong).

In 1813 the Blue Mountains were finally crossed, thus opening the wide expanses of grassy hills and plains that lay beyond to colonization and exploitation. Investigation by various explorers continued well into the nineteenth century and the names of many of these explorers are perpetuated in place names and in the names of highways, such as Blaxland, Cunningham, Eyre, Hume, Lawson, Oxley, Sturt, Strzelecki and Wentworth, among many others.

As knowledge about Australia increased and more land became available, more free settlers were attracted. The discovery of gold in the mid-nineteenth century also drew many fortune-seekers, not only attracting migrants into the country (Australia usually calls its newcomers 'migrants' rather than 'immigrants'), but also causing enormous movements of population within the country. When gold was discovered in Victoria, for example, men flooded from Tasmania into Victoria. It is estimated that perhaps two-thirds of Tasmania's non-convict workforce left in the space of two years, around 1851 to 1852. New settlements were also established in the north, south-east, south, far west and inland, many of them now remote from Sydney and quite independent of the penal colony system. The colony of South Australia, for example, based on Adelaide (founded 1836), was established for free settlers and was never a destination for convict transportation (although convicts and ex-convicts soon reached the colony as servants of pastoralists). By the mid-nineteenth century there were six separate colonies in Australia: five on the mainland, namely New South Wales (now delimited as about 10 per cent of the total area of the country), Queensland, South Australia, Victoria and Western Australia; and the separate island colony of Tasmania. Until federation, in 1901, the colonies remained separate, without any overarching Australian government. But the population continued to be highly mobile. The colony of Western Australia, for example, remained small and relatively isolated until the last decade of the nineteenth century, and had a population of less than 50,000 in 1891. But then gold was discovered, in the neighbourhood of present-day Coolgardie and Kalgoorlie (where gold is still mined today). From 1891 to 1901, the population of the colony more than trebled, to nearly 185,000. Many of the newcomers came from elsewhere in Australia, of course, and it is large movements of this kind that are part of the reason why there is so little regional variation in Australian English. We do not know whether Western Australians had developed a local style of Western Australian English by the 1890s, but if they had, they were swamped by other Australians arriving in the next few years.

Despite some fluctuations and crises caused by over-optimistic expectations and speculation, by the late nineteenth century Australia was widely regarded as a land of opportunity for anyone prepared to put some effort into realizing their dreams of a better life. Many of the early explorers and settlers paid a high price for their ignorance of conditions in this harsh continent, and certainly the Aboriginal population paid dearly for European-style development and exploitation, but the now mainly British population began to enjoy the fruits of material prosperity. All the land that was suitable for agriculture or grazing was steadily sold or leased by the Crown to locals and migrants at very low prices compared to Europe; a number of major mining sites were developed, providing work for tens of thousands of people; and local manufacturing and service industries grew rapidly in well-established cities, providing more jobs. By 1900, Sydney and Melbourne in particular were major cities of the British Empire, centres of trade and commerce, with large buildings, major port facilities and extensive suburban railways and tramways, allowing the population not only to commute to work but also to enjoy such leisure pursuits as getting to the beach or attending sporting fixtures. The situation of British migrants in this 'workers' paradise' at the turn of the twentieth century is described by Geoffrey Bolton: 'The Australians were those fortunate members of the lower orders who had broken loose from British hierarchy and were exercising their own choices about their style of life' (see Withers, 1989, pp. 13–14).

Towards independence from Britain

The rapid increase in population and a rising standard of living inevitably led to moves towards some sort of independence for Australia. Unlike the USA, however, which fought a war of independence, Australia gained its self-government in stages. Even in the nineteenth century, Britain had granted a degree of self-government to each of the colonies. Then in 1901 the colonies formed a federation as the Commonwealth of Australia. By the late twentieth century, Britain had ceased to have any legislative authority over Australia, and Australians could no longer appeal to the Privy Council in the United Kingdom, but the British monarch remained the Head of State of the Commonwealth of Australia, represented by a governor-general in the national capital, Canberra, and by a governor in each of the six states. The governor-general and governors have limited powers (similar to those of the monarch in Britain), and nowadays they are Australians, not delegates of the British Crown. To all intents and purposes, Australia is governed by Australians, by a democratically elected federal parliament, in which the government is led by a prime minister, and democratically elected state parliaments, in which the governments are led by state premiers. All legislation is enacted by these parliaments. While there is an active republican movement in

Australia, neither a majority of politicians nor a majority of citizens seems keen to abolish the monarchy.

Even after self-government and federation, Australia considered itself to have a special relationship with Britain, within the British Empire, later the British Commonwealth. In fact this special relationship with Britain often meant sacrifice by Australia, as when many Australians died in the First World War fighting alongside the British, even though Australian borders had not been threatened. But the relationship remained significant until the Second World War, and many Australians have continued to value the British model of parliamentary democracy and many other features inherited from or influenced by the mother country. But the Second World War and the period following it changed things quite dramatically.

Until war broke out in the Pacific in 1941, the Australian government and people believed that, should Australian borders be threatened, Britain would use its armed forces to assist in their defence. In fact, after the surrender of Singapore, the British concentrated their efforts on the war in Europe and North Africa and left Australia and other allies with little or no support in South-east Asia and the Pacific. While the British could argue that their own islands were seriously threatened and their resources extremely strained, the fact is that the USA quickly became Australia's great ally and protector in the Pacific. Australia served as the largest and most secure base for the war against Japanese forces, Australian armed forces co-operated with American, and Australians became used to seeing American military personnel on their streets and in their cafes and cinemas. The alliance with the USA was strengthened by subsequent agreements between the two countries, and by the participation of Australian forces alongside Americans in Korea, Vietnam, and more recently in Iraq. As Donald Horne says: 'Australians have lived with the recognition of American world power longer than any other nation outside the Western Hemisphere – since early 1942 when General MacArthur escaped from the Philippines to Darwin. Australia was the first country in the contemporary world to be saved by the Americans' (Horne, 1978, p. 82). He also comments that this dependence on American power does not seem to arouse in Australia the same bitterness it arouses in other parts of the world and that Americans could find here some of the best friends they are likely to find in an envious world.

A second cause of change in the relationship with Britain was Australian population policies, especially immigration policies. After the Second World War, Australia accepted a large number of 'displaced persons' from various non-English-speaking European countries. Later, refugees were admitted from other parts of the world, especially from the Middle East and Asia. These new Australians or their children and grandchildren do not have any attachment to a special relationship with Britain. And of course there were already many other Australians, particularly Aboriginal Australians and Australians of Irish ancestry, who had no reason to think of Britain as their mother country.

British entry into the European Community meant that Australian goods and indeed Australian citizens lost any preferential status in the United Kingdom, and this proved to be the final straw. The Australian government deprived the British of their right to automatic entry into Australia – UK citizens now had to apply for visas or permanent residence like any other non-Australians.

The Commonwealth of Australia today

Government and administration

Australia has a rather complex system of government. There are two houses of the Federal Parliament meeting in Canberra (a lower house, the House of Representatives, and a Senate), while all of the six states except Queensland have their own two houses of parliament, a Legislative Assembly and a Legislative Council, meeting in the state capital city. (Queensland has just a single house of parliament.) In addition there is a system of local elected government in each state (cities, shires, municipalities, etc.). Moreover, bureaucracy (known in Australia as the Public Service) has been no less elaborate, at least until privatization and cost-cutting began to be implemented in the 1990s. The Public Service was of course originally modelled on the British Civil Service, but had its own development in a country where, in the absence of long-established European-style communities and services, the government was often expected to organize everything and sometimes did so more pompously than effectively.

Voting is compulsory, a fact which points to that strange Australian tension between egalitarianism – we ALL vote – and authoritarianism – we vote whether we want to or not. However, many Australians do not seem to be greatly interested in politics or in changes, especially those that are not going to influence their daily lives in any significant manner. It is not surprising, then, that Australian political life tends to be dominated by particular interest groups.

On the left of the political spectrum is the Australian Labor Party, which has always been closely associated with the trade union movement. On the right are two parties which often work together in coalition: the Liberal Party of Australia, often seen to be allied with business interests, including small and medium-sized businesses, and the National Party of Australia, which used to be called the Country Party, showing its strong support from farmers and graziers and country people in general. Since the Liberals and Nationals have almost always joined to form a coalition government whenever they could, Australia's political scene is virtually a two-party system. As in the two-party systems of several other English-speaking countries, the major political parties become organizations of professional or semi-professional politicians, supported by a professional publicity apparatus, who often display more dedication to keeping their party in power than to looking after the people whom they supposedly represent, let alone to fostering open debate about the long-term future of the nation. In general, Australians are now fairly cynical about their politicians. From time to time, new groups or parties make some impact. Some have won seats in the Senate, such as the Green Party representing ecological and environmental concerns, and the Australian Democrats, who were founded, as their leader put it at the time, to 'keep the bastards honest' (the 'bastards' being the politicians from the three largest parties). And, indeed, the Democrats have sometimes held the balance of power in the Senate and have managed to force majority parties to modify their policies. Other parties have sometimes achieved successes in State elections, like the Democratic Labor Party (a breakaway from the Australian Labor Party) which held some seats in Queensland in the late 1950s, but the three large parties remain dominant. (For more information on Australian political parties, see Bambrick, 1994, pp. 148–54.)

Most Australians are not quick to talk politics but, if they do, they will often express cynicism about politicians and government. In this they are supported by the media, who criticize policy and politicians with a freedom which seems excessive to many visitors, especially those from Asia and Africa. For this reason alone, it is not certain that a referendum to change the constitution and make Australia a republic would succeed. Many Australians are suspicious of the motives of politicians who are campaigning for a republic, especially when it is difficult to see whether there would be any real change to the way in which the country is now governed and administered.

The population

For many years after the First Fleet landed with its convicts and marines from the British Isles, Australia favoured white English-speaking immigrants. There were exceptions – for example, Chinese who came to join the gold rushes, Pacific Islanders ('Kanakas') from places such as Vanuatu and the Solomon Islands brought to Queensland as labourers in the sugar cane fields, and Afghans who came as camel drivers to inland Australia (see Bambrick, 1994, p. 222). But the expectation that the British Isles would be the main source of settlers continued until after the Second World War. Then, non-English-speaking European 'displaced persons' (167,000 of them according to Horne, 1978, p. 68) were allowed to enter, and immigration was encouraged from non-English-speaking European countries, such as Italy and Greece. Substantial numbers of Europeans came to Australia, brought relatives with them or after them, and generally introduced Australia to their compatriots as a potential destination for emigration, so that an initial wave of non-English-speaking immigrants was followed for many years by a steady stream.

Two further important changes in policies took place in the 1960s and 1970s. First, the political marginalization of Aboriginal people was acknowledged and they were (finally) given the right to vote and began to be recognized as citizens who were entitled to equal opportunities within society. Secondly, the 'White Australia Policy' was abandoned and immigrants began arriving not just from Britain and elsewhere in Europe but from all over the world, including various Asian countries. As a result, contemporary Australia can claim to be a multiracial and multilingual country, its population consisting of a clear majority of native English speakers and a variety of smaller groups representing well over 100 languages and cultures from all over the world. Most of these new Australians are the result of 'period migration'. They may have been driven by particular events in their home country or by relatively poor economic conditions at home, or just inspired by the example of a few adventurous compatriots. This is how Australia has gained, for example, Chinese immigrants from Hong Kong and mainland China itself, Croatians, Lebanese, Macedonians, Poles, Serbs, Sri Lankans and Vietnamese, among many others.

Australian society today is a unique mix of the old and the new, of Anglo-Saxon, other European and Asian influences, which are reflected in family life and friendships, in the workplace and in ways of spending leisure time, in attitudes and values, in what Australians are sensitive about and what they consider to be unimportant, in the way Australians dress, what they like to eat and, consequently, in the ways they use English to express themselves and to function in their Australian environment.

As in most cultures, there are myths about Australia and stereotypes of Australians, some developed by Australians themselves, others fostered outside the country. Popular views are therefore not always accurate. The following paragraphs discuss some specific aspects of contemporary Australian society, examining popular perceptions (myths and stereotypes) against available statistical and other information, including the results of a questionnaire we administered to 40 subjects currently living in Australia (including

23 native Australians and 17 migrants and/or long-term foreign visitors).

Living and working in Australia

A popular view of Australia in other parts of the world is that life is easy there: Australia can export its wool, meat and minerals without much effort, the social welfare system is generous, the medical services are free, and no one really has to work very hard to make a living. Replies to our questionnaire suggest that this image is still very much alive among foreigners and first-generation migrants, although probably for different reasons. Seventy-one per cent of our respondents in this group said that Australians do not like hard work, and 88 per cent agreed with the statement that 'Australia is a paradise for people who don't like to work more than they have to, and like nature and comfortable living in a mild climate, heavily supported by welfare'. This widespread perception is nevertheless a stereotype, an over-generalization based on a rather small group of Australians.

As in every other society, there are rich people in Australia, some of whom have worked and still work very hard to achieve their wealth, others of whom have been fortunate enough to inherit or acquire their wealth without much effort. But there are also many hard-working people on lower incomes, and there are people who are unemployed or underemployed, some of whom live in very difficult conditions. And there are also people who make little or no effort to contribute to the economy, and who live off unemployment support ('the dole') or other social welfare benefits. Some of this last group take advantage of the very mild climate in and around the coastal cities and thus contribute to the myth – in one of its most exaggerated forms – that Australians spend every day lounging on the beach. The coastal areas of Australia can indeed be very pleasant places to live or take a holiday, but a more realistic picture of them recognizes that you need a good income to be able to enjoy them. There are some increasingly strict rules about access to social welfare and medical services, and while there are a small number who manage to deceive officials and exploit the system, many hard-working Australians are critical of 'dole bludgers' or people who 'rort the system' and may even 'dob them in' to the authorities.

Australia has been and still is one of the world's wealthiest countries, but it is not quite paradise. It is heavily dependent on international trade and investment, and fluctuations in the value of the Australian dollar can have a serious impact on Australian commerce. Even in its most affluent periods, Australia has never been without scandalously poor people, many of them Aboriginal people living in sub-standard housing on the fringes of towns and cities, but many of them non-Aboriginal Australians. Early twentieth-century Sydney and

Melbourne had slums as well as grand town halls, post offices and railway stations. Moreover, while earnings might look reasonably equitable, wealth is not entirely a matter of earnings (Withers, 1989, p. 17).

There is very little 'old money' in Australia which is not a foreign investment. Relatively few of those who have come to Australia in the last 200 years have brought much money with them. The earliest migrants were of course convicts, and many later migrants, such as the 'displaced persons' after the Second World War, had little or no money when they arrived. Some nineteenth-century migrants did come with money to invest, and the late twentieth century saw a scheme of business migration for those with substantial money to invest, but most of Australia's rich have acquired their wealth quite recently. Some Australians struck gold on the gold fields in the nineteenth century and were able to invest their money in property and commerce. Others occupied large portions of what they considered vacant land to graze sheep and cattle (the 'squatters') and later, when their right to hold the lands was recognized by the government, these large estates gave them wealth and power (as the 'squattocracy'). The twentieth century has seen a number of new and energetic migrants make it 'from rags to riches' by sheer hard work and enterprise, and a few have made money by smart operations on the stock exchanges of Australia. Consequently, most of the rich and powerful, with substantial direct and indirect influence on the cultural and political life of the country, belong to the group that Europeans often describe scornfully as the *nouveaux riches*, 'the new rich'. Many of the wealthy are of course hardly affected by changes and crises in the Australian labour market – they are part of the world financial market.

It is 'the battlers' who have been affected most severely by changes in the labour market and are painfully aware of it, as well as of the false image of Australia in this respect. Only 30 per cent of our native Australian respondents agreed that Australians were lazy and even fewer (22 per cent) agreed with the statement that Australians don't like hard work. Who are these 'battlers'? They are people for whom Australians have always had affection and sympathy, people who have to work hard, on a farm or in a factory or small business, just to make ends meet, people who see themselves at the mercy of the weather or of government policy or of decisions by a wealthy and powerful minority or by large multinational companies. Below we will look at what sections of modern Australian society fit the definition, but first we review the changes that have been happening to Australia.

The working environment of Australia has always been changing. In the nineteenth century, the growing cities were already creating their own demand for tradespeople and shopkeepers and light industry. In the twentieth century, farming, grazing and mining became less important (though by no means unimportant) and Australia became an industrial country, developing its own steel industry and a wide range of manufacturing, including shipbuilding and motor vehicle manufacturing as well as domestic appliances, clothing and footwear. Many of these industries were actually owned by overseas interests, initially British and American, and from the 1960s Japanese as well, and the profit therefore went overseas. At the same time Australia still exported substantial amounts of primary produce, especially wool, so it was possible to continue the belief that the country still depended on rural activities and that Australia still, as the saying went, 'rode on the sheep's back'.

In the latter part of the twentieth century there were even more profound changes, with a considerable shift from agriculture and manufacturing to services. But unemployment also rose (as of course in many other countries in the last quarter of the twentieth century) and fell at the beginning of the twenty-first century. Generally speaking, those who do still get and retain jobs do not always enjoy the good working conditions that were once regarded as normal in Australia. The country may still have a reputation as a 'workers' paradise' but conditions of employment have been renegotiated in many industries and, particularly in professional and administrative jobs, many people are now working long hours, often without overtime pay. The old practices of taking 'sickies' (an allowed number of days on full pay while sick, but often used simply to take time off for leisure) and extended lunch and tea-breaks, have almost disappeared, as employers will no longer tolerate them when employees are competing for available jobs. In general, getting a full-time, steady job is becoming harder each year for the young people who complete school and university, and finding a job is even harder for those in their forties or fifties who lose one job and try to get another. As a result, the ability to look for a job, write an application and perform well in a job interview has become so crucial that a new and thriving industry of teaching these skills has developed.

In the past, then, a 'battler' might have been an unskilled labourer working on a low wage, his wife at home taking care of several children, the whole family trying hard to scrape together enough savings to go for that one holiday in the year. These old-style battlers are still there, struggling harder than ever to maintain a decent lifestyle, but they have been joined by many others. As we have already seen in talking about the labour market, changes in industrial relations laws have been introduced. These have resulted in a significant drop of official unemployment numbers to 5 per cent. But the definition of 'employed' is now so generous that it includes people working part-time or on short-term contracts and hence it may be said that the situation is not improving for Australian workers. The trade unions, which often fought hard for good conditions, are not as strong as they once were, and their membership is declining; while the percentage of unemployed has dropped, the complex mechanisms of the welfare state, providing such financial support as unemployment benefits ('the dole') and compensation for injury at work ('compo'), are no longer as generous as they were. This, combined with rather high tax margins, has created a situation in which many middle-income earners, now eligible for fewer welfare benefits, have joined the ranks of battlers: after they have made all their mortgage, child-care, superannuation and insurance payments, they are left with little spare money to enjoy the kind of life that was still possible for this group of people in the 1980s.

An important characteristic of battlers in Australian eyes is that they do not whinge – they do not complain but try to tolerate or overcome their difficulties. Perhaps this is a remnant of traditional life in the bush. Those who had to build a life for themselves in the Australian bush had to face the many hardships of droughts, bush fires, floods, and so on, away from the coastal areas. The old tradition was not to complain in the face of adversity, but to try harder. During the twentieth century many of these people or their descendants came to the cities and maintained the tradition of battling on. A 'whinger', someone who complains constantly about their personal circum-stances, is accordingly an unpopular figure among average Austra-lians. Particularly unpopular are 'silvertails' (wealthy people) who complain about the high mortgage payments on their luxurious houses, 'bludgers' (people who live off welfare benefits or the generosity of others) who still bemoan their misfortune, and migrants who loudly and constantly compare Australia unfavourably with their countries of origin (especially migrants from Britain who denigrate everything Australian – 'whinging Pommies').

Finally, we should mention the tradition of 'mateship' which is peculiarly Australian. The origins of this tradition are controversial but must have something to do with the way in which white newcomers to Australia needed to help each other and rely on each other, particularly as they moved inland. As Donald Horne puts it:

> Mates are men who are thrown together by some emergency in an unfriendly environment and have become of one blood in facing it. In this sense its use is strongest in the unions and in the armed forces. Mates stick together in their adversity and their common interest. Mateship of this kind is a theory not of universal brotherhood but of the brotherhood of particular men. (Horne, 1978, p. 17)

But this traditional sense of mateship has undoubtedly dimin-ished in recent years and many Australians see it as a phenomenon that was badly tainted by sexism and racism (for mateship has often been for white men only). The old jobs that provided the model of traditional male solidarity in the trade unions – shearing, mining, the waterfront – do not employ as many people as they once did and the armed forces and the RSL (Returned Services League) no longer have the same status they enjoyed in two world wars and the years immediately following them. And the combined effects of urbanization, more employment and public roles for women, greater participation in public life by Aboriginal Australians, immigration from continental Europe and from Asia, and the growth of service industries such as tourism and finance, mean that the Aussie bloke is no longer who he was (or was thought to be).

The city and the bush

Despite the fact that the vast majority of Australians live in the seven capital cities (the national capital Canberra, and the six state capitals, Sydney, Melbourne, Brisbane, Perth, Adelaide and Hobart), the rural areas of Australia remain highly significant, in myths and images, as well as in reality. The non-urban and sparsely settled areas of Australia are commonly referred to as 'the bush', whether particularly covered in bushes or not. Thus you can talk about living out in the bush (away from the cities) or travelling through the bush or about how quiet or lonely the Australian bush is. The term 'outback' is similar, as in travelling 'outback' or living 'in the outback', but emphasizes even more the remoteness and sparse population and settlement. Consciousness of the size of Australia and the distances within the country are evident in various phrases with the general meaning of 'a long way from the city', like 'back of beyond' or 'back of Bourke' (i.e. even further inland than the town of Bourke). The 'black stump' (a tree stump blackened by fire, sometimes formerly used as a landmark or direction indicator) is a fictitious point at which civilization ends. Thus a remote cattle station might be 'beyond the black stump', while civilization is 'this side of the black stump' (as in 'the best butcher this side of the black stump').

The bush is often romanticized, whether in folklore or to promote modern tourism. Expressions like 'the Great Outback' (note the capital letters) or 'the dead heart' or 'the red centre' (for dry Central Australia where the soil and rocks have a reddish brown colour) reflect a rather sentimental view. And the romanticization is often linked to the popular conception – inside and outside Australia – of Australians as rough, independent pioneers. The country is seen as 'a land of sweeping plains, of bush-dwellers who tamed a vast continent, a manly, hardy, stoical new breed, independent, equal and free' (Withers, 1989, p. 1). Australian society is thus supposed to be egalitarian, anti-authoritarian and anti-intellectual, its thoughts shaped by the experience of its rural heritage and the wide open spaces of life in the outback, the product of the ethic of mateship among men (Edgar, 1980, p. 15). The very fact that most Australians now live in large cities (a good 20 per cent of them in Sydney alone, and nearly as many in the second largest city of Melbourne) shows that the perception of a typical Australian as a farmer or shearer conquering the outback is quite inaccurate today, even if there is some historical basis to the image.

The language also reflects the fact that the bush can be dangerous and hostile. The phrase 'to go bush', as in 'he's gone bush', can mean 'to go and live in the bush', but it may imply the abandoning of comfort and civilization, as well as some admiration for someone who wants to live a simpler life closer to nature. The phrase 'Sydney or the bush', meaning 'all or nothing', emphasizes the contrast between city and bush, and implies that the bush has nothing to offer compared with a big city. On the other hand, city people who own properties in the country may be referred to as 'Pitt Street farmers' or 'Collins Street farmers' (after major business streets in Sydney and Melbourne), implying that they know nothing of farming or life in the bush but own these properties for tax loss purposes or for some idealistic but impractical reason.

Australians who live in the large cities are often as conscious of their own city and state as they are of the nation as a whole – newspapers tend to be based on cities (note the names of, for example, the *Sydney Morning Herald* and the *Adelaide Advertiser*) even though they carry national and international news, drivers' licences and vehicle number plates are issued under the authority of the states, not the national government, and many clubs and organizations are state-based even if federated nationally. A certain regionalism is also reflected in ways of referring to geography. Thus in Sydney, 'the North Coast' refers not to the northern coast of Australia but to the coastal area in the north of New South Wales (which is actually part of the east coast of Australia). Similarly when Sydneysiders refer to 'the South Coast', they mean the coast of New South Wales in the south of the state. Tasmanians, living in the only state which is an island, refer to the rest of Australia as 'the mainland' and to other Australians as 'mainlanders', while Western Australians talk of 'the East', meaning the eastern states, particularly Victoria and New South Wales, or 'over East' (as in 'I was offered a promotion but I didn't want to move over East').

The changing face of Australian culture

There is a popular stereotype that Australians are crude and primitive when it comes to what is sometimes called high culture. This was reflected well in the responses of non-Australian participants of our questionnaire, in which only 12 per cent of the respondents believed Australians to be 'cultured'. This is, in fact, another myth about Australia and its inhabitants, which persists even though it runs contrary to available statistical evidence.

According to Withers (1989, p. 13), a survey in the 1980s showed that although almost all Australian households own TV sets and people do spend time watching commercial soaps and other programmes of doubtful cultural value, two-thirds of Australians devote some of their leisure time to reading and listening to music and one-third of them enjoy being spectators of various forms of art. Indeed, in the past, local cultural talent was not always highly valued and it was sometimes believed, even by native-born Australians, that overseas artists and performers must necessarily be better than Australians (in a phenomenon sometimes called 'the cultural cringe'). But there is now strong community interest in Australian painters, Australian musicians and singers, and Australian films and plays. In fact, for quite some time now most Australians have been taking pride in the cultural achievements of their country, without losing their interest in international artists. We have already noted that participating in 'arts' as a spectator is quite popular. Art galleries, concert halls and theatres are well attended, and so it may be said that in Australia an interest in football and an interest in the theatre are not necessarily mutually exclusive, nor are enjoyment of cricket and enjoyment of concerts. As Withers says, the majority of Australians are favourably disposed in attitudes and interests to the development of Australian cultural life.

One of the reasons for the internationalization of Australian culture may have been the adoption by the government in the 1970s of the 'Multicultural Policy', a policy of acknowledging and facilitating the maintenance of the various cultures and languages of Australia, including Aboriginal and non-English-based cultures as well as English-based language and culture. The result of this bold move has surpassed everyone's expectations: instead of a fragmented culture, where each ethnic group was pulling its own way, Australia's mainstream English-based culture has not only retained its strength, but has been profoundly enriched by all the other cultures contributing on an equal footing. Moreover, a side effect of the recognition of Aborigines as legitimate citizens, enjoying equal rights with everyone else, was a surge of interest in Aboriginal languages and culture. As a result, unlike most of their predecessors until the mid-twentieth century, many contemporary Australians have some knowledge of, and pride in, the culture of the indigenous people of the land. If you take a stroll along one of the busy streets of Sydney, Melbourne or Perth and ask 20 people to suggest a good restaurant in the area, you might be directed to 20 different places, in 20 different accents. Yet if these same people are asked what nationality they are, they will probably answer 'Australian'. The process of integration of new and old Australians has generated relatively little conflict and, in the final analysis, has been a resounding success.

In concluding this overview of contemporary Australian society, we have to agree with Donald Horne that despite considerable input from the British in the initial stages of Australia's development, to describe Australia as British would be wrong. Horne explains why:

> This new people, the Australians, fused out of old ingredients and separated in new ways, have taken British and European history to be their history (they could scarcely claim the history of the Aborigines) and have retained many of the forms of British political and social life without examining the differences. Words like 'democracy', 'monarchy', 'trades union', 'parliament', 'upper class', 'working class' and a whole terminological apparatus are used in the two countries with different meanings. Australians are not merely transplanted English. When they reach London the tens of thousands of Australians who, since the war, have migrated for a season or two to England often enjoy the theatres, the music and art shows, the natural beauties of England, its closeness to Europe, without achieving any rapport with the English. Their conversation reveals the alienation of people in someone else's country. Almost every Australian feels a sense of difference when arriving in England. (Horne, 1978, p. 78)

Living and interacting in modern Australian society

Every society has its own methods of defining an individual person, whether by the ways people are officially identified and categorized, or more informally by social conventions about how people should behave, or even by the ways in which families and friends talk to and about each other. Here we are looking at the ways in which Australians identify themselves, at the ways in which they relate to society at large and to their family and friends, and at the ways in which such relationships are reflected in communication styles and strategies.

The individual in society

When asked to give their full name for official purposes, Australians are expected to supply a first and family name, e.g. Maureen Smith, Tony Rizzi. As in many English-speaking countries, the spoken versions of first names may not always be the correct official versions. Thus Jennie or Jenny Miller is probably Jennifer Miller according to her birth certificate, Tony may be officially Anthony or Anton or Antonio, while Bob or Rob is likely to be Robert. Many Australians also have an additional given name, and this may need to be included in official documents, e.g. Maureen Beverley Smith, Andrew Harold Schmidt.

Until quite recently, Australians did not carry any kind of identity card. A passport was needed only for travel outside the country and a typical driver's licence was a printed sheet of paper with the driver's name and address and a permit number but no photograph or personal details. Then in 1987, the Federal Government proposed introducing a national identity card, with a photograph, for all Australians, arguing that such a card was indispensable in a modern society and that Australia was one of the very few countries in the world that did not have one. There were immediate and strong protests from many Australians and the proposal was dropped. A few years later, however, the traditional driver's licence was upgraded. It now has a photograph and gives not only the person's full name and current address, but also their date of birth. Since people who have not passed a driving test must also have a document like this to deal with banks and government institutions, the driving licence has in effect become an identity card, widely used to identify a person beyond reasonable doubt.

The family

Most Australians continue to value their right to enjoy some privacy and to pursue individual goals. They resent what they see as intrusions from individuals, institutions and governments alike. These attitudes are reflected in both private and public life – in the family home and relationships in it, as well as in behaviour towards authority in general and government in particular. The word 'home' is widely used and valued – people speak of 'going home' after work, rather than going to their house or apartment, while real estate agents sometimes advertise 'homes' for sale rather than 'houses', and 'home units' rather than 'flats' or 'apartments'.

Although Australia is now a highly urbanized country, with many people living in city apartments, the idea of a freestanding family home surrounded by lawn and garden, with a fence to maintain some privacy, is still very much part of the 'Australian dream'. Even if reality falls short of that dream for many Australians, the home is still commonly thought of as the place where family life can be conducted without interference from others – the Australian version of 'my home is my castle'. The average family inhabiting a dwelling like this consists of Mum and Dad and two or three children and, despite substantial numbers of single-parent families and single people sharing accommodation, this family unit remains an ideal, promoted, for example, by advertising images and television programmes.

For most non-Aboriginal Australians, the word 'family' still means immediate family, not the wider or extended family of uncles and aunts and cousins. Thus an Australian might say her family are all in Sydney (perhaps including parents and grown-up children, even if they do not live with her) but she also has relatives living quite near (perhaps an aunt and her family or a cousin and his family). It is quite rare for grandparents to live with their children and grandchildren. In some instances, the family are first- or second-generation migrants and the grandparents are not in Australia at all. In other cases, as in many other affluent societies, those who have retired have the means to live separately from their children, whether in houses of their own, retirement villages or nursing homes.

Younger Australian families seem to be following the trends of other industrialized societies, but perhaps more slowly than many. The traditional pattern of a father who works outside the home, earning the family's only income, while the mother stays at home to look after the children and run the household, has already been rivalled by a pattern in which both parents work outside the home and share child care and housework. Children get their breakfast and take a 'cut lunch' with them to school, returning around 4 p.m. to do their homework, play in the garden or watch television before having a meal and going to bed. Thus there may be relatively little contact between parents and children during the working week and, in most cases, there are no grandparents around to spend time with the children.

During weekends and holidays, most parents do devote more attention to the children. In January in particular, beaches, amusement parks, zoos and cricket matches often draw huge crowds of summer holidaymakers. Even then, however, Australians display the traditional Anglo-Saxon behaviour of 'not fussing too much about the children' or 'not spoiling the children'. While mothers may hug and kiss their young children, even up to primary school age, fathers rarely do, especially not their sons. Australian parents generally do not hover over their children, guarding them against every possible danger. Parents are usually not worried if their children swallow a little sea water at the beach, nor alarmed by minor scrapes or falls in a playground. Boys in particular are allowed and even encouraged to explore the world for themselves. A little boy who seems likely to cry because of a scratched leg may be given a hand and urged 'not to be a baby' or 'to be a big boy', rather than embraced with elaborate sympathy, and children of both sexes may be encouraged 'to be good' and 'not to make a fuss'. Phrases like 'it's all right' or 'you'll be right' or even the specially Australian 'she'll be right' (where the 'she' simply means 'it') are used not only with children and reflect a fundamental attitude which might be viewed, positively, as strength in the face of adversity, or, negatively, as a rather casual kind of optimism.

From primary school years onward, children will be actively encouraged by parents to take part in quite demanding activities, including various sports, bush walking, camping, horse riding, fishing and sailing. By the time they reach their teens, most Australian children can be quite adventurous and are generally capable of taking good care of themselves at home, at school, in the city and in the bush.

To some first-generation migrants and foreigners, whose cultures treat children and the elderly differently, Australians may seem not to care much about their families. Indeed, when we asked our questionnaire participants whether Australians had a strong family commitment, 57 per cent of native Australians answered with an unqualified yes, while only 35 per cent of first-generation migrants and foreigners believed this to be the case. In fact, with the elderly, Australians may simply be letting their parents do what they want, that is to retire independently and to continue to pursue their individual goals, which probably do not coincide with those of the younger members of their family. This does not necessarily mean that they have no interest in their parents, for they may visit them regularly, share holidays with them and help them when they are sick. They just do not usually live under the same roof with their parents. As for the younger generation, Australian parents see themselves as teaching their children to be independent from an early age and to pursue their own interests. In other words, parents are training their children to live and function effectively in a society where independence and resourcefulness are considered important.

The language within an Australian family, like that within most families worldwide, often has private aspects to it. Mothers may use their own terms of endearment to children, husband and wife may have private nicknames for each other, the family may have their own words and phrases for use within the home, whether in intimate matters to do with the body and bodily functions or in other matters that are peculiar to the household, such as routines to do with housework or games. These aspects of language are not necessarily unique or creative – they may have been acquired from parents or even picked up from a favourite film or television programme – but they are probably not shared outside the family. Even the words with which children address their grandparents may vary, from 'Grandma' to 'Gran' to 'Granny' to 'Nanna', for example, or from 'Grandpa' to 'Granddad' to 'Gramps'. As in any part of the world, there are often private jokes within the family. Members of a family may consistently and deliberately mispronounce a word at home (e.g. 'yoogly' for 'ugly' or 'tommytoe' for 'tomato') or they may have special verbal signals, such as some phrase used to warn another member of the family that he or she is beginning to sound too pompous at the dinner table.

Greetings, introductions and terms of address

Outside the family, Australians like to think of themselves as open and informal – they themselves might use the words 'friendly' or 'easy-going'. This is reflected in commonly used greetings and forms of address and introduction. Australians frequently use informal greetings, similar to those used elsewhere in the English-speaking world, 'Hello' and 'Hi', and may even use them in rather formal situations such as in shops and offices. The more formal variants ('Good morning, Good afternoon, Good evening') are of course available and are often used in formal settings. Many people associate the greeting 'Good day', pronounced informally as 'G'day', with Australia, perhaps because of characters in Australian films who seem to use it frequently. It is certainly used, in informal situations and among friends, but not all that frequently, especially in the cities, and it is probably not advisable for visitors or new arrivals to use it, in case they seem to be caricaturing Australian habits. As elsewhere in the English-speaking world, 'Good night' is not a greeting of the same kind as 'Good morning' or 'Good evening' . You say 'Good night' when parting for the last time in the day – for example, when leaving an office at the end of the working day, or when going home after dinner in a restaurant, or, if you share a house, when going to your bedroom for the night.

In contrast with some other English-speaking countries, the question 'How are you?' is often used as a (rather informal) greeting, rather than as a genuine question about someone's health. Thus two acquaintances might greet each other by both saying 'How are you!', more or less simultaneously, and with falling intonation. It is possible to reply to the question (with something like 'Good, thanks!' or 'I'm fine, thanks!') but it is not necessary to reply directly to the question at all. And it is possible to use 'How are you?' as a greeting to strangers in relatively informal circumstances.

Traditionally, Australians have tended to follow an English-style reserve about shaking hands and kissing. Older Australian men may shake hands only when being introduced for the first time or when marking the occasion in some special way – for example, when making a business deal or expressing sympathy to bereaved relatives at a funeral. Some older Australian women do not even offer their hand when being introduced and may shake hands quite rarely. Kissing when meeting or parting is traditionally reserved for relatives and very close friends, where one or both of the parties are female. (Men may kiss their very young sons or nephews or grandsons, but this stops at quite an early age. In general, men do not kiss each other at all, even two brothers or father and adult son.) Behaviour among younger Australians is changing, however, whether because of a greater willingness to show affection in public or because of the influence of non-British immigrants. Many men and women now shake hands not only when being introduced, but also when seeing each other after some interval and when parting at the end of some special occasion. Some men may hug each other on special occasions, but even younger males do not kiss each other. It is quite common now for two women or a woman and a man to kiss each other on the cheek – for example, when greeting guests for dinner or congratulating someone on a special achievement. But the pattern of behaviour is not well established and many Australians are still a little cautious. In general, it is wise for a man to wait to see whether a woman offers her hand or her cheek. Behaviour found in some parts of Europe, such as kissing each other on both cheeks, or kissing a woman's hand, is not customary.

If possible, Australians like to address each other by first names ('Hello, Maureen', 'Good afternoon, Eddie', 'How are you, Cathy', 'Fine thanks, Colin'). This seems to establish a normal, friendly relationship. In many cases, people use each other's first names from the moment they are introduced. It would seem quite awkward to most Australians to address a neighbour or a workmate as 'Mrs Jones' rather than as 'Jean', or as 'Mr Papas' rather than as 'Emil'. Some Australians do not even know their neighbours' surnames. To the surprise, and sometimes dismay, of many visitors, university students and teachers normally address each other by first names, as do many commercial and professional contacts, such as hairdressers, garage mechanics or chiropractors and their regular customers or clients. The use of title and surname ('Mrs Malouf', 'Mr Andrews', 'Dr Chan') suggests some marked distance between the people involved. Sometimes a large age gap is sufficient to create this distance. Thus your elderly neighbours may be happy for most of their neighbours to address them by first name; but they might prefer your very young children to address them as 'Mr and Mrs Berg'. Most university students might be happy to address most of the lecturers by their first names, but they may use title and surname for some of the very senior staff ('Professor Smith' or 'Dr Heinemann'). Professional settings may also suggest a necessary distance. A medical practitioner might introduce himself or herself to patients as 'Dr Benson' to establish a professional relationship. But doctors who introduced themselves in this way at a social function (instead of as 'Ruth Benson' or 'Alan Benson') would be regarded as 'putting on airs' or 'putting on the dog'.

The words 'Sir' and 'Madam' have limited use in Australia. Waiters in expensive restaurants, receptionists in high class hotels or airline booking staff, for example, may use these terms of address to older customers ('Would you come this way, please, Sir?', 'Could I ask you to wait a moment, please, Madam?', 'Please be at gate 16 by 11.30, Madam'). But even in these contexts, Australian service staff nowadays generally prefer to use the customer's name, once they know it. Thus the hotel receptionist, having booked you in and learned your name, may say 'I hope you enjoy your stay, Ms Henderson', or the airline check-in officer, having seen your ticket and issued your boarding pass, may say 'There you are, Mr Garcia, gate 16 at 11.30'; and the staff of one of the domestic airlines regularly address passengers by their first name. It is important to realize that 'Sir' and 'Madam' are not general ways of softening a request or making it polite. The use of 'Sir' and 'Madam' by ordinary members of the public, especially to younger people, will strike most Australians as foreign. So if you want to request something of a stranger in public, use words like 'excuse me' and 'please', frame a question rather than an order, and do not address people as Sir or Madam:

> 'Excuse me, could you tell me how to get to Martin Place, please?', 'Excuse me, could I come past you, please?' or 'Excuse me, would you mind moving your bag, please?'

Sport and gambling

In our questionnaire all the Australian respondents and 82 per cent of non-native respondents agreed with the statement that 'Australians have a strong sense of pleasure'. Both groups of respondents also agreed that Australians are 'sporty types' and 'nature lovers'. And, indeed, leisure continues to be an important part of Australian life. The weekend is highly valued as an escape from the routines of work, and many Australians end the working week with 'Have a good weekend!' and begin it by asking fellow workers 'Did you have a good weekend?'. And if there is a public holiday on a Friday or a Monday you can enjoy a 'long weekend'.

Sport is of course famously popular in Australia – national and international sporting events dominate commercial TV channels over weekends and, even on some evenings during the working week, some sporting events get very good ratings. Considering its relatively small population, Australia has often performed outstandingly well in such sports as cricket, rugby, swimming and tennis and many Australians who are involved in sports as participants, spectators or organizers can be quite passionate about it. Sport is also a common topic of conversation, especially among men. We have already mentioned the Australian reluctance to talk about politics and religion, and sport does provide a safe topic. Metaphors from sport are quite common, though of course not unique to Australia. In sports such as tennis and golf, it is important to 'follow through', i.e. complete a hitting movement properly, and this gives rise to more general use of 'following through' as an expression for completing a task properly. In football, the goal posts are of course fixed in place.

If the posts were moved closer together or further apart, it would create unexpected changes in the playing conditions. Hence a politician or a boss who keeps altering the rules or the priorities, may be accused of 'shifting the goal posts'. In cricket, the aim is to score runs, and the current total is shown on a scoreboard. 'To know the score' means to understand the situation and to know what is required; 'to have runs on the board' means that you have made some progress or achieved some success.

The co-operative team spirit of games like cricket and football, in which players depend on each other and must work together, is highly valued in Australian culture. In football, manoeuvres in which several players co-operate to score a goal are often cheered and applauded, and the players themselves will give credit to 'the team play' rather than focusing on the one player who actually scored the goal. From cricket in particular come expressions like 'fielding a team' (bringing a group of people to a task), 'going in to bat for someone' (to play one's part to help someone, to support someone) and 'carrying one's bat' (continuing to bat undismissed, even though other players are being dismissed, hence accomplishing a lengthy and difficult task). In cricket it is also important to 'back each other up'. When the ball is thrown in towards the centre of the field, for example, one team member should normally be in position to catch it. But in case he misses or fumbles the ball, other team members should if possible move round behind him ready to stop or retrieve the ball. This notion of 'backing each other up' readily extends to general usage.

In general, Australians like 'fair play', in sport and in life at large. People should compete with each other honestly and without special advantage or privilege (not that all Australians are fine examples of fairness). A noisy audience might be asked to give the speaker 'a fair go', or someone who wants a fair opportunity might ask for 'a fair crack of the whip'.

Apart from the general availability of sporting facilities, such as swimming pools, cricket ovals and football fields even in smaller country towns, an important factor contributing to sporting achievements is the active interest which most parents and schools show in competitive sport at all levels. All schools, including primary, require their students to participate in school teams in a variety of sports on a regular basis. Thus during the school year at least one of the parents in each family with children regularly spends Saturday mornings and early afternoons driving children to various inter-school competitions ('bussing', as it is popularly known). Many parents are also involved as trainers, referees or organizers. Moreover, national or professional football, swimming, tennis and cricket teams take an active interest in this kind of activity, often sponsor tournaments and, in the process, fish for new talent.

Cricket is popular all over the country in the summer months and the Melbourne Cricket Ground (MCG) is the largest cricket ground in the world, able to accommodate nearly 100,000 spectators. During the winter months various forms of football are played and watched. Rugby League Football (played also in northern England but hardly anywhere else in the world) is popular in New South Wales and Queensland. Australian Rules Football (unique to Australia, as the name suggests, and often referred to as AFL, short for Australian Football League, or more colloquially as 'Aussie rules') developed most strongly in the other states, namely Victoria, Tasmania, South Australia and Western Australia, where it is the dominant code of football. But teams from New South Wales and Queensland do now play in the AFL and have some popular following. Despite its peculiarly Australian origin, Australian Rules Football, as an organized sport, is as old as British-style football. (There are written rules of Australian football dating from a game played in Melbourne in 1858.) British style football is also played in Australia, and Australians take some interest in the widely publicized events, such as the English Cup Final and the World Cup, but when Australians speak of football (or colloquially footy) they mean Rugby League or AFL, depending on which state they are from. British football is 'soccer'.

Sporting events such as major cricket and football matches, especially grand finals and test matches (certain international games), are probably as significant to many Australians as Australia Day and Anzac Day. They attract large crowds of supporters, dressed in club colours, waving banners and club flags, singing songs written specially for their clubs and generally cheering their sides passionately.

Finally, horse-racing is a national pastime for many throughout the year. As in England, there are numerous horse races held throughout Australia, but the most famous is the Melbourne Cup, run on the first Tuesday of November. The day is a public holiday in Melbourne. Linked to some extent to the interest in horse racing and other competitive sports, but extending to many other areas as well, is the Australian passion for gambling. It is estimated that the average expenditure per adult per year is around $500 (about £200). Horse racing is a common avenue for betting. Also popular are lotteries, some of which are owned or controlled by state governments, including 'instant' tickets known as 'scratchies' since the purchaser scratches panels to reveal whether the ticket is a winner. Lottery tickets are widely available – for example, at many newsagencies. Gambling has probably become even more widespread with the opening of large casinos in all major cities. Gambling metaphors, such as a 'safe bet', 'long odds' and 'odds-on', are found in ordinary discourse about risks and probabilities, as in 'it's odds-on he'll say no' or 'I wouldn't mind betting John will put his name down for that'.

Functions, parties and celebrations

What we have said so far may seem to have given prominence to sport and gambling, but of course there are many other leisure activities pursued by Australians at home and away from home which deserve mention in a review of this type, such as the way Australians celebrate various occasions and holidays, as well as what types of entertainment and other indoor and outdoor activities are popular.

Australia Day, on 26 January, commemorates the founding of the first British colony at Sydney Cove and has become more popular in recent years as organizers have tried to hold crowd-pulling events such as ferry races and parades of sailing ships on Sydney Harbour. Citizenship ceremonies are also often scheduled for Australia Day. Like the first Governor of Australia and his officers, who spent the evening of 26 January 1788 drinking the health of the royal family, many of the participants of the Australia Day celebrations linger on in pubs or public parks, often consuming large quantities of alcohol (but usually not toasting the royal family).

ANZAC stands for the Australian and New Zealand Army Corps, formed during the First World War, and Anzac Day commemorates the landing of Australian and New Zealand troops at Gallipoli in Turkey on 25 April 1915. Many Australian soldiers died there and the day has become a memorial to all Australians who died in war. Religious services are usually held at dawn, followed by a veterans' march. After the march, most of the veterans gather in local pubs or RSL (Returned Services League) clubs. These reunions are often accompanied by heavy drinking and drunkenness.

Christmas and Easter are observed as religious occasions, but Christmas is also a time of family celebration. Many families will make a point of getting together on or around Christmas, even if they live some way away from each other and rarely see each other during the year. There is of course no white Christmas in Australia. Both Christmas and New Year's Day, which is also a public holiday, happen in the middle of the hot summer and long school holidays. Since many people go away from home for holidays during this time and there is a much smaller demand on shops and businesses, many businesses and offices close between 25 December and 2 January. Some factories may close for longer than this and cities become quite deserted, while the majority of Australians fill country roads, beaches, caravan parks, hotels and motels, mainly along the coast. The last evening of the old year (New Year's Eve) is frequently marked by fireworks displays and by partying in public parks in the cities as well as in holiday venues.

As can be seen from the above, Australians generally love a good party and they like to get together with friends and relations to celebrate various occasions. Some occasions, such as weddings, more important wedding anniversaries or the baptism of a new baby, are

105

shared with most other cultures, although, again due to the climate, many of these and other occasions when Australians entertain at home take place in the garden and the meal is usually cooked on a barbecue. This makes Australian parties organized in private homes much less formal than in some other countries – people come wearing clothes that are of good quality but definitely casual in style, and they move around the patio and garden, drinking beer or wine to which they often help themselves from portable coolers called 'Eskies' where the drinks are stored on ice. The adults, including the hosts, do not have to run in and out of the kitchen, since the meal is being barbecued outside, and the adults can therefore enjoy leisurely conversation with each other, while the children play various games or sports in the garden and, generally speaking, take good care of themselves without bothering the adults too much. There are usually a few older boys and girls who can make sure the little ones don't get hurt and have something interesting to do.

Another interesting feature of such parties, especially those organized for larger groups of people with some common interest (for example, parents of children playing some sport in the same school team), is the custom of bringing something to drink and 'bringing a plate'. (The plate of course should have some food on it!) This makes the organization of such gatherings much easier on the hosts, as the preparations and expenses are shared by all who come. It is not surprising that barbecues and other open-air parties are popular and frequent.

Finally, unlike most peoples living in colder climates, where parties are organized inside the home in much more formal settings, and certainly unlike most British people, Australians seem to share with some southern European cultures a fairly relaxed attitude towards themselves and their guests. While people are told when the party is taking place and what time it starts, no one seems to mind some guests arriving up to an hour late or to make much fuss when some guests leave much earlier than others. Of course Australians do sometimes have more formal dinner parties, and the conventions are correspondingly stricter (you might bring a bottle of wine to a dinner party, but even in Australia you don't bring a plate of food nor do you wander uninvited into your hosts' kitchen!). And Australians are not as tolerant when it comes to social conversation. As in most English-speaking cultures, Australians tend to avoid controversial topics and they disapprove of expressing your opinions in a forceful way or arguing during social gatherings (see the following section).

When they are not throwing a barbecue party, Australians love to go out to eat. Depending on their financial means and the occasion, people go to fast food outlets or bistros or restaurants of lower or higher standard. And it must be said that, thanks to large intakes of migrants from many different countries, Australian cities offer a stunning variety of high-quality food styles in both cheaper and more expensive restaurants. When larger groups meet in a restaurant to celebrate someone's birthday or promotion, or just to enjoy the food, the custom of everyone sharing in the bill makes it much easier for groups of friends to do it quite often.

In general, Australians value egalitarian friendliness more than lavish hospitality. At a barbecue or dinner party, while it is of course important that there is enough food and drink, hosts will not make a point of having far more food than is necessary, and there is no disgrace if the food is all finished by the end of the meal. Hosts will generally take some responsibility for offering food and drink ('Please do start', 'Will you have some more wine?') but will often issue a general invitation ('Please help yourselves') and guests will indeed do so, especially at outdoor barbecues or parties. There is no ritual of urging people to take more or eat more, while guests politely decline until pressed two or three times. In other words, offers to have more are genuine and the guest is free to decline or accept as he or she wishes. Of course this freedom brings a certain responsibility: if guests are free to help themselves, they should keep an eye on how much food there is and be aware of what looks like a fair share.

If a guest declines an offer of food or drink, they usually do so with some polite reference to their satisfaction – for example, 'No thanks, I've done very well already', 'No more for me, thanks, it was beautiful food', or 'I really couldn't eat any more, thanks, wonderful food'. Strict laws against driving under the influence of alcohol mean that most hosts will not press guests to drink excessively, and if they do, guests will often use the law as a justification – for example, 'No more to drink, thanks, I'm driving', or 'No, I mustn't have any more wine, thanks, I've got to drive home tonight'.

Australia has drinking places similar to English pubs. Australians commonly refer to these as pubs but the official term is hotel, which means that the word hotel is sometimes ambiguous between the kind of high-rise hotel for tourists and business people in the cities and the traditional pub. The local pub is as much of an institution in Australia as it is in England, but there are differences. For example, Australian pubs rarely have the old British-style signboards and names (like the Red Lion or the Grafton Arms) and they tend to be named for their location or their owners in the Irish style (as, for example, Eastwood Hotel, Railway Hotel or Jackson's Hotel). In cities there is usually at least one pub within walking distance of most homes, and if you 'go bush', you may find that a dot and name on the map turns out to be a small town centred on a post office, a petrol station, a general store and a pub, these facilities perhaps serving a farming community spread over a wide circle around the town. The traditional Australian pub was for men, who drank mainly beer and yarned with their mates, but women are now allowed in all areas of pubs, and many pubs are trying to attract wider clienteles – for example, by offering a range of meals in various styles or running a night club with music and dancing in the evenings. Beer is still popular but is no longer the obligatory alcoholic drink for men, and Australia now has a good reputation for its wines. Most pubs offer wine for sale by the glass, as well as a variety of beers, spirits and soft drinks.

Everyday conversational encounters

As we have already mentioned, Australians are generally willing to exchange friendly greetings and casual conversation with each other. Neighbours might talk to each other in this way, as might people who share the same workplace and even sometimes people standing next to each other in a queue or sitting next to one another at a sporting event. But there are important qualifications to this friendliness. In the first place, a false image has been created by some films and television programmes of an easy-going (and possibly not highly cultured or intelligent) Australian who cheerfully says 'G'day' to everyone he or she meets. Australians themselves are aware of this kind of overseas image and sometimes resent it. While it may once have been common practice in country areas to greet everyone you see – and still is in remote areas where there are relatively few people – it is certainly not customary in the densely populated cities to greet or speak to those with whom you rub shoulders on buses or trams or in lifts or shopping centres.

Second, a willingness to exchange pleasant conversation is not necessarily friendship in a deeper sense, and Australian openness is balanced by the sense of privacy we have already referred to. Thus suburban neighbours might habitually greet each other and exchange remarks about the heat, the lack of rain, the building of a new road in the district and suchlike, but they may not invite each other inside their houses (except very occasionally, perhaps for an evening of drinks shortly before Christmas) and they will generally avoid 'intrusive' topics to do with one's age or income or political affiliation. Australians will defend such practices by saying that if you want to attend church, join a political party or consult an accountant about your finances, you are free to do so. And most people have some close friends to whom they can speak relatively freely and openly. But you should not presume on casual acquaintances.

The ability to carry on a professional or social conversation requires not only linguistic skills but also some knowledge of what is considered acceptable and unacceptable in conversational exchanges in the context of a given culture. Generally speaking, Australians seem to follow the British model of trying not to appear authoritarian, pushy or excessively disagreeable in discussing matters professionally or socially, unless encouraged by circumstances to do so. Thus they will not readily initiate discussion of politics or religion, or indeed of personal finances. Anyone who quickly and openly declares a political stance or who speaks freely of their own income and wealth is likely to be judged as 'coming on too heavy' or 'shooting a line'. Indeed, a whole range of phrases demonstrate the Australian distaste for any talk that suggests self-importance or self-praise. Males in particular may condemn another man for 'big-noting himself', 'having tickets on himself' or 'shooting off his mouth'. More vulgarly, they may dismiss what they see as excessive and exaggerated talk as 'bullshit', sometimes slightly less crudely abbreviated to 'bull'. A man who achieves a reputation for boastful and unreliable talk may therefore be known (but not usually in public) as a 'bull artist'.

The devices that Australians use to soften or qualify an expression of opinion in order not to sound authoritarian may seem overelaborate to outsiders ('I suppose you could say that . . .', 'I would say that . . .') but it is important to Australians to avoid direct disagreement most of the time. So they may either hedge, making their disagreement sound tentative ('Well, I think I see it a bit differently' or 'Yes, I know what you mean, but wouldn't you say that . . .'), or they may accompany their disagreement with an apology ('No, I'm sorry, I disagree' or 'I'm afraid I don't see it that way'). Self deprecation may strike the outsider as artificial but is again an important device to take away the bluntness of a disagreement: 'Maybe I'm being stupid but I don't think that . . .' or 'Well, I'm very old-fashioned, so I think that . . .' or 'Nobody's going to like me for saying this, but . . .'.

When an Australian does veer towards bluntness or aggressiveness in conversation, others may indicate their disapproval in apparently light-hearted or humorous ways: 'Well, you've put your cards on the table, haven't you, Bill!', 'I think Sandra's finished off that topic for us, hasn't she!' or 'Well, Colin, you've given us all plenty to think about there!' After all, to express your disapproval too bluntly in public would mean that you were doing precisely what you were disapproving of! A consequence of these constraints on social discourse is that many non-Australians may find conversation in Australia tame and trivial, not vigorous and challenging.

This does not mean to say that Australians are ineffective in resolving public issues. On the contrary, by skilfully applying such techniques as letting everyone have their say without interruptions or open brawls, putting forward motions and voting on them, Australians sometimes manage short but fruitful meetings that lead to specific solutions. As elsewhere of course, this is often possible only because the most controversial matters have been discussed before the meeting by smaller groups who may make their stance known and exert some influence over the meeting and any voting. The technique of predicting or arranging the voting in advance, particularly before political meetings, is sometimes called the 'numbers game' and a man who is expert in arranging things is a 'numbers man'. This often means that the meeting itself can be conducted without bitter confrontation and overt hostility (even though there may be real differences of opinion beneath the surface). Similarly, in professional encounters in which no voting takes place, say meetings between business people or between service providers and their clients, any suggestion or proposal is usually expressed politely but consistently, and may be matched by an equally politely expressed counter-proposal. By making sure that conversations of this type involve turn-taking, people usually manage to reach a compromise solution.

Similar techniques are applied in social conversation at private parties, barbecues and other unofficial gatherings, although, as we have already seen, some topics, such as sport, gardening or children, are considered more interesting and safer than others. From the point of view of some cultures, this may make Australian social conversations sound very boring. There are at least two important reasons for avoiding controversial topics outside groups of family or close friends. One of them, which seems to be shared with the British, is the wish not to appear opinionated or pushy. This, however, accounts for the manner of speech, rather than the choice of topics. Second, the purpose of social conversation, especially in relaxed settings during a weekend, is mostly to share information or to seek or give advice on matters of mutual leisurely interest. The average Australian wants to leave worries and serious issues alone from Friday evening until Monday morning. The television programming responds to this very well: the evening news on Friday and Saturday usually contains relatively little political news (but often plenty of sporting news) and there are few serious current affairs programmes shown at weekends.

Many people form their opinions about the degree of friendliness and warmth of representatives of other cultures on the basis of encounters involving professional, social or incidental conversations with them. In this context, it is interesting to note that Australians like to think of themselves as warmer and more friendly, more down-to-earth and honest and definitely less patronizing than the British. In fact, 70 per cent of the Australian respondents in our questionnaire considered the British to be proud, 61 per cent considered them to be serious and cold, and only 48 per cent considered them friendly. These perceptions are strongly supported by our non-Australian respondents, who have had encounters with both cultures: 65 per cent considered the British to be proud, 82 per cent serious and 59 per cent cold; only 23 per cent considered them friendly.

We can probably assume that the above figures are based more on social and incidental than professional exchanges, which are quite similar in most English-speaking cultures. What seems to be the case is that many (although not of course all) British people tend to retain at least some of the professional standards and the famous 'stiff upper lip' even in social conversations. This causes them to come across as cold at times, but it also allows them to discuss more serious matters socially in an agreeable fashion. Australians, on the other hand, seem to prefer resorting to safe topics and shedding some of the pomp and principles for the weekend, which allows them to speak more forcefully (to many non-English cultures this comes across as more bluntly or more honestly) about things like the performance of the Australian cricket team, the effectiveness of a new variety of garden fertilizer, or the increasing traffic congestion in the neighbourhood. This is also probably what Donald Horne meant when he commented on Australian conversational customs as follows:

> ... remarkable openness of manner impresses – and sometimes appals – those who are used to social stiffness or deference. Truth is sometimes blurted out with a directness that can disgust those who come from more devious civilisations. A cult of informality derived from a deep belief in the essential sameness and ordinariness of mankind reduces ceremony to something that is quietly and self-consciously performed in a corner. (Horne, 1978, p. 19)

Friendly and not-so-friendly encounters with strangers

Something that has often puzzled visitors and migrants going shopping in Australia is the tradition of having to wait one's turn. Even if there are not many customers, they will have to wait while the Australian shop assistant follows the rule of serving one person at a time. Although this behaviour may seem inefficient or even lazy, especially to those from other countries who have seen sales staff dealing with several customers at a time, Australians consider it impolite to walk away from someone in the middle of a conversational exchange, which is considered finished only when the whole of the transaction is complete. Moreover, as we have already said, Australians generally do not want to appear pushy, and walking away to serve another customer before the first one has completed business might look like a tactic to force the first customer to hurry up and make a decision.

As in other English-speaking countries, the dialogue between the shop assistant or cashier or attendant and the customer may seem very polite, especially when it comes to requesting and refusing things in the process. Direct imperatives are not common in the speech of Australians. It is possible, among family and very close friends, to give direct orders: 'Come over here', 'Put the plates on that table', 'Don't leave that garbage in the kitchen, take it outside to the bin.' But even where a close relationship allows such directness, commands may still be softened by tags, as in 'Come here, could you?' or 'Don't put that down there, will you?'

Once you move away from family and close friends, it becomes essential to avoid direct imperatives in spoken English. The most common strategy is to turn an order or request into a question. Thus 'Leave the papers on the table' becomes 'Could you leave the papers on the table?' or 'Would you leave the papers on the table?' or, even more politely, 'Would you mind leaving the papers on the table?' The addition of 'please' is of course a further way of signalling politeness, but Australians sometimes use 'thanks' where other English speakers might use 'please', as in 'Could I have a look at the book over there, thanks?' It is common to hear Australians buying tickets, for example, with such requests as 'A single to Central, thanks' or 'Two adults for cinema 3, thanks'. Failure to use this style of interaction – for example, by simply saying 'Put the book over there' or 'Give me a single to Geelong' – will sound abrupt or aggressive.

There are well defined and restricted contexts in which it is normal to utter imperatives, such as when an army officer gives orders or a trainer takes a fitness class through their exercises. But here there is a clear understanding that someone is in a position of authority or acting as an instructor. Outside such contexts the use of imperatives is generally likely to be offensive. And of course sometimes people intend to be offensive, when they angrily abuse another driver or tell someone to get out of their way. Here the use of the imperative, as in 'Watch what you're doing!' or 'Get moving!' or 'Don't just stand there!', is itself part of the indication that these are exceptional utterances expressing anger and impatience.

Similar considerations apply to refusing a request or demand. Even people with authority may apologize for a refusal: 'I'm sorry I can't agree to that', 'I'm afraid there are no seats left on that flight', 'I'm very sorry, we don't have funds for that purpose.' Even someone who tries to beg a cigarette or money in the street may be turned away with 'Sorry' or 'Afraid not' rather than just a blunt 'No'.

Interestingly, English (not only in Australia) does allow imperatives in written texts like recipes and instruction manuals (where other languages may for various reasons avoid them): 'Slice a large onion', 'Remove the plug from the socket', 'Insert the tab into the slot', and so on.

The reluctance to appear pushy also makes Australian shop assistants, service providers and public servants seem as if they do not really care, especially when they are asked directly to provide advice. When it comes to giving advice, Australians seem to behave differently, depending on whether they are being asked for information or being asked to help in a decision. Australians – generally speaking – will readily supply information but if they feel they are being asked to assist in making a decision, they tend to seem unhappy about the request itself and to make some effort not to be involved.

Thus Australians can be extremely friendly and forthcoming when it comes to practical advice on little everyday matters, such as street directions, explaining how a device works or where one can go to obtain professional assistance, as well as on the more important practicalities of settling down in Australia or in a new neighbourhood. They seem to share this feature with Americans, perhaps because both cultures have been through a pioneering period, when advice of this type was vital. This may be one of the main reasons why both Americans and Australians are viewed as friendly by migrants from other cultures. They not only give advice of this type freely and willingly, but they also tend to follow up on their advice and offer assistance when necessary. You usually have to ask for this advice, however. For fear of appearing pushy, Australians are usually quite reluctant to volunteer advice of this type unless they are asked for it. Important advice for members of other cultures visiting or settling in Australia is therefore: if you have a practical problem and do not know how to go about solving it, do not hesitate to ask.

The attitude of an average Australian is quite different, however, when it comes to making decisions for other people. This is well illustrated by the typical behaviour of Australian shop assistants: information about products will be supplied readily but special care will be taken to present it in the form of several choices and to avoid any hint as to what decision should be taken. This is caused not only by the desire not to appear aggressive or self-important, but also by a deeper belief, held dear by most Australians, that everyone should not just be free to take their own decisions, but that responsibility for those decisions and their consequences is a personal matter that should not be interfered with by others. Thus, for a visitor or new arrival looking to make a decision, the advice is the opposite of our previous comment: if you have a problem reaching a decision, do not ask for help in making that decision. Your questions may cause embarrassment and may even be considered rude. The chances are that every effort will be made not to give direct or useful answers.

What we have said above applies in shops and in most situations where you are acquiring goods or services, including small businesses, travel agents, government and private offices, and doctors' and dentists' surgeries. The general impression of a person coming from another culture might at times be that services in Australia are second rate, mainly because they can be slow and quite restrained when it comes to assisting the customer or client in a choice of items or services. On the other hand, it must be said that most Australian service providers somehow manage not only to get their customers to decide what they want, but also to deliver the services requested on time.

Australian values and attitudes

Australian society cherishes similar basic values to most other cultures belonging to the Western world, although Australia's history and the temperament of its peoples have caused some of the values to become more important than others. The aim of this section is to give the reader some insight into the Australian system of values and thus help you to understand and appreciate the way Australians interpret the world around them.

Australian nationalism

Australia has been very fortunate in that from 1901, when the colonies became a federation, its self-determination has never been seriously questioned or threatened, nor has any belligerent neighbour claimed parts of the continent as rightfully theirs. Except for the Second World War, when Australia might have been invaded by the advancing Japanese, all the wars in which Australian soldiers have taken part have happened quite far away – Europe, Africa, Korea, Vietnam and the Middle East – and these wars were only indirectly connected with the security of Australia. Australians are fiercely patriotic as both competitors and spectators in sport, but they hardly ever talk about the other, more traditional sense of patriotism.

This does not mean that Australians are not patriotic. But patriotism has no Australian war of independence, no Australian imperial history (other than involvement in the British Empire) to feed on. Australian nationalism is mainly reflected in its sporting performance against other countries, in its changing attitudes towards Britain and in strong reactions to criticisms of Australia and Australians by foreigners. But, unlike many other nationalisms around the world, Australian nationalism is of the friendlier kind and does not habitually interlock with aggression or threats against other countries.

Australian English

Most Australians in the early twenty-first century accept that their culture and language are distinctively Australian and they do not see any need to apologize for this. It was not always so. In the first half of the twentieth century, for example, it was common for Australians to criticize Australian ways of using English. Dame Nellie Melba, who was born in 1861 and died in 1931 after a long career as one of Australia's most famous singers, spoke of Australians' 'twisted vowels' and 'distortions and slackness of speech' (Mitchell and Delbridge, 1965, p. 66). A correspondent to the *ABC Weekly* in 1942 reflected the desire of many Australians to identify with Britain and the British Empire: 'There is not, and should not be, any difference in standard English as spoken here, in the Motherland, or elsewhere in the Empire …' (*ibid.* pp. 67–8).

This was the era of what has often been called 'the cultural cringe'. Many Australians seemed ashamed of local features and local talent. It was thought that what came from overseas, especially from the centre of the British Empire, must be better than anything originating in the former colonies. In this era, Australian English or Australian language often meant vulgar language or swearing. Even in the 1970s, one Australian publisher was reluctant to publish a general English dictionary with a title like *Dictionary of Australian English*, for fear the title might be taken to mean this was a dictionary containing only slang or colloquial expressions. During this period, then, British English was being presented as the standard for Australians. The ABC (Australian Broadcasting Corporation, founded in 1932 as the Australian Broadcasting Commission) was in its early days modelled quite closely on the British BBC and, like the BBC, it favoured British Received Pronunciation (RP, see Chapter 2) in its announcers – though it didn't always achieve that ideal. Even today, when attitudes have markedly changed, many Australian actors, voice teachers and singers still regard RP as a kind of ideal pronunciation, even though most of them do not expect Australians to use it most of the time.

Australian attitudes to Britain

There is some popular animosity between English and Australian people. The English will make jokes about Australians being heavy-drinking, ill-mannered descendants of convicts; Australians can be no less scathing in their jokes about the pretentious, complaining and dirty English. The Australian colloquial term for an English person is a 'Pommy' or a 'Pom'. This term is probably better defined as 'someone from the United Kingdom', as it may refer to Scottish or Welsh people but not usually to the Irish. The term may sometimes be used endearingly, as in the generally light-hearted reference to England or the UK as 'Pommyland', as well as in derogatory expressions like 'whinging Pommy', for an English person who complains constantly. Jokes about the dirtiness of the English reflect the fact that

Australians have developed a concern for personal cleanliness and regard daily showering as a minimum requirement for civilized living in a warm climate, while the English, in a colder climate, have, at least until recent years, not given the same priority to showering or bathing. The Australian prejudice is reflected in expressions like 'My throat is as dry as a Pommy's bath towel' or in jokes like 'Where do you hide your money from a Pommy? – In the bathroom, under the soap.'

Despite such hostility, whether light-hearted or more serious, Australia remains tied to Britain in formal ways, as well as by the mere fact that millions of Australians are of British origin. The Head of State of Australia is still Queen Elizabeth II, although her role in Australia is almost entirely ceremonial, performed through the Governor-General of Australia and through the governors of each state. Australian legislation still nominally requires royal assent; land owned by the government is still commonly referred to as crown land; the Australian navy and air force are still the Royal Australian Navy and the Royal Australian Air Force; and many institutions carry the title 'Royal' as a mark of honour, from the Royal Easter Show (an annual agricultural show and fair held in Sydney) to the Royal Flying Doctor Service, which provides medical services by plane in remote areas of the country. And the Queen's Christmas address is still televised in Australia each year.

Many older Australians, including some born in Britain and some who served in, or remember, wars in which Australians served in the name of the Queen, are reluctant to see Australia sever all its ties with Britain. British programmes, such as comedy series and historical dramas, are often shown on Australian television; cricket matches between Australia and England draw large crowds; and major sporting events from Britain, even some that include no Australian participation, such as the annual soccer cup final, may be broadcast live from Britain. Eventually, however, Australia will become a republic and it will be interesting to see what changes, if any, in attitudes will follow. It is possible that, having totally discarded any symbols of dependence on Britain, Australia might actually become more affectionate towards the source of its very existence, its language and many elements of its culture.

Religion

The largest churches in Australia are the Roman Catholic Church, the Anglican Church of Australia (linked with the Church of England) and the Uniting Church (an amalgam of what in Britain were called 'dissenting' or 'nonconformist', i.e. non-Anglican, churches). Roman Catholics are a notably higher proportion of the population than in the UK, partly because of the numbers of Australians of Irish origin and partly because of post-war immigration from strongly Catholic areas of Europe. Most Australians have a nominal commitment to Christianity, although for many of them it is no more than that: they may get married in a church, have their children baptized, perhaps even send their children to a Sunday school, and be farewelled in a church funeral, but not enter a church for months at a time. But even though a minority of Australians seem to be seriously committed to attendance and participation in church life, surveys always seem to indicate that a majority of Australians have some kind of belief in God and in life after death.

As in many European countries, the influence of the church was once much stronger than it is now. In retrospect, many Australians now judge that influence to have been repressive, but it is debatable how far the churches were responsible for the kind of Puritanism prevailing in Australia in the past and how far they simply reflected contemporary notions of respectability and restraint. And much of the good that was done by churches – charitable work in an era without social services and education, for example – is often forgotten. Nowadays those who are too zealous or outspoken about religion may be called 'holy Joes', those whose aim seems to be to stop other people enjoying themselves may be condemned with the label 'wowsers'. Against these holy Joes and wowsers, Horne sees 'a counter-balancing paganism among ordinary people' (Horne, 1978, p. 24). Putting it more philosophically, he comments: 'Belief in the dignity of man, in the human potential and in the value of human life is almost universal. The official beliefs of Australians are essentially humanist and those parts of Christianity that fit this belief are retained' (*ibid.,* p. 46).

From the nineteenth century there have been other minority religions – Judaism, for example – but post-war immigration, from Europe and the Middle East, and now from Asia, has increased the diversity of Christian churches as well as adding non-Christian religions. Immigrants from eastern and southern Europe, the Middle East and Asia have brought flourishing Orthodox churches, as well as growing Muslim and Buddhist communities.

Liberty, equality and fraternity the Australian way

Australia is still known in many parts of the world as the 'workers' paradise' and, indeed, it seems to be one of the few examples of countries and communities that have put the ideals of liberty, equality and fraternity into practice with some success. As we mentioned above, Australia's independence has not been seriously challenged so far and hence it is civil liberties of the individual, the right to privacy and to a decent income and, most of all, the right of individuals to decide about their own affairs, that seem to be cherished by an average Australian. This is reflected in typical attitudes to rules and authority.

Australians are perhaps no different from most people in the world in having a love-hate relationship with authority, but the history of Australia has given a particular local twist to this tension. Most people welcome authority when it makes for an ordered, efficient life, when justice is upheld and crime is punished; but they can also find authority intrusive, restrictive and repressive. Strong government has often been considered essential in such matters as keeping order and contributing to the development of the country – through the building of schools, hospitals, roads and railways, for example. But government authority is also easily identified with a bureaucratic desire to organize people and society in ways that stifle freedom and individuality. Putting things in their Australian historical context, firm authority may be necessary to get the bush tamed and cities built – but firm authority can also be used to run the country like a penal colony or a military camp, a vision to which most Australians do not warm.

In the eyes of an average Australian, the government is elected not to tell people what to do, but to provide everyone with secure jobs, high quality medical services, good education and to maintain order. The police force is there not to interfere with what people wish to do, but to arrive quickly and assist in case of emergencies and when the law is broken. And the local council is often regarded as a nuisance or a menace. The council wants its quarterly fees ('council rates'), they are too nosy about what people do on their own land and they have too many regulations which they insist on enforcing against the will of the people. What they should concentrate on is organizing the weekly rubbish collection and improving local streets, parks and services.

In social life these attitudes translate into a measure of restrained orderliness, a kind of rough-and-ready compromise between strict regulation and rampant individualism. On the streets of the cities, Australians show a kind of easy-going respect for each other, but without any particular courtesy. At a bus stop, people will rarely form a strict queue in the orderly manner still seen in some parts of Britain; but they generally have a sense of fairness, with some deference to older people, and they avoid pushing and squeezing if they can. But where people are forced to queue, as where railings or barriers oblige them to in a post office or at an airport, they usually accept it. Attempts to 'jump the queue' are generally considered unfair, though an Australian is more likely to give you a dark look or make a quiet comment on your behaviour than to abuse you loudly or threateningly.

Drivers observe most of the traffic rules which they judge sensible. But many of them regularly exceed speed limits when they think it reasonable to do so and most of them see nothing wrong in making an illegal manoeuvre (say an explicitly prohibited turn at an intersection) if there is no other traffic or police car around. To drive the long way round, simply in order to observe the traffic signs, when there is no other traffic on the road in the middle of the night, would seem silly to many Australians. Nevertheless, behaviour which makes life difficult for others may be criticized. In general, pedestrians and drivers do not remonstrate with each other, and there is, for example, much less sound of car horns in Australian cities than in many cities of the world. But thoughtless and disruptive behaviour such as blocking an intersection, so that other road users do not get their 'fair go', may well incur noisy abuse.

This famous Australian phrase, 'a fair go', says much about the Australian way of pursuing the ideal of equality and about how egalitarian attitudes prevail through government and society, in community life and at the level of individual behaviour. Of course not everyone in Australia is equal – and some Australians have a selfish and vested interest in inequality – but an appeal for a fair go is always likely to draw a good response from most Australians.

Both state and federal governments tend to 'play things by ear', listening carefully to numerous interest groups, big and small, so that no one can complain that someone else is getting preferential treatment. More importantly, however, since the majority of Australians believe in giving everyone equal chances of having an income and access to medical and other basic services, Australia has, over the years, developed into a welfare state in which the working population heavily subsidises the unemployed, the sick and the aged through the taxation system. And, even though everyone complains about high taxes, and some politicians have campaigned for savings in public spending and won elections, no political party has so far seen it as advantageous to promise the complete abolition of welfare payments or the compulsory national medical insurance system (Medicare).

Egalitarian attitudes are reflected in community life as well. Class distinctions are not prominent or emphasized, nor are there serious tensions caused by racial or religious divisions. Again, this is not to say that there are never any assaults or violent incidents or riots in Australia – but, in comparison with many countries in the world, Australia is calm and relaxed about its internal diversity. Everyone deserves a fair go and a chance to do what they wish as long as it does not interfere with others. It is thanks to such attitudes that Australia was able to introduce a policy of multiculturalism in the 1980s and, by and large, to make a success of it.

A less attractive aspect of egalitarianism is that Australians often seem suspicious of people who stand out as more successful than others, people who enjoy unusual power or wealth or status, especially if these people give the impression that they consider themselves better than others. Such people are known as 'tall poppies' and are generally disliked. While they are successful, people will make derogatory comments about them, in a process sometimes called 'cutting down the tall poppies'. When they run into trouble, the tall poppies can expect little sympathy or support.

Finally, egalitarian attitudes are reflected in personal relations in everyday encounters, at work and on public occasions. While Australian bosses have all the authority they need to carry out their job and often enjoy income and privileges that are way above the average, they tend to present themselves as ordinary people. Many of Australia's wealthiest business people will appear on television in casual (though expensive) clothing and will use an accent and vocabulary that are indistinguishable from those of their employees. At functions organized for staff, a boss will often mix with staff and talk to them on an equal footing. Many Australian politicians likewise try to come across as ordinary Australians. They are often photographed in situations that might risk being undignified, such as on the beach or taking exercise or greeting passers-by in a shopping mall, and it seems they value their exposure as ordinary people above dignity or formality. In fact, many people who are at risk of being tall poppies seem to go out of their way to appear not to be. Famous sportsmen and sportswomen visit school teams to share their skills in a pleasant and relaxed manner; highly paid and famous TV and radio personalities try to appear friendly and ordinary while conducting interviews or reporting events; the richer parents at school make a point of fraternizing with the parents of the poorer kids on an equal footing. In short, everyone seems to be trying hard to be a 'dinkum Aussie' – and most of the time, despite the real disparities in power and income, it seems to work!

It should not come as a surprise that a relaxed egalitarian society, enjoying all the basic civil rights, subscribes en masse to the ideology of fraternalism. From the point of view of an average Aussie there is little to fight about and plenty to gain by being 'good mates' with others involved in the same kind of activity or sharing the sense of belonging to the same group. In their easy and relaxed way, Australians are also known to have warm and friendly attitudes to newcomers in most situations, be it other Australians arriving at a camping ground at the seaside or foreigners who have just migrated to Australia and are joining a neighbourhood. These attitudes, so characteristic of everyday life in Australia, are also exhibited when Australians go on overseas trips. As Max Harris puts it:

> Mateship became an attitude to human relationship, an easy readiness to strike up contact with fellow human beings in a warm and casual way. This often strikes outsiders as evidence of vulgar over-democratisation ... In fact the Australian has a rough

but ready capacity for immediate affection, a quality which, oddly for an Anglo-Saxon breed, he shares with some of the Mediterranean people. (in Horne, 1978, p. 20)

Tasks and exercises

1. What social classes or groups can be distinguished in the society of your home country? How do they compare with the divisions within the Australian society?

2. Explain the meaning and origin of the following words and expressions:
   - displaced person
   - battler
   - dole bludger
   - silvertails
   - squattocracy
   - whinger
   - sickie
   - Pitt Street farmer
   - the bush
   - outback
   - back of beyond
   - the red centre
   - beyond the black stump
   - Aussie bloke.

3. How do you understand the words 'mate' and 'mateship'? Do you have an equivalent term or concept in your native tongue? Does it mean the same thing as in Australia?

4. Contemporary Australia is a multiracial, multicultural society. Such societies are often divided because of racism, prejudice and lack of understanding between people. Use your knowledge of Australia, your home country, and any other countries you know, to discuss ways of eradicating or reducing racism or prejudice.

5. Major newspapers in most countries have entertainment guides at least once a week, often in the Friday edition. Try to gain access to an Australian newspaper, e.g. the Friday editions of the *Sydney Morning Herald* or *The Age* (you can use the Internet if you do not have access to an International Press Club or Australian Consulate). Look for the entertainment guide, read it carefully, then answer the questions below:

a) List all types of entertainment advertised and/or reviewed in the entertainment guide.
b) Are all the types of entertainment listed available in your country?
c) Is there any entertainment offered free of charge? What is it?
d) Which of the types of entertainment seems to be most popular in Australia? Is it the same as in your country?
e) What are the differences between the entertainment scene in your country and in Australia?

6. What information are people normally expected to provide in your country when asked to identify themselves for official purposes? Comment on the similarities and differences between your country and Australia.

7. What kind of an identification document (if any) are you expected to be able to provide on request in your home country and what information does it contain? Compare this document with the Australian driver's licence.

8. Make a list of all the relatives you would consider to be your close family. How does your list compare with the Australian concept of a close family?

9. Do parents in your home country treat young children the same way as Australians treat theirs? What are the differences?

10. Fill in the questionnaire below by marking appropriate boxes against each statement, then discuss the results with your fellow students and teacher.

Statement	Your country	Australia
Parents should support their children until they complete their tertiary education.	☐	☐
If a young couple are not able to buy their own home, their parents should invite them to live with them.	☐	☐
If parents are better off than their children, they should help them financially.	☐	☐
If the children are working, they should contribute financially to the household.	☐	☐
Brothers and sisters should help financially family members who are less well off.	☐	☐

Grandparents should help with the care of their grandchildren on a regular basis.	☐	☐
When parents grow old and can no longer look after themselves, they should live in a retirement village.	☐	☐
All important decisions should be discussed first with one's parents.	☐	☐
All important decisions should be discussed first with one's brothers and sisters.	☐	☐
Parents and children should maintain close contact and help each other.	☐	☐

11. Is it customary in your home culture for people to spend their old age in retirement villages and old people's homes? What do you think about this Australian custom?

12. Discuss with your teacher and fellow students in class your answers to the questions below:
a) How do you feel about using your English teacher's first name in and outside class?
b) Would you feel comfortable introducing your English teacher to your friends using his/her first name only?
c) How do you feel when much younger or much older people than yourself address you by your first name in English?

13. How would you address the following people in your home country and in Australia:
- your spouse
- a close friend
- a doctor
- a university lecturer
- an elderly neighbour
- your grandfather
- a stranger?

14. Explain the meaning and usage in the Australian context of the following words and phrases:
- easy-going
- good afternoon
- g'day
- how are you
- putting on the dog.

15. Do gatherings of family and friends in your country involve more or less bodily contacts (kissing, embracing, patting, hand-shaking, etc.) than among Australians? Comment on differences.

16. What is the most popular sport in your country? Which of the popular Australian sports are also popular in your country?

17. How does a team win a game of cricket? Find out as much as possible about the game. (But if you know nothing about it, be warned that it is a long and complicated game. Most games last for at least six hours and some international matches last five days!)

18. Explain the meaning of the following words and expressions as they are used by Australians:
- follow through
- shifting the goal posts
- to know the score
- a fair go
- football
- the MCG
- bussing
- a safe bet
- scratchie
- long odds
- AFL.

19. What are the most important holidays celebrated in Australia?

20. Why is Australia Day a national holiday and when is it celebrated?

21. Mark the statements below as either true or false for your home country culture, then compare your answers with what you have learned about Australian party customs from the text.

Party customs	True	False
It is quite all right to be late for a barbecue or a picnic party.	☐	☐
You may be expected to bring a present for the host or hostess even if it is not their birthday or another occasion of this type.	☐	☐
You may be expected to bring food to a party.	☐	☐

The hosts should supply enough food for everyone. ☐ ☐

The hosts should supply enough drinks for everyone. ☐ ☐

The hosts should make every effort to make the guests feel good at a party. ☐ ☐

After the food and drinks have been laid out, the guests should be allowed to decide for themselves how much and when they wish to eat and drink. ☐ ☐

The guests should be repeatedly encouraged to eat and drink. ☐ ☐

If guests say they do not want any more to eat, it would be impolite not to encourage them to have some more. ☐ ☐

If guests say they have had enough to drink, they should be repeatedly encouraged to drink more. ☐ ☐

22. Do you have a venue similar to the English and Australian pub in your country? If not, where, if at all, would alcoholic drinks be available?

23. Make up a list of subjects you would consider attractive for a conversation at a party in your home country. Compare your list with typical Australian party conversations as described above. What differences have you noticed? Can you think of any reasons for these differences?

24. In many cultures around the world, debating 'hot' issues at parties and social gatherings is not only acceptable, but seems to be a favourite pastime. What are your views about it?
a) Do you think it is a good idea to debate serious issues socially, at a party?
b) Do you enjoy getting intellectually and emotionally involved in debating controversial topics?
c) How important is it to you whether you win or lose a debate?
d) What are the Australian customs in this respect?

25. Look at these two obviously incorrect statements and think about how you would disagree with them in your native language:
• The earth is not a globe; it is flat like a dinner plate.
• Top-of-the-range Ford cars are more expensive than Rolls Royces.

Write down a few different ways of disagreeing with each of those statements in your native language, then translate them into English preserving the flavour and tone they have in your language. Would your translated responses be acceptable to Australians without any modifications?

26. Why do you think native Australians consider many non-English-speaking Europeans rude (e.g. the Dutch, Germans, Hungarians, Poles and Russians, among others)?

27. Under what circumstances would Australians use the following phrases:
- John came on too heavy about the unions last night, I think.
- Did you believe him? Don't! He's a bull artist.
- Why, you've put your cards on the table, haven't you, Geraldine?

28. Write down what you would say in your native tongue if you wanted the following people to hand you an expensive looking vase:
- Your father's youngest brother (your uncle, only five years older than yourself)
- Your good friend
- Your spouse
- Your boss at work
- Your employee at work (you are the boss)
- A shop assistant (you are a customer).
Would your requests be acceptable in Australia if translated literally? If not, what would you have to change?

29. John, one of your fellow students, has asked you to lend him your car for the afternoon. You have agreed but, soon after he started driving you home, you noticed that he is a very bad and reckless driver. Think of three ways of telling John quickly that you have changed your mind. Would you say the same in your mother tongue and in English? What would be the differences?

30. Martha Miller is a relatively new migrant to Australia. She is in a hardware store talking to Henry Baldry, a shop assistant in the paint department. Read the conversation, then answer the questions below.

HB: Hello, can I help you?
MM: Yes, I need a 1 litre can of white paint for my kitchen ceiling. What paint would you recommend?

HB: Yes, we have several brands of ceiling paints, they are all on this shelf here.

MM: So which one should I take – I see some of them are more expensive than others.

HB: Yes, they are priced differently – this one here is the cheapest 'no frills' variety and then you have different brands at different prices.

MM: So which one is the best? Is the most expensive brand the best?

HB: Well, it's difficult to say, they are all more or less similar. Of course the dearer brands might last longer. I haven't had any complaints from customers who bought the 'no frills' variety, though.

MM: So, would you say the most expensive brand would last the longest?

BB: It should. Then, again, a lot depends on the way you prepare the ceiling before you put the paint on. Even the 'no frills' one will last if you do a good job of it.

MM: Should I buy the 'no frills' variety then?

BB: I didn't say that. Oh, excuse me, I have to serve this other customer. Why don't you browse for a while – I'll come back if you need any further help.

Frustrated, Martha buys the most expensive brand and leaves the shop.

a) Which variety of paint was the shop assistant trying to recommend?
b) Did he answer any of Martha's questions directly?
c) Did he actually recommend the 'no frills' variety in a direct way?
d) If so, did you guess that that was the variety he recommended?
e) Would this conversation run a similar course in your home country? What would be the differences?

31. The text above discusses a number of values held by Australians. What are the most important values held by your native culture? Make a list of those values, using single words or phrases that reflect them well. Having prepared a list like this for your home country culture, browse through the text and write out a similar list of Australian values.

32. Compare the two lists and discuss differences between them in class or in an essay.

References

Bambrick, S. (ed.). (1994) *The Cambridge Encyclopedia of Australia.* Melbourne: Cambridge University Press.

Borrie, W.D. (1989) 'The Population', in Hancock 1989, pp. 119–42.

Brown, R.G. (1989) 'Social Security and Welfare', in Hancock, 1989, pp. 44–69.

Clark, M. (1986) *A Short History of Australia.* Melbourne: Penguin.

Crittenden, B. (1989) 'Education in Australia: Conformity and Diversity', in Hancock, 1989, pp. 70–93.

Edgar, D. (1980) *Introduction to Australian Society. A Sociological Perspective.* Sydney: Prentice-Hall of Australia.

Encel, S. and Byron, L. (eds). (1984) *Australian Society. Introductory Essays* (4th edition). Melbourne: Longman Cheshire.

Goodnow, J. Burns, A. and Russell, G. (1989) Australian Families: Pictures and Interpretations, in Hancock, 1989, pp. 23–43.

Hancock, K. (ed.). (1989) *Australian Society.* Sydney: Cambridge University Press.

Horne, D. (1978) *The Lucky Country. Australia in the Sixties* (revised edition). Sydney: Angus and Robertson.

Jones, F.L. (1989) 'Changing Attitudes and Values in Post-war Australia', in Hancock, 1989, pp. 94–118.

Jose, A.W. (1914) *History of Australasia from the Earliest Times to the Present Day.* Sydney: Angus and Robertson.

Lacour-Gayet, R. (1976), *A Concise History of Australia.* Melbourne: Penguin.

Miller, J.D.B. (1989) 'Australia in the World', in Hancock, 1989, pp. 228–43.

Mitchell, A.G. and Delbridge, A. (1965) *The Pronunciation of English in Australia* (revised edition). Sydney: Angus and Robertson.

Withers, G. (1989) 'Living and Working in Australia', in Hancock, 1989, pp. 1–22.

5 Canada – the Winter Half of North America[1]

Magda Stroińska and Vikki Cecchetto

If some countries have too much history, we have too much geography. (Prime Minister Mackenzie King, 1936)

Introduction

The word 'Canada', adopted from the Huron-Iroquois *kanata* ('village') was allegedly first used by Jacques Cattier to refer to a settlement that later became Québec City, and to the surrounding territories. Later, the word was used to refer to New France, until the British conquest of 1759 when it was replaced by the word 'Québec', referring to the colony north of the St Lawrence River and the Great Lakes. In 1791, Britain divided this territory into Lower Canada and Upper Canada, which corresponds to the modern distinction between Québec and Ontario. In 1841, these lands became the Province of Canada, made up of Canada West and Canada East, joined later, in 1867, by Nova Scotia and New Brunswick to form the Dominion of Canada. Confederation then moved west, adding Manitoba and the Northwest Territories in 1870, followed by British Columbia in 1871: Canada now stretched from sea to sea. Prince Edward Island joined Confederation in 1873; Yukon Territory in 1898; Alberta and Saskatchewan in 1905. The last province to join Confederation was Newfoundland (with Labrador) in 1949.

If we were to choose just a few features to describe Canada, we would probably select the vastness of the Canadian territory, its scarce but diverse, multicultural population and its often extreme and unpredictable climate. Despite short but hot summers, the tempera-mental nature of the Canadian weather remains towards the cool end of the scale, with its blizzards, snow, ice storms and freezing rain. Québec singer Gilles Vigneault sings: '*Mon pays ce n'est pas un pays, c'est l'hiver.*' It is a country, where, as the poet Alden Nowlan says: 'a man can die simply from being caught outside'. Yet Canadians rarely complain about the weather and it is not a popular topic for small talk, although it remains a popular 'opener'. The weather is either good, and then does not deserve to be mentioned, or it is a serious problem that requires solidarity and mutual co-operation, not discussion.

The second largest country in the world (surpassed only by Russia), Canada occupies that part of North America east of Alaska and north of the 8,892-km-long border with the USA at the 48th parallel, including some islands of the adjacent Arctic Archipelago. Although Canada's motto is officially 'From sea to sea', it should really be 'From sea to sea to sea' since Canada is bounded on three sides by water. In the north lies the Arctic Ocean and in the north-east Baffin Bay and Davis Strait, in the east is the Atlantic Ocean and in the west the Pacific Ocean.

The territory of Canada is 9,922,330 sq. km, with more lakes and inland waterways than any other country in the world. A large percentage of the Canadian territory (close to 9 per cent) is covered by bodies of fresh water and it has been estimated that Canada holds one-seventh of the world's fresh water. Of the five Great Lakes, only one

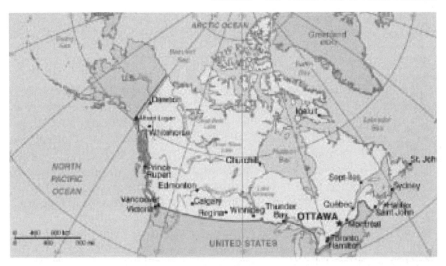

(Lake Michigan) is not partly in Canada, the others are all stretched along the Canada–US border. There are also 31 other lakes with a surface area of over 1300 sq. km, not to mention the myriad other smaller lakes dotted over the Canadian landscape. Among the great rivers, the most famous one is the St Lawrence, which has its source in the Great Lakes and empties into the Gulf of St Lawrence. Other great rivers include the Fraser and the Columbia which empty into the Pacific; the Mackenzie and the Peace which flow into the Arctic Ocean; the Nelson, Saskatchewan and the Red rivers which empty into Hudson's Bay; and the Ottawa and Saguenay rivers which flow into the St Lawrence.

Most of the over 33 million Canadians inhabit the southern part of the country (or more precisely a long, relatively thin 150-km band to the north of the Canadian–American border). Because of the harsh climate and the physiographic make-up of the country, only about 12 per cent of the land is suitable for agriculture. This leaves vast territories in the central and northern portions sparsely inhabited. The average population density is about three persons per sq. km, a statistic that makes Canada comparable to Australia, which actually has an even lower population density, with around 2.5 persons per sq. km. The United States has almost the same territory as Canada but the population is almost ten times higher! If one compares the population density in North America with the density of almost 250 persons per sq. km in Great Britain, 189 in Italy and 336 in Japan, for example, one can understand why some visitors from overseas feel overwhelmed with so much open and uninhabited space.

Politically Canada is a federation of ten provinces and three territories, each with their own legislature and administration. Starting from the east coast and travelling to the west, the provinces are as follows: Newfoundland (capital St John's), Nova Scotia (Halifax), Prince Edward Island (Charlottetown), New Brunswick (Fredricton), Québec (Québec City), Ontario (Toronto), Manitoba (Winnipeg), Saskatchewan (Regina), Alberta (Edmonton) and British Columbia (Victoria). The south-eastern coastal provinces of New Brunswick, Nova Scotia and Prince Edward Island are sometimes referred to as the Maritime Provinces, while Atlantic Canada designates these provinces plus Newfoundland and Labrador (the official name of the last province changed in 2001).

The three territories are: the Yukon Territory (capital Whitehorse), which is governed by a federally appointed commissioner, assisted by an elected executive council and legislature; the Northwest Territories (Yellowknife), governed by a federally appointed commissioner and an elected assembly; and as of 1 April 1999, Nunavut (meaning 'our land' in Inuktitut) with the capital Iqaluit. The new territory is governed by the Tungavik Federation of Nunavut, the Inuit government. While having an area of almost one-fifth of Canada, the population per square kilometre in the Nunavut area is approximately 0.01.

As in the United States, towns and cities are often listed or mentioned with their province following, for instance: the national capital of Canada is Ottawa, Ontario, situated along the Ottawa River west of Montreal with a population of about 1 million in the Ottawa-Hull metropolitan area. Other major cities are Toronto, Ontario (the largest city, financial, manufacturing and cultural centre for English Canada), situated on the shores of Lake Ontario, with over 5 million inhabitants in the metropolitan area; Montreal, Québec (port, commercial and cultural centre for French Canada), with over 3.5 million inhabitants; and Vancouver, British Columbia (shipping, railway hub and fishing and forest products centre), with a population of over 2 million. Other important centres are Edmonton and Calgary in Alberta (a province noted for its petroleum, cattle and farming resources), Regina, Saskatchewan (known for its oil and natural gas, potash, kaolin, sodium sulphite, bentonite and agriculture), and Winnipeg in Manitoba (a major wheat market and railway hub).

It is no wonder that the environment, nature and all its aspects have played and continue to play a paramount role in shaping Canadians' attitudes towards each other as well as the varieties of Canadian English and conversational style.

The people of Canada

Canada has a rich and varied racial and ethnic make-up, with two major groups and a number of smaller ethnic communities. Traditionally, the two major cultural and linguistic groups are people of British origin and people of French origin. While the descendants of the

British are spread throughout the country, French Canadians live mostly in Québec. Large French-speaking groups can also be found in Ontario and New Brunswick. (The francophone area of the Maritime Provinces is sometimes called Acadia, after the name of an early French colony. Some of the Acadians migrated to Louisiana in the eighteenth-century and their language became the basis for Louisiana Creole – 'Cajun' is a shortened eighteenth century pronunciation of Acadian.) The francophone population of Canada, supported by federal programmes, cultivates the French language and its culture and traditions, and maintains a separate system of education. Since Canada is officially a bilingual nation, all government services and offices function in both languages throughout the country.

In the 2001 Census of Canadians, one of the surprising results was the fact that 39 per cent of those questioned indicated 'just Canadian' as their ethnic origin. 'As more young people consider themselves ethnically fractioned – half of this and a quarter of that – fewer will have a strong connection to an ethnic group other than Canadian. [. . .] The very term "ethnicity" is an awkward one, but it fits: We are creating a new multiracial, multicultural, boundary-free ethnic group called "Canadian"' (Mendelsohn, 2004, pp. 60–1). According to the Census, of the 30 million inhabitants of Canada, over 17,350,000 respondents listed English as their mother tongue; 6,703,325 listed French; over 850,000 listed Chinese, now the third language in Canada; almost 470,000 listed Italian; almost 440,000 listed German; with Polish, Spanish, Portuguese and Punjabi accounting for over 200,000 speakers each. Completing the roster of non-official languages spoken in Canada we find: Arabic (199,000), Tagalog (174,000), Ukrainian (148,000), Dutch (128,000), Vietnamese (122,000), Greek (120,000), Cree (73,000) and Inuktitut (Eskimo – 29,000), with other non-official languages accounting for another 1,506,965 speakers. (According to the Statistics Canada web page: 'Mother tongue: the first language learned at home in childhood and still understood by the individual at the time of the census'). Different groups arrived at different times and often formed ethnic pockets. For example, there are many Ukrainians in the Prairies and many Italians in the Toronto, Montreal and Vancouver areas. In the last decade, there has been a dramatic increase of immigration from non-European nations, which adds to the higher percentage of visible minorities in the new Canada. (See, for example, Anderssen, Valpy *et al.*, 2004.)

Canada's official multicultural policy has had an impact and continues to have implications for the educational system as well, which has to respond to the challenges of having over 60 languages spoken by students within the Canadian system. Instruction in these languages, which represent more than 70 ethnocultural groups (Heritage Language Instruction), is widely available in many communities throughout Canada. Although education is a provincial responsibility, the federal government, through the Canadian Heritage Ministry, funds projects promoting multicultural research, ethnic histories and other documentary resources, as well as the development of courses or institutional change designed to bring all Canadians to an understanding and appreciation of other cultures. As we shall see later in this chapter, this multicultural richness has had an impact on the varieties of English spoken in Canada and on the heritage languages themselves. One of the nice things about such a diverse ethnic make-up is the fact that there are all kinds of restaurants serving ethnic food and, as Canadians like to celebrate with food, eating out is a favourite Canadian pastime.

The First Nations people make up just over 3 per cent of the Canadian population and the group is slowly growing. Some people from outside North America, as well as a fair number of North Americans themselves, seem to have the impression that all Native people speak the same language or various dialects of the same language. This is a stereotype of the kind fostered by many older Hollywood movies about the American Wild West. The reality is different. The Native people in Canada, who can be divided into some 600 groups, are predominantly but not exclusively members of the Algonquian group (mostly speaking Cree or Ojibwa); other groups represented in Canada are the Iroquoian, Salishan, Athapaskan and Inuit. The tribal associations, together with linguists and elders, are currently doing much work to preserve, analyse and consolidate many of the Native languages, which are in danger of being lost. Many schools on the reservations are now teaching both the language and the culture of the First Canadians as well as English. Many university students of linguistics are able to take courses in indigenous languages as part of their curriculum.

Black Canadians do not constitute a large segment of the Canadian population (just over 2 per cent), although, back in the eighteenth century, Canada was the country of destination for many slaves fleeing the United States through an operation called the Underground Railroad. Many of them settled in Ontario near the towns of Chatham and Sarnia, and in the province of Nova Scotia, which had abolished slavery in 1787. This had marked the beginning of the end of slavery in the entire British Empire, making Canada a close haven for the American runaways.

The ethnic and linguistic diversity of, Canada is also reflected in the religious make-up of the country. The largest religious group, Roman Catholic, is most strongly represented in the Province of Québec, with nearly half of the Catholic population of Canada. Of the remaining Christian-based religions, Protestants account for over 8.5 million Canadians, Christian Orthodox for almost 500,000, and other

Christian-based faiths for almost 800,000. The next largest religious groups are Muslims (almost 600,000) and Jews, Buddhists, Hindus and Sikhs (approximately 300,000 adherents each). Over 15 per cent of Canadians do not consider themselves religious and are not churchgoers. Because of this diversity of denominations and attitudes, religion is not a popular topic of conversation. But being of a different denomination from your conversation partner has no negative connotations and is in no way seen as a problem, as religion is mostly considered a private matter. There is a religious division in the school system, and parents may often be heard discussing the advantages and disadvantages of public (non-denominational) and separate (Roman Catholic) schools and schoolboards, but such discussions are generally not specifically religious.

Canada is not only a country of immigration but also one of emigration. The destination of emigrants is most often the United States, so much so that in an article, Rick Marin declared:

> Canada has produced some of America's funniest comedians, actors, writers, directors – a veritable army of renegade humour professionals. Without them, there would have been no *Saturday Night Live,* no *SCTV,* no *Spy* magazine, no *Ghostbusters,* no *Wayne's World* ... Thanks to their near undetectable accent and their proximity to the United States, Canadians have insinuated themselves into the pop culture of the United States ... (in Olive, 1996, p. 218)

Canada is the country of origin of many Hollywood stars, some very popular. Examples include Pamela Anderson (best known from the TV series *Baywatch*), British-born but Canadian-raised Mike Myers (known through the *Austin Powers* movies and as the voice of *Shrek*), Jim Carrey (*Mask, The Truman Show* and *The Eternal Sunshine of the Spotless Mind*) and the late comedian John Candy. Arguably one of the most popular and respected US TV news anchors was a Canadian: Peter Jennings hosted the ABC *World News Tonight* from 1978 until his death in 2005. Canadian music stars who have become famous worldwide include singers Céline Dion, Alanis Morissette and Avril Lavigne, as well as Bryan Adams, a singer, guitarist and songwriter, and the singing poet, Leonard Cohen. Interestingly, while Canadian actors and musicians often choose to pursue their careers down south, American film crews come to Canadian cities to shoot urban film footage, as it is less expensive than in the US. Canadians, then, have much to brag about; they are just too polite to mention it!

The origins of Canadian English

The English language in Canada, Canadian English, is a record of the various events and peoples who have made Canadian English

> what it now is ... The vocabulary, the grammar, the pronunciation
> of a language or variety of it is never the product of chance. It is
> the product of history ... (Scargill, 1977, p. 7)

The history of Canadian English, like Canadian history in general, is a
history of immigration. The first English-speaking settlers – as
opposed to English 'migrant workers' who had been coming to these
same shores for fish and furs since the sixteenth century – came to
Canada after 1713 when the Maritime Provinces, Newfoundland and
the Hudson's Bay region became British possessions under the Treaty
of Utrecht, which ended Queen Anne's War. By the end of the
eighteenth century, British Canada was composed of four distinct
regions, with different immigrant and linguistic populations:

- Newfoundland, consisting mainly of fishing settlements
  peopled by settlers from Ireland and south-western England;
- the Hudson's Bay Region, where English and Scottish
  companies competed for the fur trade;
- Acadia, renamed Nova Scotia, New Brunswick and Prince
  Edward Island, which had been populated by Scottish and
  Irish settlers as well as by United Empire Loyalists from the
  New England states after the American Revolution;
- New France, renamed Québec, where by the Québec Act of
  1774 the British rulers guaranteed the French colonists their
  traditional language, civil law and religion. The Constitution
  Act of 1791 also split Québec into two distinct regions
  according to language: Lower Canada, which was mainly
  French (the present province of Québec), and Upper Canada,
  which was mainly English (the present province of Ontario).
  The bulk of United Empire Loyalists (about 50,000) fleeing to
  British-held territory after the American Revolution settled in
  Upper Canada.

These, then, are the foundations of Canadian English: eighteenth-
century American speech plus influences from a number of specific
languages. McCrum *et al.* comment on the inception of this new variety
of English as follows:

> Every revolution – and the American Revolution was no exception
> – has its casualties. The Loyalists, those who backed the British,
> were driven into exile partly by mob violence and partly by the
> desire to protect their investments. Some went to England, some to
> the West Indies, but the majority fled north to Canada, and settled
> in the part that is now Ontario. This was the beginning of a
> separate Canadian English. (McCrum *et al.*, 1996, p. 244)

The speech patterns of the Loyalists, who, fleeing from New York and
Pennsylvania, settled in Ontario and then spread into the western part

of the country, became the foundation of what developed into so-called 'General Canadian English'. (The term General Canadian was coined by Avis, 1973, quoted after de Wolf, 1992, p. 2). The Maritime Provinces on the East Coast have always displayed a greater variety of English speech patterns, partly because of their isolation from the central portion of Canada and partly because of settlement by diverse groups such as Gaelic-speaking Scots. The speech of Newfoundland was also affected by longer adherence to British rule – it did not become self-governing until 1855 and joined Confederation only in 1949. The Western Provinces were heavily settled by immigrants from Northern and Eastern Europe, especially people of Icelandic, Ukrainian and German origins and adherents of religious sects such as the Mennonites and Doukhobors (from the Russian 'spirit wrestlers') during the early part of the nineteenth century. British Columbia had a large influx of Asian settlers at this time – mainly Chinese – hired to work on the railway.

English in Canada today

> I speak Ontario English; I don't admire it, but it's all I've got; it's better than affectation.
>> (Stephen Leacock, Canadian humorist and economist)

Many people believe that Canadian English is not a language in its own right but rather a variety of American English. In fact even some Canadians may have doubts about the status of their English, for, until quite recently, they had to consult either British or American dictionaries for word usage. The *Canadian Dictionary of the English Language: An Encyclopaedic Reference* (1997) was followed by Canadian editions of other dictionaries, e.g. the *Oxford Canadian Dictionary*, the *Gage Canadian Dictionary*, the *ITP Nelson Canadian Dictionary of the English Language*, and the *Oxford Canadian Thesaurus*. These resources all claim to offer the most authoritative and reliable Canadian tools for checking spellings, pronunciation and definitions. Canadians can also consult – although it is not a complete and exhaustive dictionary – the *Oxford Guide to Canadian English Usage* (1997) by Margery Fee and Janice McAlpine from the Strathy Language Unit at Queen's University.[2]

Some researchers have long defended Canadian English's claim to 'language' status, or at the very least 'varietal' status. Avis defines Canadian English as neither American nor British, different from them in terms of vocabulary, syntax and pronunciation (Avis, 1955 and 1956). As Eric Partridge says: 'Canadians have a very distinctive variety of English, far more different from that spoken in Britain than is the English spoken by Australians; yet Canadians – so imperceptibly, so constantly has the process operated – "just get on with the job"; having this very different English, they therefore do not feel the need to have it at all' (Partridge, 1951, p. 61).

This lack of concern for the language among English-speaking Canadians may be one of the reasons why many of them have little sympathy for the demands of French Canadians who want to give French so much attention (see McRoberts, 1997 on the question of Canadian unity). Another reason is obviously the fact that English is and will likely remain the dominant language of the country and it is usually the linguistic minority that tends to be more protective of its cultural and linguistic heritage. Given the increase in immigration during the past decade and for the foreseeable future, native English speakers, though, are becoming increasingly protective of and interested in knowing more about their language. Even CBC, the national radio broadcaster, now has a weekly programme devoted to aspects of the English language – *Words: Woe & Wonder* – where the editor of the *Oxford Canadian Dictionary*, Dr Katherine Barber, is a frequent guest. As well, the network has a resident Broadcast Language Advisor.

Is there one homogeneous variety of language spoken in Canada? Some authors claim that Canadians (unless they are trained phoneticians) are unable to identify in conversation the province or region of origin of their fellow Canadians without asking them specifically. This, however, seems to be the view represented rather by non-Canadian authors. Canadians are usually well able to identify fellow Canadians in an English-speaking crowd and many believe that they can identify the origin of other Canadian speakers. While Professor Higgins, the expert on pronunciation in Shaw's *Pygmalion*, would have found Canadian dialects rather boring, Canadians find it very convenient and reassuring that they may travel for many days without really noticing much linguistic variation.[3]

In its broad sense the term Canadian English refers to the several regional varieties of English spoken in Canada. For historical reasons, the type of English associated with southern Ontario, formerly Upper Canada, has become the basis for a national norm, an imperfectly described but recognized standard across Canada. This type, which may be designated 'General Canadian', has a phonemic system and a number of subphonemic features which, along with certain distributional characteristics, give General Canadian much of its special character (Avis, 1986, p. 215).

Although some linguists see Canadian English as a homogeneous entity (e.g. Avis, 1973; O'Grady and Dobrovolsky, 1996), many others (e.g. Chambers, 1975; Warkentyne, 1973; Clarke, 1993), interpreting the results of the 1972 Survey of Canadian English, conclude that there are three major dialect areas: Newfoundland; Eastern Canada, which includes Ontario and the Maritime Provinces; and Western Canada, from Manitoba west. In addition, six linguistic enclaves are also recognized: the Ottawa Valley 'twang'; Lunenburg, Nova Scotia; Montreal English; the Red River Valley; Saskatchewan and southern Alberta; Vancouver, British Columbia. It is nevertheless true that, especially taking into account the huge territory of Canada, Canadians speak with an astonishing uniformity, although the Americanization of Canadian English is a fact no one would dispute.

The assumption about the apparent homogeneity may, however, have been a result of an insufficient amount of research devoted to speech variation in Canada (see Clarke, 1993). In recent years there have been a number of studies devoted to speech variation across Canada, with detailed work produced on many small linguistic islands, both urban and rural – for example, on Vancouver (de Wolf, 1992) and Newfoundland (Paddock, 1982). The data from older studies on regional variation (Chambers, 1975 and 1979) are still valid, since changes have not been noted in the pronunciation and syntax, but rather in vocabulary. There has been a wealth of new research on all aspects of Canadian English, from phonetics to pragmatics to new linguistic phenomena. We include just a representative sampling of the available publications: Brinton & Fee, 2001; Chambers, 2002; McKinnie & Dailey-O'Cain, 2002; Tagliamonte, 2005.

It should be mentioned here that, while the regional variation in the speech of people born in Canada remains rather intangible, there is great variation in English language usage due to the steadily growing number of Canadians who speak a language other than English at home. These people can be divided into two important categories. The first one is the group of the First Nations, who are the original inhabitants of the North American territory. The second group is constituted by recent and previous immigrants, who settled in Canada but kept their language and customs, as provided for by the Canadian Multicultural Law. Unlike the 'melting pot' of cultures and languages just 'south of the border',[4] Canada allows and even encourages new settlers to keep their traditions and language alive. As art critic Arnold Edinborough maintains, 'Canada has never been a melting pot; it is more like a tossed salad' (Colombo, 1998, p. 27). Immigrants are offered help in learning English but they are also given support in teaching heritage languages. Although in times of economic stress, Canadian tolerance for immigrants may be tried, polls suggest that the level of acceptance of the newcomers is considerably higher than in many other countries (e.g. the results of the *Maclean's* magazine/CBC's *The National* telephone poll of 1,200 Canadian adults, reported in the 29 December 1997 issue of the *Maclean's* magazine). This may be due to the fact that Canada is still far away from its optimum population level and so immigrants are not seen only as intruders. This view was reiterated in the latest survey on Canadians' attitudes to new immigrants reported by Anderssen & Valpy, 2004.

We shall not consider here the English language used by the first, and in some cases perhaps even second, generation of immigrant Canadians, the so-called 'hyphenated' Canadians such as Italian-Canadians, Polish-Canadians and German-Canadians. We are looking at Canadian English in its native version, i.e. in the form that is used in official media, literature, education, and as it is used by those Canadians who consider it as their mother tongue. It is nevertheless interesting to note briefly that English has had a major influence on all the immigrant languages now used in Canada, and in some cases English words or structures have been borrowed and incorporated into the immigrant language to such an extent that the language has acquired a name of its own, like 'Italiese' for Canadian Italian or 'Kitchener Deutsch' for Canadian-German. Thus 'Italiese' uses words like *fattoria* for 'factory' and *carro* for 'car' (compare this with the Standard Italian meanings of 'farm' for *fattoria* and 'cart' or 'wagon' for *carro*). With similar evidence of English influence, an Italiese speaker may say that something *fa senso,* 'makes sense', whereas Standard Italian would say that something *ha senso,* 'has sense'. Likewise Kitchener Deutsch has *Marmelade* in the English sense of 'marmalade' (whereas in Standard German the word refers to any kind of jam or preserve, not just marmalade) and reveals structures like *ich habe freunde gemacht,* 'I have made friends' (compare Standard German *ich habe mich mit ihnen angefreundet,* 'I have befriended them').

Features of Canadian English

> The differences are mainly of vocabulary and pronunciation. There is no distinctive Canadian grammar. (McCrum *et al., 1996,* p. 245)

The most striking feature of Canadian English pronunciation is known technically as Canadian Raising, a feature affecting the vowels in words such as 'ice' and 'right', and 'house' and 'scout'. As if to underline the relatedness of American and Canadian speech, the same feature is found in some parts of the USA, most notably in Virginia and South Carolina (Bloomfield, 1975, p. 6; Trudgill, 1985, p. 35; see Chapter 2 for details).

Another feature which separates Canadian pronunciation from most British and American accents is lack of contrast in Canada between the vowels of 'cot' and 'caught' or 'collar' and 'caller'. For most Canadians pairs of words like these are identical in pronunciation.

Although there are not many differences in pronunciation between American and Canadian English, it is nonetheless interesting to note that most Canadian students react negatively when American transcription of pronunciation is presented as the norm (for example, in introductory phonetics or linguistics courses at Canadian universities, when American textbooks may be used). There are certainly some features in which Canadians seem to lean towards British rather than American pronunciation patterns. For example, Canadians seem to show a greater tendency than Americans to retain the glide in words like 'student', 'due', 'nuclear' (pronouncing these words in the typical British way, rather than as the usual American 'stoodent', 'doo', 'nooclear'), but certainly not 'nukular', favoured by President George W. Bush and justified by some American linguistic textbooks, cf. Finegan, 2004, pp. 447–8.

In morphology there are few if any real Canadianisms and the younger generation seems to be preferring American variants, such as past tense forms 'shrunk' (rather than 'shrank') and 'sneaked' (rather than 'snuck').

A further morphological feature which has been noticed recently in the speech of some Canadians, especially in the central region, has been the use of the third-person, present tense '-s' verb marker extended to other persons as a past tense marker when reporting past events, as in: 'And I *says* to him last night ...', meaning 'And I *said* to him last night ...'. This usage (which is found in regional English in Britain) has already been documented in the popular speech of Newfoundland (Paddock, 1982, Story, 1982). Given the substantial internal migration from the Maritime Provinces to Ontario in the last 25 years, this feature may be due to this influence, but since it is also a feature of Black English, it could also be another example of American influence.

Canadian English is not substantially different from American English when it comes to syntax, but many Canadian speakers do have one syntactic feature that is shared with British English, namely the treatment of the verb 'have' in yes-no questions (O'Grady and Dobrovolsky, 1996, p. 526). Canadians can ask questions like 'Have you any jam?' and give replies like 'No, I haven't' or 'Yes, I have'. Typical American usage here has questions like 'Do you have any jam?' and replies like 'No, I don't' or 'Yes, I do'. Nevertheless, with ongoing Americanization, Canadians are increasingly familiar with the American usage.

A true Canadian syntactic feature is the use of 'as well' (meaning 'also, in addition') sentence-initially to link two sentences (de Wolf, 1992, quoting after Chambers, 1975, p. 38): 'He told Mary to be careful. *As well,* he asked all of us to help her.'

Conversational style

Stephen Leacock, a renowned Canadian satirical author, commented on Canadian English in 1936 as follows:

> We used to be ashamed of our Canadian language, before the war, and try to correct it and take on English phrases and say, 'What a ripping day', instead of 'What a peach of a morning', ... and 'Oh, rather!' instead of 'O-Hell-Yes'. But now since the Great War ... we just accept our language and are not ashamed of it. We say 'yep!' when we mean 'yep!', and we don't dare try to make out it's 'yes', which is a word we don't use; and if we mean 'four' we say so and don't call it 'faw'. (quoted in McCrum *et al.*, 1986, p. 247)

Perhaps the most famous of the Canadian idioms or fillers (as 'eh', 'like' and 'you know' have sometimes been called) is the universally applicable 'eh'. Some speakers use this extremely frequently, at the end of many of their spoken sentences. It is true that 'eh' is found also in both British and American English, but not with the same frequency as in Canadian English. It is also interesting to note that this 'eh' is multifunctional. It is found in questions, with the same function as a tag: 'It's cold outside, eh?' (more or less equivalent to 'It's cold outside, isn't it?') and 'Late night last night, eh?' (more or less equivalent to 'You had a late night last night, didn't you?'). But it also has the function, in narrative, of allowing time for listener comments, if the listener wishes to make them: 'I moved in on goal, faked a shot, and then shot the puck in, eh,' or 'I got picked up by this old couple, like 65 or 70 or so, eh'. At this point the listener can comment with something appropriate such as: 'No guff!' or 'Right on!' or 'Ya, in your dreams!' depending on the degree of belief held by the listener in what has been said.

One of the most commonly used words in the English language spoken by the young generation, not just in Canada but throughout the English-speaking world, is undoubtedly *like*. In March 2005, the on-line *Newsletter* of the International Student Centre at the University of Toronto published a guide to correct and incorrect 'Use of "like" in everyday speech: What your grammar teachers never told you' (although, as linguists, can we be 'prescriptive' about such a popular lexical item?). It states that 'we use it in the ways that our English teachers taught us, but also in ways that make our English teachers – and parents, and bosses, and editors – crazy'. The author, Vicky Burrus, Coordinator of the English Conversation Program at the University of Toronto, distinguishes between the use of *like* as a filler in situations where the speaker is hesitating, wants to use a hedge or is emphasizing something (e.g. '*I was*, like, *walking down the street ... there was this*, like, *guy ...*'), and the special quotative use of *like* when reporting someone's words or describing his or her thoughts, behaviour or actions (e.g. '*I was* like, "*Wow. What's going on here?*"') (cf. Burrus, 2005). For more information on this particular linguistic phenomenon in Canadian English, cf. also Blyth, Recktenwald & Wang, 1990; Chambers, 1986; Romaine & Lange, 1991; Poplack, Walker & Malcolmson, 2005 and Tagliamonte & D'Arcy, 2004.

It is worthwhile mentioning at this point that 'eh', 'like' and 'you know' do serve specific functions and are not just random thoughtless intrusions. In a study of university students in Hamilton, Ontario (a survey conducted for a course taught by V. Cecchetto in 1997), we found that speakers sometimes use 'like' to indicate that they recognize the doubtfulness of what they are saying or that they lack evidence, as in utterances such as 'If I start studying right about now and go until tomorrow morning around nine, I'll be [studying] *like* twelve hours' or 'Swiss chard? That's *like,* that's *like, like* the past tense of char'. 'Like' may also be used, for instance, to put together two clauses which are grammatically different, as if the speaker is thinking of something that has been forgotten and wants to insert it in the present utterance without forming a new sentence: 'But that's not the same as, *like,* you are not talking about them' or 'You can, you could, *like,* using "like" is okay, just not in that way.' 'Like' may also appear sentence-initially, as in '*Like* he thinks I can read that!', uttered by someone annoyed by another person's illegible handwriting.

Visitors to Canada seem to be impressed by the politeness of Canadians. The writer Umberto Eco has commented on Canadian behaviour as follows: 'Everybody who has enough coins can photocopy a book of even 700–800 pages. The patience of the Canadians is infinite: they can wait until I reach the 700th page before complaining' (Olive, 1996, p. 172). And this politeness is evident in language too: 'In this city [Toronto] of 3 million people ... buses carry the apologetic sign "Sorry ... Out of Service"' (Olive, 1996, p. 174). The fact that Canadians use 'please' and 'thank you' and structures such as 'could you ...' or 'would you ...' or 'do you mind ...' relatively frequently, even in customer–client interactions, is often remarked upon by others, both by people in other countries who encounter travelling Canadians and by visitors to Canada, especially Americans.

Like their American cousins, Canadians use a number of formulaic structures that do not always mean what they say. One of the most frequent and best known is the utterance 'Let's get together for lunch' which is really a ritualistic way of saying 'Goodbye' and does not necessarily imply a commitment to meet for lunch. Similarly, when someone says, in response to a request in a telephone conversation, 'I'll get back to you', they may mean simply that they can't deal with the problem and that they want to end the conversation in a way that seems polite. Frequent among young people, especially teenagers and those in their early twenties, is the multifunctional expression 'Hellooo?!', which, depending on the preceding utterance, can mean anything from 'Are you listening to me?' to 'Are you really asking/telling me this?' or 'You have got to be kidding!'

'Wacky Canadian words and sayings' are the topic of a number of best-selling (in Canada) books. In *Speaking Canadian English: An informal account of the English Language in Canada,* Mark Orkin describes 'the kind of language which you never learned in school but which everyone talks when he is being himself' (excerpt from the cover). In Western Canada, there is a different perspective on the language: for example, in the prairie provinces, where friends and neighbours might be many miles away, to 'go back and forth' means that you are close friends; or a small child might be described as 'knee-high to a grasshopper'. In *Casselman's Canadian Words* and *Casselmania* (from which the following expressions were taken), Bill Casselman tries to show the richness of the sources for sayings that are deeply rooted in Canadian culture and tradition. For example, 'I'll give you what Paddy gave the drum' is clearly of Irish origin and 'He's tighter than a crofter's lease' is Scottish, while 'Thin? I've seen more meat on a hockey stick' originated with the national sport of ice hockey. Metaphors like 'He's so weak he couldn't pull his finger out of a lard pail', or 'far as ever a puffin flew', are part of the conversational style as much as a relaxed manner. Some British visitors may find Canadian (and American) greetings and expressions exuberant, but most Canadians would probably say it is just part of their enthusiasm for life!

Between Britain and the USA: the example of Canadian spelling

Canadians are often conscious of being, in a cultural sense, in between Britain and the USA. They may be torn between the two opposing tendencies, one from 'over 'ome' and the other from 'south of the border'.

In matters of spelling, Britain and the USA have reached a number of different conventions, as with words ending in '-our', like 'labour, honour' (in their British spelling, or 'labor, honor' in their American spelling; see Chapter 2 for more details). For Canadians, torn between two big brothers, spelling is an area of considerable inconsistency. While the British norm is still considered an official standard, the everyday proximity of the USA and extensive trade with that country make American spelling a useful concession and sometimes a necessity. Until recently, many Canadians followed British spelling because it was what they had learned at school and what was accepted at university. Today, children may still learn to use British spelling at school, but as soon as they leave school, and often also while still there, find themselves surrounded by American newspapers and magazines, American books and movies, American television programmes and American spelling on the Internet.

Canadian spelling is therefore a mixture of influences. A noticeable loyalty to British practices may be due to a desire to be different from the big brother south of the border, rather than to a true preference for the British norm.

Canada has seen its own ventures in spelling reform. One notable attempt to simplify the spelling was made in 1885 with the publication in Port Hope, Ontario, of the *Fonetic Herald,* a periodical 'devoted tu Orthoepi and Orthografi'. The introduction to this journal read as follows:

> Its chief object wil be to elucidate and exemplify the *simplicity* and *practicability* of amending English orthografy on a fonetic basis. It shal not be the organ ov any party, sect or society; nor advocate any particular alfabet or other views, but wil treat the whole subject az one ov linguistic science, and therefore tu be approacht in the spirit ov general science, always unbigoted and cosmopolitan. Orthoepy, a sister subject ov orthografy, shal receiv a larj shar ov attention, az wil also, in les degree, etymology. (see Orkin, 1970, p. 151)[5]

The *Fonetic Herald* survived some four years and disappeared in 1889. Since then, spelling reform has not been much of a topic of discussion in Canada. Canadian spelling has remained conservative and, as Orkin puts it, 'even such mildly reformed expressions as *nite, thru, foto, sox, burlesk* and the like which have become part of American journalese – although lacking any academic imprimatur – are never used in Canada, not even on the sporting page. Our spelling resists reformation and remains as it was in the beginning, unsimplified' (Orkin, 1970, p. 152).

Because of the uncertainty in spelling caused by interference from American English or lack of fluency, there is a ready market for spelling guides, especially on-line, such as, for example, the Canadian Press website. Thus many Canadians still write 'cheques' rather than 'checks' and pour maple 'syrup' rather than 'sirup' over their pancakes. But they do prefer American 'airplane' to the British 'aeroplane' and they use the British spelling only on special occasions, as, for instance in the name of the Air Canada's frequent flyer programme, called 'Aeroplan'.

Three out of four Canadians prefer to use the British name of the last letter of the alphabet, 'zed', rather than the American 'zee', but equally many use the American pronunciation of words such as 'tomato' or 'schedule'. Canadian English also favours the 's' spelling in words like 'recognised, analysed, plagiarised'.

Canadians do not like to be corrected and are not likely to correct anyone, even though this does not necessarily mean they are tolerant of errors. Because of substantial, relatively recent immigration, non-native English is widely heard in the media and on the street. People in Canada are generally more adept and willing to make an effort to understand non-native speakers than people in many other countries, and consequently non-native speakers are less likely to have to repeat themselves before being understood. But aversion to correction may become aversion to correctness, as Victoria Branden (1992) tries to warn the readers in her book *In Defence of Plain English: The Decline and Fall of Literacy in Canada.*

Canada through its vocabulary

> And while many believe that little differentiates Canadian culture from American culture (a reasonable assumption since we watch their movies and their television programs, eat at their restaurants, consume their goods and listen to their music), the language of Canadians reveals just how unique a nation we inhabit. (Thay, 2004, p. 5)

The First Nations peoples have of course left their mark on Canada in names and words. As noted earlier, the name of the country itself can be traced (via French) to *kanata,* a word for 'village' in a now extinct Iroquoian language.[6] Many Canadian place names are also of Native origin, including the names of four provinces: Ontario, an old Iroquois word meaning 'shining waters'; Québec, meaning 'the place where the water narrows'; Manitoba, derived from two words *minne toba* meaning 'water prairie'; and Saskatchewan, from a Cree word *kisiskatchewan,* meaning 'the river that flows swiftly'. Many other topographic names are of Native origin, including: Toronto, Ottawa, Saskatoon (from the Cree word *misaskwatomin,* describing a particular berry), Mississauga, Nanaimo or Niagara Falls ('thundering waters'). The combination of French and Indian place names (as in Sault Sainte Marie, Ontario or Lac La Biche, Alberta) and many traditional place names from the Old World (Paris, London, York) gives a special flavour to travelling in Canada. Not far from Brantford, Ontario, there used to be a road sign with the names of two nearby cities, London and Paris (both in Ontario, of course, and less than 200 km or 125 miles apart). There were so many cars stopping to take a picture of it that police probably removed it. Or perhaps it was stolen by a tourist who saw it as a good joke.

Words for some native Canadian plants and animals and for some objects and tools have been taken over from Native languages: 'chipmunk, woodchuck, racoon, opossum, toboggan, kayak, canoe, caribou' and many others. On the west coast, from Salish, come the words for different types of salmon from 'coho' to 'sockeye' (from *sukkegh)* to the 'Chinook salmon' (from the name of a tribe that once lived on the Pacific coast). Sport fishers in northern Ontario try to catch 'muskellunge' or 'muskie' (from the Ojibwa word for the fish). Some of these words underwent significant phonological changes, and their present form may suggest English meanings that were never part of their earlier meaning. This process of folk etymology is illustrated by the word 'woodchuck', which derives from Algonquian *otchek,* unrelated to either 'wood' or 'chuck'.

The Indigenous peoples of Canada are themselves referred to in a number of different ways. The term 'Aboriginal', once associated particularly with indigenous Australians, has recently begun to be used to refer to the first inhabitants of North America. In 1982, the Canadian Charter of Rights and Freedoms introduced the phrase 'the aboriginal peoples of Canada'. Since then, the expression has been accepted, but only as an adjective and capitalized. Other forms listed in the *Guide to Canadian English Usage* include Native people(s), Indigenous people(s), Status Indian, Registered Indian, Treaty Indian, Non-Status Indian, First Nations, First Peoples and Amerindian. Individual nations of course promote their own names – for example, the *Inuit* (with the singular form *Inuk*). The word 'Indian', originally reflecting Columbus' erroneous assumption that he had landed in India, may have lost its general popularity but it is still the only way to make a clear distinction between the three major categories of the Aboriginal peoples in Canada, namely Indians, Métis and Inuit (see Fee and McAlpine, 1997, p. 7). With the growing push for self-realization and self-identity, the Native people in Canada prefer to use the terms: 'Indigenous' or 'First Nations'.

The effects of immigration are also evident in the language. Even the nickname for a Canadian, 'Canuck' (or 'Jack Canuck' or 'Johnny Canuck'), comes, according to one explanation, from the name of the Irish province of Connaught, a name used by French Canadians for the Irish (Orkin, 1970, p. 165). But another view is that it is derived from the Iroquoian *kanuchsa*, 'a resident of a *kanata*' (Scargill, 1977, p. 22).

From their historical origins, expressions take on new meanings, as the following examples taken from Scargill (1977) and *A Concise Dictionary of Canadianisms* (1973) illustrate. Thus 'to stake a claim' may have had its origin in the language of the miners during the Fraser River Gold Rush in the nineteenth century, but nowadays one can stake a claim to an idea, to an object or even to a member of the opposite sex! Equally, 'to hit pay dirt, to pan out, to strike it rich' (all successes on the gold fields) and 'to get down to bedrock' or 'to be washed out' (with their negative implications) can now be heard applied to all manner of endeavours, even Bill Gates' latest try at launching new products ('Windows '98 didn't quite pan out!').

We conclude this section with some examples of phenomena and activities that have been particularly important in the history of Canada. The languages of the first European visitors and settlers are the origin for many of the words that Canadians now use in daily life.

Fishing drew some of the first European visitors and the Portuguese provided the name *Labrador*, the mainland region of Newfoundland, from their word for 'farmer or worker'. There are also some interesting names for fish products in Atlantic Canada: 'Digby chicken' is a small smoked herring while 'Digby chips' are herring fillets. Dried 'caplin', from the French name for the small smelt, are used to fertilize Newfoundland gardens. And cold winter mornings in Newfoundland can produce 'sish' in the harbour (a cross between slush and ice) and in the spring fishermen do not look forward to seeing 'growlers' (large formidable icebergs) in the bay.

The fur trade brought Canada its first 'travelling salesmen', the French *coureurs de bois* who brought the furs by canoe to the Hudson's Bay Company post or back to Montréal. They had to make 'portages' over 'rapids' and, to keep themselves warm, they wore 'duffle' (heavy woollen cloth from Duffel near Antwerp). The Indians would trade furs for duffle cloth in order to make 'duffle socks' to put inside moccasins. In the north, travel was by 'dog travois' before the larger and more elaborate dog sleds or sledges were used with dog teams. The familiar cry of 'mush', to urge the dogs forward, is from the French *marche*.

In the forests, always an impressive feature of Canada's geography, logs were moved along 'corduroy roads', made by laying logs in an arrangement that looked like the ridges in corduroy cloth. Loggers brought the logs downstream by 'rafting' (tying logs together in a barge-like configuration or 'boom') and 'driving' (managing the logs as they floated down at high water, usually in the spring). When not working, the men lived in 'shanties' in the bush and ate 'shanty cakes' (coarse bread) and drank 'shanty tea' (a very strong tea).

For sport, the loggers sometimes played an Algonquian game, which the French called *lacrosse* (describing the shape of the sticks). Another Indian game renamed by the French, hockey (from *hoquet,* a 'shepherd's crook') has now become a worldwide phenomenon. (Note that in Canada, the word 'hockey' always refers to ice hockey and never to field hockey.) In the summer, if local arenas are closed, children play 'street hockey'. Many hockey terms such as 'face-off, blue-line, puck', as well as the more aggressive 'spearing, boarding, slashing' (for which a player will spend time in the penalty box), have become household words. Some, like 'face-off', now have extended meanings, so that you can 'face-off' against an opponent in any contest whether sporting or otherwise.

Still in the area of sport, Canadians have their own name for what the British call 'trainers' and the Americans 'sneakers'. In Canada these shoes are usually called, unassumingly, 'running shoes'. Like their American and Australian cousins, Canadians play football with an oval ball and soccer with a round one.

The Prairies provided rich agricultural land for many immigrants and settlers from other areas of Canada. The land was so extensive that the 'back forty' acres was that part of the farm farthest from the 'homestead'. Today, more modestly, the 'back forty' may still describe the small vegetable plot or garden that many people have behind their homes. The early settlers built 'sod shacks' and often burned 'buffalo chips' (buffalo droppings) for warmth. Cattle were watched by 'cow-punchers', who would get their food from the 'chuckwagon'. Once a year there would be a 'roundup' to bring the cattle to the railway head to be shipped to market. And when all the work was finished, any excess energy could be devoted to a 'rodeo' or 'stampede'. The most famous is the Calgary Stampede, advertised as The Greatest Outdoor Show on Earth. It was inaugurated in 1912 and became part of the annual Calgary Exhibition in 1923. The event takes place every July, combining a rodeo with a variety of other festivities. Even the name of Calgary's modern sports complex proudly reflects the 'cowboy way of life' in the Prairies: it is called the Saddledome.

A number of popular books, such as *A Concise Dictionary of Canadianisms* and *Weird Canadian Words: How to Speak Canadian*, list some 10,000 words and expressions with Canadian origins. Among them are words such as 'loonie' ($1 coin with a loon on it), 'toonie' ($2 coin, by analogy), 'Timbits' (originally tiny doughnut holes from Tim Hortons,[7] which now denote doughnut holes in general), 'snowmobile', 'Medicare',[8] 'kayak' ('man's boat' in the Inuit language) and 'Canadarm' (Canada's contribution to NASA's programme of space exploration). To leaf through these pages is an interesting way to learn about Canadian history.

msn English - the language of the young generation

Every generation feels the need to mark and delimit their identity through specific language use. Young Canadians, not unlike their friends in other developed countries, are spending a lot of time on-line – whether on the Internet or on a mobile phone – and this new reality is having a significant impact on the language they are using. Even though e-mail has been around for more than a decade and chatrooms have been known for a while, it is instant text messaging that is having a particularly dramatic impact on the way young people are communicating. One might suggest that the distances that separate people in Canada may have something to do with the popularity of the Microsoft Network Messenger (*msn*). Even children that go to the same school may be living 50 km apart and *msn* is the cheapest and fastest way to stay in touch or exchange questions about homework.

One might ask whether *msn language* should be considered a variety of English or whether it should be seen as a separate language because of its use of other modes of communication: visual, through the emoticons (or smileys) and display pictures, and physical, through the 'winks' and 'nudges'. However, most of the *msn language* is based on spoken English transformed into new shorthand. Like other in-group codes, it abounds in abbreviations, such as 'lol' for 'laugh out loud', 'brb' for '(I'll) be right back', 'b4' for 'before' or 'nvm' for 'never mind'. Another popular technique of word formation is clipping, which produces such forms as 'bro' and 'sis' from 'brother' and 'sister' or 'rents' from 'parents'. Some words change their spelling in order to reflect the preferred pronunciation, e.g. 'kewl' instead of 'cool', which originated in the popular television show *South Park* but was also used in some text-based adventure games in the 1990s.

Msn language or Internet slang exists predominantly in the written form and its shorthand shape is dictated by the requirements of instant communication. In a face-to-face encounter, there is no need to use expressions such as 'lol' as they can be easily replaced with real laughter. Interestingly, however, some of our undergraduate students report that they have already heard people use this particular abbreviation, or some of the other ones, e.g. 'jk' for 'just kidding', in spoken language. This suggests that these code 'words' mark the group membership and are used not because they are formally functional (short) but because they are socially functional (mark their users as in-group members). As such, *msn English* is a marker of the young generation but it remains to be seen to what extent different English-speaking countries develop different varieties of this Internet slang. There is no comparative research available even though *msn English* attracts attention and evokes curiosity among the general public. *The Walrus*, a Canadian magazine launched in 2003, claims that *msn language* is 'the latest street lingo [that] springs from the computer keyboard and is changing the form of the written word' (Foran, 2004).

The confusion between the spoken and the written language is at the centre of the linguistic developments that characterize the language of the young generation. On the one hand, there are phenomena that are limited, so far, to spoken language, such as the use of the multi-purpose word 'like'. Teenagers who overuse it in the spoken language are perfectly capable of switching it off in writing. But another peculiar linguistic construction, which obviously results from an incorrect interpretation of the spoken form, is the usage of *would of* instead of *would have/would've* (or *must of* and *should of*), as in this title on an Amazon website: *DVD's that even Jesus would of loved* (note also the wrong use of the apostrophe). This unfortunate but common error is now creeping into the written language and, unlike 'like', into students' academic essays.

The ever-changing and generational nature of slang can be illustrated by the new words to signify a positive evaluation of someone or something. From 'awesome' and 'sweet', popular just a few years ago, the new 'in' words (mostly among males) are 'sick' and 'solid'. Unsuspecting adults may be surprised by soccer fans cheering on their favourites with 'Jason, you are sick!' or 'That was a sick cross!'

Living and interacting in Canadian society

Canadian conversational style is a compromise between the British tradition and the egalitarian tradition born from the pioneer mentality of settlers adjusting to a new environment and social reality. As in all English-speaking countries, British tradition shows in the reserved nature of conversations, especially in the case of any potential disagreement. The new settlers' mentality, on the other hand, makes people look at others as equals and speak without the 'stiff upper lip' and class-consciousness that are often caricatured in depictions of the British English style.

In the previous sections we had a brief look at Canadian society and Canadian lifestyles. Here we shall discuss how some of the social and societal factors affect ways in which Canadians talk to each other. We will examine how they greet each other and how they address each other in various settings and situations, the ways in which they converse and the ways in which they express their opinions and emotions. And even though there may be nothing that Canadians do and others don't, the overall combinations result in a specifically Canadian way, something that makes Canadians easily recognizable and generally liked.

Greetings, introductions, forms of address

Canadians use the informal greetings 'Hello' and 'Hi' with more frequency than some other English speakers and use them even in rather formal settings. Thus, the chair of the department at the university may open a departmental meeting with a cheerful 'Hi' without being accused of ill manners. The more formal variants, such as 'Good morning', 'Good afternoon' and 'Good evening', are also available and would be used when addressing larger audiences, in more formal situations.

The greeting is usually immediately followed by a question 'How are you?' (or something similar like 'How are things?' or 'How are you doing?' or informally 'How ya doing?', 'What's up?', 'How's it going?'). It is also possible to greet someone with one of these questions, without any 'Hi' or 'Hello', or perhaps preceded by an emphatic 'Oh!' to express joy or surprise in seeing the other person. These exchanges are 'ritualistic' in nature, the questions about someone's health are semi-genuine and it is not customary to answer the question absolutely. No matter how the speaker is feeling, whether well or unwell, the answer to 'How are you?' is usually positive: 'Great' or 'Fine, thank you' or 'Not (too) bad' or, sometimes, 'Surviving'. The second part of the exchange then consists of the addressee asking the same question of the speaker. The ritualistic nature of these exchanges is underlined when either the sequencing or the vocabulary of the exchange is not respected: there is hesitation and the conversation abruptly ends in silence and embarrassment since no one knows where to go from there. In small towns, people who are not directly acquainted may say 'Hi' or 'Hello' to each other when passing in the street.

In shops, you may be certain to be asked 'How are you today?' almost as soon as you enter and it would be considered odd not to answer, even though everyone involved knows it is not a serious question about the customer's health but a way for the customer to feel more comfortable and confident in asking for help in the store since now both parties have 'broken the ice'. In a shop setting, a brief exchange about the weather would also be commonplace. Since many stores are located in large shopping malls, sometimes underground, the salesperson may be genuinely curious about the weather outside. With a much lower population density in Canada, shops are only crowded (which again is a relative term) just before Christmas and so you may be the first customer in a while. Low population density may also explain the general politeness of the sales personnel in Canada. Every customer is indeed valuable. This also accounts for the fact that if a customer has to wait to be served because the salesperson is busy with another customer, the person waiting will almost certainly be served promptly. This is not always the case in more crowded places and so Canadians travelling to, say, London, may feel that some English shop personnel are impolite and inconsiderate.

In social encounters generally, older Canadians have tended to follow an English-style reserve about shaking hands and kissing: they tend to shake hands when being introduced for the first time or when the occasion needs to be marked in some special way – for example, when finalizing a business deal or congratulating someone on some achievement or expressing sympathy to bereaved relatives at a funeral. Kissing (normally when one or both parties are female) when meeting or parting is usually reserved for members of the family or very close friends. Men will usually kiss only their very young sons or nephews or grandsons, but this generally stops at quite an early age, after which a vigorous handshake while clasping the opposite shoulder is the preferred way of showing affection or other strong emotion.

The greeting behaviour among the younger generations is at present quite fluid. Given Canada's multi-ethnic make-up, greeting rituals from many traditions are now frequently seen in Canadian society. It is therefore not unusual to see friends or colleagues (male and female) greet each other or part from someone with a kiss on one or both cheeks or even a hug. Among high school and college/ university students it is not unusual to see hugs when greeting or parting from friends of the same or the opposite gender, nor is it unusual to see males exchange a 'hugging handshake' or 'specialized' handshakes or hugs to indicate group adherence, whether because of ethnicity or interest. (This is especially true at the high school level with youth groups.)

Like most other North American English speakers, Canadians prefer to address each other by first names and consider this the only natural form of address in many settings. Thus equal-status colleagues at work use first names even if there are age differences and they often do so from the moment they are introduced. It would also seem odd not to address a neighbour by their first name – for example, 'Hi Lorna' or 'How are you Phil?' – and quite often children too use first names when talking to neighbours with whom they are on friendly terms. The exception may be when addressing elderly people. In these situations, using forms like 'Hello Mrs Tiegs' may be considered more appropriate but not compulsory. Within the family, kinship terms may be used with first names, 'Thank you, Uncle David' or 'Good night, Auntie Mary'.

At school, students usually address teachers as 'Mrs Hill' or 'Mr McDonald'. The form 'Miss' without last name as used in Britain, as in 'Good morning, Miss', is also common in Canada. At university, professors and instructors are usually addressed by using their last names with the title: 'Thank you, Dr Thomas' or 'Yes, Professor Lawson'. The form 'Professor' may be used when addressing or talking about faculty members who do not have a PhD but hold the title of a professor. Some first-year students may address faculty with 'Miss' or 'Sir', which is reminiscent of the patterns they were used to in high school. Younger faculty in most Canadian universities have taken to having students address them by their first names, marking a democratization of campuses. It should be mentioned here that the words 'staff' and 'faculty' have a specific meaning when applied to the personnel at a college or university. 'Staff' refers to technical and administrative employees of the university while 'faculty' refers to the teaching members of the university. Thus while you may go to a staff club in Britain, you would be going to a faculty club in Canada.

When you visit a professional, such as a doctor (even if it is at the emergency department of a hospital where the staff does not know you), a lawyer or chiropractor, or a service professional such as a hairdresser, manicurist or aesthetician, you will most likely be addressed by your first name. This is due not to some form of disrespect but as a conscious way of putting you at your ease for what is to come (whether pleasant or unpleasant!). In other cases – for example, with a garage mechanic or service station attendant – if you have been their regular customer for some time, title and surname are used ('I can have that done by today, Mr Jones'; 'Will that be a fill-up, Mrs McNabb?'). Otherwise, usually no address form is used ('Fill 'er up?', 'Will that be a fill-up?').

Social encounters

> You can always tell a Canadian by the fact that when he walks
> into a room, he automatically chooses to sit in the most
> uncomfortable chair. It's part of our genetic affinity for discomfort
> and self-denial, which has formed the Canadian character as
> clearly as our geography. (Peter C. Newman in Olive, 1996, p. 48)

Canadians, like most other English-speakers, try to avoid being pushy
or disagreeable in discussing matters both in professional and social
settings. They may be shocked by what some other national groups
consider a conversation, as for them it may rather look like an
argument. They may therefore misjudge other nationalities (for
example, Poles, Italians or Germans) who may say what they think
without the polite hedges. Canadians will rarely initiate discussion on
topics that may be considered controversial or too personal unless they
are talking to close friends. It is therefore not common to discuss
political affiliations or ask for whom one has voted or is going to vote
in an election. Personal finances are also rarely the topic, unless it is
relevant for some reason. It is an established tradition in many
companies or offices that, when a person is in an especially difficult
situation (because of a death in the family, accident, divorce, etc.), the
co-workers may discuss ways of helping the friend in need financially
by making contributions to a special fund.

Among close friends, however, all topics may be discussed. This
is particularly true among female friends. Topics such as personal
health and marital problems are no longer taboo and may be discussed
with the level of detail that would in turn be shocking in some other
cultures. But discussing such topics outside the circle of close friends
would be judged as inappropriate.

A safe topic for a social conversation among young people of both
sexes and among men is sport. Women, too, discuss sport but their
discussions often focus on the sporting activities of their children.
Most children play hockey, soccer, softball, baseball, volleyball or
basketball, often all year long. If they play soccer, for example, they
can play indoor soccer in the winter and in the spring start to play
outside. There is house league, as well as travel teams and rep teams
that represent the town outside. In the winter, both boys and girls may
play hockey and many do figure skating. Parents waiting for their
children usually socialize, drinking coffee (usually Tim Hortons!)
together and chatting about everything. Young women (and sometimes
men − but only those at the college/university level will admit it!)
frequently discuss the latest instalments of the popular soap operas or
the latest fashion trends or the latest dance/music craze. Although
most would not admit it openly to others, there is also quite a bit of
gossip (not frequently of a malicious nature) that is engaged in by both

154

sexes, especially among teenagers and young adults, which continues sometimes even in the workplace.

Canadians do not like meetings and these are kept to the minimum. Most things can be resolved without meetings and, with e-mail, without personal contact between the people involved. Meetings are often just an occasion for voting on matters previously discussed. They are usually short – at the university they rarely run for more than one teaching period of 50 minutes, as it is difficult to find a time slot convenient for everybody involved. At some meetings coffee and cookies or doughnuts are available, but this is an exception rather than a rule, and so there is no incentive to have meetings as a form of social gatherings. The one contradiction to this is a recent phenomenon – which is really a reintroduction of previous traditions – the church social gathering or the community social gathering. Since Canada is beginning to deal with an ageing population who have a lot of time (and in many cases money) and nothing to do, both the churches and community centres have begun to hold social gatherings (such as teas, euchre or card game parties and quilting bees) for these sometimes lonely older members of society.

Direct imperatives are not common in the speech of English-speakers and Canada is no exception. Even at home, orders are usually softened with 'please', put in a question form, or have the verb form omitted: 'Please wipe your shoes before you enter', 'Could you call your sister to the table?' or 'Dinner time!'.

Once outside the circle of home and friends, Canadian English tends to follow the rules of English usage and direct imperatives are often avoided, especially in a superior–employee situation. The order or request may be attenuated either by transforming it into a question – so that 'Leave the letters on my desk' becomes 'Could you leave the letters on my desk?' , 'Would you leave the letters on my desk?' or very politely 'Would you mind leaving the letters on my desk?' – or by adding 'please', as in 'Please leave the letters on my desk'. When one of these devices is omitted, the result sounds impolite, abrupt or aggressive or may denote anger or dissatisfaction, which is one of the reasons that mothers are constantly correcting their children when they produce such utterances. Nonetheless, there is a growing tendency in North American English to just such types of exchanges, perhaps because of the growing breakdown of common civility not only among young people but also among adults. Witness the increasing number of incidents of aggressive and rude public behaviour at sports events, behind the wheel of a car, on public transportation or more recently even among airline passengers.

Given Canada's vast dimensions and multicultural nature, there will be many occasions when someone will have to ask for advice from a fellow Canadian. When the advice requested results in an exchange of information – how to get to the Parliament Buildings, where to get information on tax questions, how to install an electronic timer or what to bring if invited to someone's home for dinner – most Canadians are forthcoming and offer the advice in a friendly manner, perhaps attenuated with an 'If I were in your place, I'd ...' or 'If it were up to me, I would ...' when they feel the advice is coming too close to telling someone what to do in a given situation.

When the request involves advice of a more personal nature, then it depends on the relationship between the people involved and on the topic to be dealt with, whether advice will be given or not. In many cases the cultural background of the people involved will have an impact on whether advice outside the ethnic circle is sought or given.

Given the Canadian characteristic of politeness, it is expected that expressions of apology would be quite frequent and this is in effect what happens. Most refusals are prefaced by an apology, as in 'I'm sorry but ...' or 'Sorry, I can't come with you right now' or 'I'm really sorry that I can't give you anything for the Church bazaar this time'. Even the modern scourge – the ubiquitous telephone salesperson or telemarketer – is discouraged with a polite 'No, thank you' or 'Sorry, we make no commitments over the phone'. Even buses are polite in Canada and say 'Sorry, Out of Service' when on their way to the garage. In this aspect of social interaction, Canadians have no special exchanges different from other English-speakers.

Canadians consider themselves and are usually considered by others as warm and friendly and this extends to visitors, who are generally welcome in Canada. There are no bad feelings about any national group. Unless someone is clearly a tourist on a short holiday, questions of the sort 'So, how long are you here for?' are never asked. It may be assumed that visitors may want to stay. The immigration process is well defined and all one needs to do is follow the steps. As Canada still accepts a large number of new immigrants every year, illegal immigration is minimal, although in the last few years there has been an increase in the number of refugee claimants, both legitimate and bogus, given Canada's generally lenient stance towards refugees. At times of economic stagnation people may not like the idea of increasing the number of people hunting for jobs, but few Canadians would dispute the need for immigration.

Parties, celebrations and other social gatherings

Canadians like to party, at any time and with any excuse. As Marlene Dietrich remarked: 'Like the Swedes, the Canadians have un-northern temperaments. Such capacity for enthusiasm!' (Olive, 1996, p. 167). Christmas and Easter are the two most popular Christian holidays. Jews celebrate Hanukkah at the same time of the year as the Christian

Christmas, and Passover at the time of the Christian Easter. Other religions observe their holidays but they are not recognized nationwide as work-free days. Nevertheless, in regions with significant ethnic groups, scheduling of exams at university often takes into account other religious holidays, and at elementary and high school, holy days of other faiths are acknowledged.

Canadian national holidays, such as Victoria Day (Monday preceding 24 May), Canada Day (1 July), Labour Day (first Monday in September) and Thanksgiving (second Monday in October) are usually good opportunities to meet with family and friends. Perhaps with the exception of Thanksgiving, these holidays usually have warm weather and people often gather outside and have barbecues in their backyards. Thanksgiving is a more traditional family holiday, with turkey, stuffing and pumpkin pie. It comes some three weeks before the children's favourite holiday, Halloween (31 October), and so pumpkins are a popular theme in October. They are often used to decorate the front porches, along with colourful Indian corn and potted mums. On Halloween, after dark, most children, wearing scary or funny costumes, go from home to home 'trick and treating'. They are often accompanied by an adult, who walks with them but stays at a distance, just keeping an eye on the children. Most people welcome the children and offer them sweets, apples or small change. Children know that they may only knock on the door if the house has some Halloween decorations and the lights are on. Those who do not wish to be bothered by (sometimes hundreds of) children may simply leave the lights off.

Mother Nature also takes part in the festivities at this time of the year. After the first frost during the second half of September and the sunny part of October we are in Indian Summer, the time when trees start turning bright yellow, orange and red. A visit to Canada at this time of the year explains why the red maple leaf is the Canadian emblem – Canadian red maple trees do turn bright red!

Canadians often celebrate with friends and families as well as with the neighbourhood. Such holidays as Victoria Day involve fireworks and are sometimes celebrated by a group of neighbours. These are very relaxed occasions, often with everybody bringing food and beverages. It is not uncommon for guests to wear shorts and T-shirts, especially on particularly hot and humid summer days. Food and drink are usually plentiful but you are not forced to eat and drink, as would be the case in some other cultures.

Canadians are hospitable and caring hosts and enjoy throwing parties. There is usually nothing lavish about Canadian parties, especially those held in the summer, outside in the backyard or garden. There is always enough food and drink but rarely far more than may be expected as necessary. Hosts may encourage guests to help themselves or may serve them but without being pushy. There are no rules of politeness of the kind that require you first to decline food before being persuaded to eat, and it is fully acceptable to take what is offered. It is also perfectly appropriate to decline with a simple 'No, thank you, I had enough' or a more evasive 'Maybe later'. Guests show their politeness by complimenting the hosts about food and sometimes asking for recipes. Thus you may hear many expressions of admiration and praise, such as 'This custard is delicious – how do you make it?' or 'Your chicken wings are fantastic – what spices did you add to them?' or 'Where did you get these shrimps? They taste better than those they have at Sobey's.'

Eating out is very popular in Canada and many people meet friends in various eating or drinking places rather than at home. In restaurants where a server would serve you, the use of a formal versus casual style of service, and consequently address, will depend on the restaurant type. Some so-called family restaurants, such as the national chains of East Side Mario's, Samuel's, Kelsey's, Swiss Chalet or Pizza Hut, welcome children and have all kinds of attractions available for them ('kids eat free' nights, colouring books, etc.). There, the serving personnel (usually high school or college/university students) may greet guests addressing them with 'guys', as in 'How are you tonight, guys?'. In formal restaurants, such as those in high-class hotels, 'Sir' and 'Madam' would be used.

Serving personnel usually introduce themselves: 'Hi, my name is Cathy and I will be serving you tonight' and ask about drinks first, leaving you time to read through the menu. They would then be back to tell you about the 'specials' recommended that day. In a restaurant setting, 'special' is not what is 'on sale' but what is particularly recommended. The specials may be printed on a separate sheet inserted in the regular menu or read out by the server. If the list of specials is quite long, there is nothing wrong with asking the server to repeat it. Eating out is a much-celebrated activity and this includes giving the guest a long list of options once they have decided about the basic dish. Main courses usually come with the option of being served soup or salad (with a choice of soup and a list of options for the salad dressing). The next stage is the selection between French fries (what the British call chips), rice, baked potato (with sour cream, butter, etc.) or possibly pasta. If you have ordered a steak, which is one of the more popular selections and which is usually more than a person can eat, you will have to face a choice between rare, medium and well done – or any combination of two such as medium–rare or medium–well done or very well done (but eating a very well done steak is according to some people like eating shoe leather). Some five minutes after the selections arrive, the server will check whether everything is all right. Eating out is supposed to be a pleasure and if anything is not as expected, there is no problem with asking for something different, complaining about or returning the food. This, though, does not happen very often, as food is usually good and plentiful. In many establishments free refills of soft drinks or coffee are offered. A 10 to 15 per cent tip (gratuity) is either left on the table or added to the total amount of the bill by the customer. Sometimes, if the service has been especially good or the server very friendly, a bit more is added.

While eating out (for dinner or lunch) is very popular and relatively inexpensive, sometimes people do not have the time for a meal and therefore a suggestion of getting together for a drink is often considered appropriate. There are a number of different types of 'watering holes' available where drinking beer or having some other alcoholic beverage would be considered morally and gender neutral. In small towns there still remain the vestiges of the local bar which was always a working-class, male-dominated environment and the more genteel 'lounge' where ladies were admitted, but through a separate door and only if accompanied. But the multicultural nature of Canadian society, especially in the larger cities, has also had an impact on drinking establishments. Although quite different from its British counterpart, the pub is frequent in city neighbourhoods, as well as the European type coffee house which serves either only speciality coffees and teas or a combination of these and alcoholic beverages and light meals. In addition, a recent phenomenon has been the introduction of 'theme' bars, such as sports bars or jazz clubs or cigar lounges or patios (during the summer months) where patrons can get together over a drink and look at the latest sports events, listen to some live music or sample different types of cigars or 'kill some time' before commuting home, all in a fairly relaxed, informal environment.

Young Canadians certainly love to party. High-school students have their school dances, some of which, called *semi-formal* (or *semi* for short), involve getting dressed 'to excite', sometimes according to a theme. Even though the legal drinking age in Canada is 19, teenagers and young adults alike often get together at parties that involve alcohol. In big cities they may go to bars or clubs, some of which do not sell alcohol and so do not require any ID. A popular party format is the so-called *keg party* (or *kegger*). This is defined as a party involving lots of beer that is provided, of course, in the form of kegs. The www.keg-net.org website claims that 'virtually EVERY college student has been to at least one keg party!' and offers 'to shed light on many of the issues surrounding these ever-popular beer guzzling bashes!' In the country or in smaller towns, there are also *bush parties*, organized out in a field or in the woods, often with bonfires. Young people are generally more responsible about drinking and driving than their parents' generation and most people arrive and depart in taxis or have designated drivers who refrain from drinking. Driving safely is a very serious issue in Canada, not only because of alcohol but mostly because of severe weather conditions that affect everyone.

If we were to eavesdrop on the conversations at these parties we would most likely be hearing talk about the latest encounters by the local professional or even college/university sports team – hockey or basketball teams in winter, baseball teams in spring and summer, and football (Canadian football not soccer!) in the fall – or talk about the developments in the latest instalments of the daytime soap operas (*The Young and the Restless, Days of Our Lives, Another World* and *The Bold and the Beautiful* are the most popular), or a discussion of the last episode of the night-time shows (*American* and *Canadian Idol, Survivor*, and other 'reality' shows).

The attitude to alcohol is not uniform throughout Canada, depending on how strong the religious or cultural traditions are in the community or province. The Puritan or Baptist heritage is against alcohol and, as a result, until quite recently there were some towns and city neighbourhoods in Canada which were legally 'dry' – no alcohol was served in public establishments. For instance, it is an offence in Ontario to consume alcohol in a public place other than at a restaurant/bar where it is served, so there is no drinking in parks or in the squares. A court case was witnessed where a man, stopped by the police while walking down the street with a bottle of alcohol in his hand, had his driver's licence suspended although he had not been driving a car at the time. There is, however, also a very practical reason why drinking is looked at in a negative way. In order to get almost anywhere in Canada, even in the same small town, one needs to drive. Many people spend a good part of their day on the road. The speed limit on major highways is 100 km per hour (about 60 mph), not because the roads are not suitable for faster driving, but because it is possible that the truck driver in front of you may have been on the road for the last twelve hours. Compared to the narrow and winding roads of Britain, Canada offers hundreds of kilometres of wide, straight and generally well-kept highways. Since practically everybody drives, public transportation is less well developed.

As guests would most likely have to drive home, drinking excessively would be considered irresponsible by most people and hosts are actually obliged to make sure that no one drives home after having too much to drink. A reference to driving is a perfect justification for declining a drink. What frequently happens is that one member of the group, whether a spouse or one of the group of friends, elects to be the designated driver and refrains from the consumption of alcohol so that they would then drive everyone home.

Canadian values and attitudes

Personal social values

> In a world darkened by ethnic conflicts that tear nations apart,
> Canada stands as a model of how people of different cultures can
> live and work together in peace, prosperity, and mutual respect.
> (Former US President Bill Clinton)

Canadian society at the beginning of the twenty-first century is a very
different one from even two decades ago. As Erin Anderssen and
Michael Valpy (2004, p. 15) say in their article 'Face the Nation',

> ... Canada is changing, becoming more urban, ethnically mixed,
> competitive, secular and media-savvy ... There is a new Canada,
> one with a clear identity, and for the young men and women now
> between 20 and 29 years of age it is the only Canada they have
> ever known.

For Canadians, the 'wake-up' call came in 1995, the year of the
Québec Referendum, when they realized that they could have lost the
country as they knew it; and decided to work to keep what they had.
Since then, there has been a new feeling of confidence in who they are,
helped by the fact that other nations and the UN had recognized
Canada's positive society and lifestyle even before Canadians did.
What has emerged is a Canada proud of its tolerance towards others,
of helping others in need, of extending the nation's abilities to keep the
peace and work toward the democratization of other nations, and even
the events of 9/11 have not significantly changed Canadian values. The
outward manifestation of this new identity was, surprisingly, a beer
commercial: the Molson 'I AM Canadian' rant. For the first time,
Canadians were not willing to accept the stereotypes that had
traditionally been applied to them and stood up to say what they
were not.

> *Hey.*
> *I'm not a lumberjack or a fur trader, and I don't live in an igloo or*
> *eat blubber, or own a dog sled, and I don't know Jimmy, Sally or*
> *Suzy from Canada, although I'm certain they're really, really nice.*
> *I have a Prime Minister, not a President. I speak English and*
> *French, not American, and I pronounce it 'about', not 'aboot'.*
> *I can proudly sew my country's flag on my backpack. I believe in*
> *peacekeeping, not policing; diversity, not assimilation; and that*
> *the beaver is a truly proud and noble animal.*
> *A tuque is a hat, a chesterfield is a couch, and it is pronounced*
> *'zed'; not 'zee' – 'zed'!*
> *Canada is the second largest land mass! The first nation of*
> *hockey! And the best part of North America!*
> *My name is Joe! And I am Canadian!*
> *... Thank you.*

In addition to the more typical spin-offs like T-shirts, mugs, car bumper stickers etc., others also used the format: I AM Australian (for the Sydney Olympics, another beer commercial, for Fosters), I AM Albertan, I AM British Columbian, to name just a few.

The liberalism of the New Canada – identified as social liberalism by the *Economist* in 2003 – is the result of at least two decades of conscious change on the part of the government of Canada and Canadians in general and may be traced back to the frontier value of freedom. These liberal social values were enshrined in the Charter of Rights and Freedoms signed by Queen Elizabeth II in 1981, and have made Canada a vanguard twenty-first-century nation, envied by others: engaged globally (in peacekeeping, humanitarian aid and dealing with global environmental issues), socially liberal (with gay rights, same-sex marriage, Medicare, approved medical use of marijuana) and culturally diverse (through the Multiculturalism Act and the embracing of continued immigration). Canada (18 per cent of the population is foreign-born) and its major cities (Toronto 44 per cent; Vancouver 38 per cent; Hamilton 24 per cent; compare Miami 40 per cent; Sydney 31 per cent; New York 24 per cent) are among the world's most culturally diverse communities.

This New Canada breaks other traditional stereotypes attributed to it: 79 per cent of the population live in urban centres, with four metropolitan areas (Greater Toronto, Montreal, Vancouver and the Calgary-Edmonton Corridor) accounting for 50 per cent of the total Canadian population; women are in the vanguard in the New Canada (they are the most highly educated and the most socially liberal group); new immigrants fairly quickly and successfully adjust to their new homeland and are among the more ambitious and patriotic citizens. Nobody is suggesting that problems in all these areas of social life do not exist in Canada, but on the whole there is a concerted effort to find equitable and mutually satisfying solutions, rather than imposing them.

The New Canada is also less involved in traditional institutions. Many Canadians are disenchanted with government and associated institutions: for example, support for a national media network – the CBC – dropped, as well as belief that Air Canada should be saved. This dissatisfaction with political parties translates into lower voter participation in elections at all levels of government. Similarly, there is a decrease in Christian-based church participation, but an increase in non-Christian denominations due to growing immigration.

The issues which are most important to this new Canadian society are not so much the material trappings of success but the quality of that success: job security is valued over salary; time with the family is more important than more money; the possibility to live freely as one wants is more precious than material goods. No matter what their income bracket, Canadians agree that it is important to support charities and they do so, or at least say that they do. The percentage of people who believe that one should donate to charitable organizations independently of income ranges from 70 per cent for the under-$20,000 group to 81 per cent for the over-$80,000 group. In 1996, there was a significant increase of 11.5 per cent in the amount of money donated to charities. It may be explained by a combination of elements, such as a generally stronger economy, tax incentives for people making donations and the feeling of responsibility for those less fortunate in the face of government cuts to social services. This increased social awareness is also at the basis of an increased volunteerism on the part of all ages of society, from the young students engaged in cleaning up the garbage along the shores of creeks, rivers and lakes, to the retired craftspersons donating time and expertise for the erection of subsidized housing through the Habitat Foundation, to the young college graduates helping illiterate adults learn to read and write. Canadians' commitment to those less fortunate than themselves is shown most clearly whenever a natural or man-generated disaster happens: they respond immediately with both practical/tangible (e.g. food, water, blankets, a place in their own home) and monetary/ spiritual aid (e.g. ministers, doctors and other 'care' professionals – psychologists, counsellors etc.).

Despite their conviction that fitness is important, Canadians do not exercise enough, and spend too much time driving their car, flipping TV channels with their remote control or surfing on their computers. Fully 65 per cent of Canadian men and 52 per cent of women are overweight according to statistics from the Canadian government. An even more alarming trend in the last few years has been the sharp increase in childhood obesity rates: in 2004, 20 per cent of children 2–17 years of age were deemed overweight. With indications that diet and lack of exercise have played an important role in this increase, many school boards in Canada have banned soft drinks and fast food from school cafeterias and vending machines; and have moved to reintroduce a 'gym' period in the school day.

From an amateur and professional sports viewpoint, though, Canada can hold its own with many other nations, not only as far as hockey is concerned, but also in alpine skiing, figure skating (Elvis Stojko was four times world figure skating champion), kayaking and snowboarding. It should also be mentioned that one of the most popular world sports, basketball, was developed in Montreal and that for two consecutive years, 1992 and 1993, a Canadian team, the Toronto Blue Jays, won baseball's World Series.

Given the modern world's preoccupation with health and the trend of returning to nature, as well as fighting pollution in all of its forms, 47 per cent of Canadians say that they are becoming more receptive to the idea of seeking alternative health-care professionals than they were in the past. OHIP (the Ontario Health Insurance Progamme) responds to this by offering coverage for many chiropractic or homeopathic treatments.

Canadian 'nationalism'

> Not bad for a Canadian, eh? (Skier Steve Podborski, on winning the World Cup 1982, in Olive, 1996, p. 46)

Canadian nationalism is like their other characteristics: reserved. They do not tend to become 'flag wavers' unless they are out of the country and being mistaken for Americans or one of their national or professional sports teams is playing. In these circumstances they become just as vehement in their defence of their homeland as anyone else. Canadian courage in defence of their country has never been called into question and Canadian soldiers distinguished themselves in both World Wars as being the first into the fray and were often used as advance troops in the areas of heaviest fighting. Canada is a member of a number of international defence organizations including NATO, OSCE (Organisation for Security and Co-operation in Europe), NORAD (North American Aerospace Defense Command), and OAS (Organisation of American States) which is responsible for the defence of member nations in North, Central and South America. In talking about Canadian nationalism, we would like to make a distinction between 'ethnic' and 'civic' nationalism. What will be talked about in this section is civic nationalism: the commitment to the nation by all citizens when its identity or security is threatened. Canada also has its share of ethnic nationalism (witness the ongoing problem with French Canada), but this never interferes with the fulfilment of international commitments by the nation or the support and defence of Canada by its citizens outside the borders.

But in an international context Canada is almost unique for its commitment to peacekeeping and this has given Canada, a mid-sized nation militarily, a powerful voice, as a *Washington Post* headline pointed out (3 December 1997, p. A01): 'Canada's Global Clout Grows as Its Army Shrinks'. Since the end of the Second World War, Canada has participated in more than 40 peacekeeping missions, of which 35 were as part of the United Nations Emergency Force. (This Force was first established in 1956 to respond to the Suez Crisis and was the brainchild of a Canadian politician and diplomat, Lester B. Pearson, who won the Nobel Prize for Peace for this initiative.) Apart from sports figures, the only other recent 'heroes' in the Canadian public's mind have been peacekeepers: Major General McKenzie, the leader of the UN operations in Bosnia; Lt Gen. Romeo Dallaire, the Commander of the UN Peacekeeping Troops in Rwanda who defied the UN order to pull out and leave the civilians to their fate; and the Canadian soldiers, among them the first female soldier, who have died in Afghanistan. Major General McKenzie's public popularity was so great that two major political parties, the Liberals and Conservatives, tried to convince him to run for Parliament for their party.

Canada's 'clout' was felt in December 1997 when, after a year of behind-the-scenes work, Foreign Minister Lloyd Axworthy hosted in Ottawa the signing by more than 100 nations of the Treaty to Ban Landmines. And this is not the only front on which Canadian diplomacy is working, as the *Washington Post's* Howard Schneider has pointed out:

> If there is a new world order emerging from the fall of communism and the rise of international trading blocs, then look for a Maple Leaf stamp of approval on it. With borders secured by two oceans, a polar cap and its long-standing alliance with the United States, the country is pursuing an agenda rare in history: aggressive demilitarisation combined with an expansive foreign policy. (Schneider, 1997, p. A01)

Canada's commitment to international demilitarization and peacekeeping and its over-50-year record in responding to civil strife, humanitarian assistance and election monitoring around the globe prompted the government to establish the Lester B. Pearson Canadian International Peacekeeping Training Centre in Cornwallis Park, Nova Scotia.

Canadian 'Non-Americanism'

Blair Fraser, a Canadian journalist, was probably right when he wrote in 1967 that 'without at least a touch of anti-Americanism, Canada would have no reason to exist. Of all general definitions of the Canadians, this is the most nearly valid: twenty million people who, for anything up to twenty million reasons, prefer not to be American' (Olive, 1996, p. 114).

Perhaps the social value that characterizes Canadians the most is their 'non-Americanism'. They are very quick to point out that they are different from their neighbours to the south. Canadians pride themselves on their civility (although this is in flux with the younger generations as we have pointed out above) and on the cleanliness of the cities that can be found in Canada as opposed to the abruptness and filth found in large cities in the United States. Canadians also see themselves as different from their American cousins as far as lifestyles are concerned: they consider themselves to be more laid back and not as stuffy as the British but also not as arrogant and aggressive in all things as Americans seem to be. Perhaps the best way to sum up the ambivalent attitude to the US is the 1996 words of journalist Don Gilmour:

> We have often defined ourselves as not being Americans. We lack their gift for mythology and instead of rallying around the image of Johnny Canuck or Lester Pearson, we see ourselves as quieter, less parochial, and more peaceful than our neighbours. The act of defining oneself by a negative is the easiest and most attractive method. We identify the worst habits in others and note that while we aren't perfect, at least we don't have race riots or food shortages or drive-by shootings, etc., although we are making headway in all of those areas. (Olive, 1996, p. 53)

Many people outside North America are unable to distinguish Canadian English from American English, and often mistake Canadians for Americans. Canadians usually react to that with an immediate correction and stress their Canadian origin, somehow assuming it to be better and more acceptable abroad. It is a generally accepted opinion that Canadians are liked everywhere and have no particular enemies. Thus, if they happen to be mistaken for Americans, they find it important to make sure to correct this.

The best country in the world

> When I'm in Canada, I feel this is what the world should be like.
> (US actor Jane Fonda)

The United Nations Human Development Index repeatedly cites Canada as one of the top five places in the world to live. In 1995, a World Bank study named Canada the world's second wealthiest society after Australia, using calculations based on resources and investment in education and social programmes. Canadians live one and a half years longer on average than Americans and the country has a lower infant mortality rate, all this with lower spending on health care (9.7 per cent of the GDP as compared to 14.2 per cent in the USA in 1994). Recent economic difficulties may have affected this picture but most people, even in Canada, believe that Canada is still a good place to be.

The New Canada has come a long way in the past two decades but there is still much work to be done if the dream of the free, harmonious and multicultural nation envisioned by Pierre Trudeau is to become a solid reality. As Governor General Michaëlle Jean, a Haitian immigrant from Montreal, said in her installation speech in September 2006, 'We must eliminate the spectre of all the solitudes and promote solidarity among all citizens who make up the Canada of today.' (Maclean's, 23/01/06, p. 23).

Tasks and exercises

1. Why don't Canadians talk much about the weather? Is the weather a popular topic or conversation opener in your culture?

2. What is the most frequently used 'filler' characteristic of Canadian English?

3. Another filler frequently used by Canadians is the word 'like'. Look at the sentences below and the word 'like' inserted in places, then explain the effect the word has in each context:
a) I looked out of the window and, even though it was quite dark, I saw (like) a fairly large animal sitting on a tree.
b) My mother told me it must be our neighbour's cat and that I should go and get it off the tree and bring it home. (Like) She thinks I've got nothing better to do than to take care of our neighbour's cat.
c) Nevertheless, I went out to investigate, (like) I'm not afraid of cats, but I never discovered what it really was, since by the time I got downstairs it was gone.

4. Not all language expressions, such as ritualistic phrases, metaphors, sayings, mean exactly what they seem to mean at first glance. Look at the list of Canadian expressions given below and try to explain what they mean and what would be the correct context or contexts to use them in. Then think of ways of expressing the same feelings, ideas or meanings in your native tongue:
- Let's get together for lunch.
- I'll get back to you.
- To go back and forth.
- Knee-high to a grasshopper.
- Thin? I've seen more meat on a hockey stick.

5. Explain the origin and/or usage of the following Canadian words and phrases:
- Canada
- Manitoba
- Saskatoon
- Niagara Falls
- Paris
- chipmunk
- racoon
- toboggan

- kayak
- Canuck
- duffle cloth
- corduroy roads
- Digby chips
- Digby chicken
- back forty
- buffalo chips

6. Provide at least three names of First Nations who inhabited Canada before it was colonized by Europeans.

7. Explain the meanings and usage of the following expressions connected with Canadian history:
- to hit pay dirt
- to strike it rich
- to stake a claim
- to get down to bedrock
- to be washed out

8. How would you greet the following people in Canada and how would you do this in your native culture? What are the differences between your native and Canadian customs in this respect?
- your boyfriend/girlfriend
- your boss at work
- your university lecturer
- your cousin
- your mother
- an elderly neighbour
- someone your age you do not know very well
- a customer in a shop

9. How would you address (by first name, surname or title) the following people in Canada?
- colleague at work
- elderly neighbour
- your uncle Ben
- a school teacher
- a university lecturer
- a university professor
- a dentist
- a priest
- a lawyer
- a physician

10. Would all of the above people address you the same way you addressed them?

11. Would the above people be addressed the same way in Britain and Australia? What, if any, would be the differences?

12. Name three topics that would be considered too controversial by Canadians to be discussed at a party. Would these topics be considered equally controversial in your native culture?

13. Do close friends discuss personal and intimate details such as personal health and marital problems in your native culture? How about Canadians?

14. On the basis of what you have read above, would you agree that Canadians are 'warm' and 'friendly'? Why do you think so?

15. The questionnaire below compares party customs in your native culture and in Canada. If the statement below is true, put a tick in the box; if the statement is false, leave the box empty. After you finish filling in the questionnaire, compare the party customs in Canada and your home country.

Party custom	Canada	Your country
You should arrive exactly on time	☐	☐
You may be expected to bring a present for the hosts	☐	☐
You may be expected to bring some food with you	☐	☐
You may be expected to bring a bottle of drink with you	☐	☐
There will be much more food than necessary	☐	☐
The hosts will actively encourage people to eat more	☐	☐
The hosts will insist on serving large quantities of alcoholic beverages to the guests	☐	☐
You may be expected to show your appreciation by expressing admiration for the food served	☐	☐

16. Compare the behaviour of serving personnel in fast food outlets and formal restaurants in Canada and in your home country. Comment on the similarities and differences.

17. If you wanted to have a glass of beer, wine or spirit outside the home, where would you be able to get it in Great Britain, Australia, Canada, New Zealand and the United States?

18. What are shops selling alcoholic beverages called in Australia, Great Britain, Canada, New Zealand and the United States?

19. Make a list of the most important values in your native culture, then use the text to draw up a similar list of Canadian values and comment on the similarities and differences.

Notes

1. An expression attributed to the Canadian Prime Minister, Joe Clark (Olive, 1996).
2. The Department of English at Queen's University had received from J.R. Strathy an endowment to promote the use of correct English in Canada. In 1981, the Unit began the compilation of a computer corpus of samples of Canadian English. The *Guide* is a direct result of that undertaking. Another dictionary, the *Canadian Oxford Dictionary*, edited by Katherine Barber, was published in 1998, and is based on 'five years of work by five Canadian lexicographers examining almost 20 million words of Canadian texts held in databases' (from the preface, p. viii).
3. We must keep in mind that Canada is officially a bilingual country and in a large portion of the Canadian territory (i.e. Québec) French is spoken, as well as in other pockets throughout the country (Manitoba, New Brunswick).
4. Americans are sometimes surprised to realize that for Canadians, the USA is 'south of the border'. In the USA, this expression is reserved for Mexico and may have slightly pejorative or patronizing connotations.
5. Any discrepancy in the orthography of *orthoepi* and *orthografi* between the title and the reported text is attributable to the original citation appearing in Orkin.
6. Another more fanciful origin for the name of the country would have it deriving from the disgusted expression of early Spanish explorers upon seeing the winter snow and ice instead of gold and riches: 'Aca nada!', 'Here nothing!' (Orkin, 1970, p. 162). Another joke attributes the discovery of Canada to Germans who gave the empty land its name Kanada ('Keine da!', 'No-one there!').
7. Tim Hortons coffee shops have been a tremendous Canadian

success story. Established in 1964 in Hamilton, Ontario, by hockey star Tim Horton and entrepreneur Ron Joyce, the coffee and doughnut (vs US spelling donut) chain is the largest in Canada and has now expanded to the USA. It is most notable for its coffee, Timbits, bagels, soups and sandwiches. Most Canadians consider it an essential part of the Canadian identity and a symbol of 'home'. Because of this association, in 2006, Canadian soldiers stationed in Afghanistan asked for and succeeded in getting a Tim Hortons franchise for their base in Kandahar.

8. Medicare, universal public medical coverage, was first introduced in 1962 by Tommy Douglas when he was Premier of Saskatchewan (in 2004 he was voted the greatest Canadian) and extended to the whole nation in 1968 by the federal government. Canadians pride themselves on the establishment and continued existence of Medicare and it is cited as one of the major reasons for Canada's high ranking in world evaluations of a positive living environment. It is also one of the most striking differences between Canada and the USA.

References

A Concise Dictionary of Canadianisms (1973) Toronto: Gage Educational Publishing Ltd.

Adams, M. (1997) Sex in the Snow: Canadian Social Values at the end of the Millennium, Toronto: Viking Press.

Anderssen, E., Valpy, M. et al. (2004) The New Canada: A Globe and Mail Report on the Next Generation, Toronto: Globe and Mail/ McClelland & Stewart.

Anderssen, E. and Valpy, M. (2004) 'Face the Nation', in Anderssen, E., Valpy, M. et al. (2004) The New Canada: A Globe and Mail Report on the Next Generation, Toronto: Globe and Mail/McClelland & Stewart, pp. 15–25.

Avis, W.S. (1955) 'Speech differences along the Ontario–United States border, II Grammar and Syntax', Journal of the Canadian Linguistic Association, 1.

Avis, W.S. (1956) 'Speech differences along the Ontario–United States border, III Pronunciation', Journal of the Canadian Linguistic Association, 2.

Avis, W.S. (1973) 'The English Language in Canada: A Report', Current Trends in Linguistics 10, 40–74.

Avis, W.S. (1986) 'The Contemporary Context of Canadian English', in Allen, H.B. and Linn, M.D. (eds), Dialect and Language Variation, New York: Academic Press.

Bloomfield, M. W. (1975) 'Canadian English and its Relation to Eighteenth Century American Speech', in J.K. Chambers (ed.) (1975).

Blyth, C., Recktenwald, S., & Wang, J. (1990) 'I'm like, "say what?!": A new quotative in American oral narrative', *American Speech* 65/3: 215–27.

Brinton, L.J. & Fee, M. (2001) 'Canadian English', in Algeo, J. (ed.), *The Cambridge History of the English Language, Volume VI: English in North America*, Cambridge: Cambridge University Press, pp. 422–40.

Branden, V. (1992) *In Defence of Plain English: the Decline and Fall of Literacy in Canada*, Willowdale, On: Hounslow Press.

Brook, G.L. (1973) *Varieties of English*, Macmillan, London and Basingstoke.

Burrus, V. (2005) 'The use of "like" in everyday speech: What your grammar teachers never told you', at http://www.isc.utoronto.ca/newsletter/mar05.htm, consulted on 20 May 2006.

Canadian Oxford Dictionary (1998) edited by K. Barber, Toronto, New York, Oxford: Oxford University Press.

Canadian Dictionary of the English Language: An Encyclopaedic Reference (1997), International Thomson Publishing, Toronto.

Casselman, B. (1995) *Casselman's Canadian Words: A Comic Browse through Words and Folk Sayings Invented by Canadians*, Toronto: Copp Clark.

Casselman, B. (1996) *Casselmania: More wacky Canadian words and sayings.* Toronto: Little, Brown and Company (Canada) Ltd.

Chambers, J.K. (ed.). (1975) *Canadian English: Origins and Structures.* Toronto: Methuen Press.

Chambers, J.K. (1979) *The Languages of Canada*, Montreal: Didier.

Chambers, J.K. (1986) 'Three kinds of standard in Canadian English', in Lougheed, W.C. (ed.), *In Search of the Standard in Canadian English*, Kingston, ON: Strathy Language Unit Occasional Papers 1: 1–15.

Chambers, J.K. (2002) 'Maple Leaf Rap', *Language Magazine*, vol. 1, no. 9, May, 37–9.

Clarke, S. (ed.) (1993) *Focus on Canada*, Varieties of English Around the World Series, G11, Amsterdam, Philadelphia: John Benjamins.

Colombo, J.R. (1998) *Quotable Canada: A national treasury*, Philadelphia/London: Running Press.

De Wolf, G.D. (1992) *Social and Regional Factors in Canadian English: A Study of Phonological Variables and Grammatical Items in Ottawa and Vancouver.* Toronto: Canadian Scholar's Press.

Finegan E. (2004) *Language: Its structure and use*, Boston: Thomson-Wadsworth.

Foran, C. (2004) 'Language: MSN Spoken here', at http://www.walrus-magazine.com/article.pl?sid=04/01/13/ 1755252, consulted on 20 May 2006.

Gage Canadian Dictionary (1997). Toronto: Gage Educational Publishing Company.

Kretzschmar, William A., Jr (2003) 'Linguistic Atlases of the United States and Canada', in Preston, D. (ed.), *Needed Research in American Dialects*, Durham, NC: Duke UP, for American Dialect Society, pp. 25–48.

Fee, M. and McAlpine, J. (1997) *Guide to Canadian English Usage*, Toronto, New York, Oxford: Oxford University Press.

McCrum, R., Cran, W. and MacNeil, R. (1986) *The Story of English*. New York: Elisabeth Sifton Books, Viking Penguin Inc.

McKinnie, M. & Dailey-O'Cain, J. (2002) 'A Perceptual Dialectology of Anglophone Canada from the Perspective of Young Albertans and Ontarians', in Long, D. and Preston, D.R. (eds), *Handbook of Perceptual Dialectology*, Volume 2, Amsterdam, Netherlands: Benjamins, pp. 277–94.

McRoberts, K. (1997) *Misconceiving Canada: the Struggle for National Unity*. Toronto, New York, Oxford: Oxford University Press.

Mendelsohn, M. (2004) 'Contradictions in the New Canada' in Anderssen, E., Valpy, M. *et al.* (2004), *The New Canada: A Globe and Mail Report on the Next Generation*, Toronto: *Globe and Mail/* McClelland & Stewart, pp. 280–5.

Microsoft *Encarta 97 Encyclopedia*. Microsoft.

O'Grady, W. and Dobrovolsky, M. (eds). (1996) *Contemporary Linguistic Analysis* (3rd edn). Toronto: Copp Clark Ltd. Olive, D. (1996) *Canada Inside Out*. Toronto: Doubleday Canada Ltd.

Orkin, M.M. (1970) *Speaking Canadian English: An informal account of the English Language in Canada*. Toronto: General Publishing Company Ltd.

Paddock, H.J. (ed.). (1982) *Languages in Newfoundland and Labrador*. St John's, Newfoundland: Memorial University. Partridge, E. (1951) *British and American English since 1900*, London: Scargill, M.H. (1977) *A Short History of Canadian English*. Victoria, E.C.: Sono Nis Press

Poplack, S., Walker, J. & Malcolmson, R. (2005) 'An English "like no other"?: Language contact and change in Québec', to appear in *Canadian Journal of Linguistics*.

Romaine, S. & Lange, D. (1991) 'The use of *like* as a marker of reported speech and thought: A case of grammaticalization in progress', *American Speech* 66/3: 227–9.

Schneider, H. (1997) 'Canada's global clout grows as its army shrinks', *Washington Post*, 3 December, p. AO1.

Story, G.M. (1982) 'The dialects of Newfoundland English', in H.J. Paddock (ed.) (1982).

Tagliamonte, S & D'Arcy, A. (2004) 'He's *like*, she's *like*: The quotative system in Canadian youth'. *Journal of Sociolinguistics* 8/4: 493–514.

Tagliamonte, S. (2005) 'So Who? Like How? Just What? Discourse Markers in the Conversations of Young Canadians', *Journal of*

Pragmatics: An Interdisciplinary Journal of Language Studies, vol. 37, no. 11 (November), 1896–1915.

Thay, E. (2004) *Weird Canadian Words: How to Speak Canadian*, Edmonton, Alberta: Folklore Publishing.

Trudgill, P. (1985) 'Dialect mixture and the analysis of colonial dialects', in H.J. Warkentyne (ed.) (1985), pp. 35–45.

Warkentyne, H.J. (1973) 'Contemporary Canadian English', *American Speech* [1971] 46, 193–9.

Warkentyne, H.J. (ed.) (1985) *Papers from the Fifth International Conference on Methods in Dialectology.* University of Victoria, E.C.: Department of Linguistics.

http://www.canada.qc.ca – web page for Statistics Canada and Government of Canada information.

http://www.cajunculture.com/Other/acadian.htm – web page for Cajun historical and cultural information.

6 New Zealand or Aotearoa – Land of the Long White Cloud

Dianne Bardsley

Chapter overview

New Zealand was the last country in the world to be discovered and settled by humankind. It was also the first to introduce full democracy. Between those two events, and in the century that followed the franchise, the movements and the conflicts of human history have been played out more intensively and more rapidly in New Zealand than anywhere else on Earth.

(Michael King, The Penguin History of New Zealand, 2003)

Early history

It is likely that Maori and Moriori ocean voyagers discovered and settled the islands that make up New Zealand, around the thirteenth century. Bringing the Polynesian dog known as the *kuri,* and the Polynesian rat *kiore* with them, the Maori people found no indigenous terrestrial mammals in their new land other than two species of bat. The land was rich, however, in indigenous birds, both winged and flightless, freshwater and marine fish, shellfish, lizards, frogs and various insects. While there is ample evidence of the richness of the primordial natural environment upon Cook's arrival in 1769, approximately half of the land's numerous bird species were already extinct. The introduction of the *kiore* and *kuri* had catastrophic effects for bird life in particular, and the *moa*, a unique flightless bird that grew to a height of more than three metres, became a victim of Maori moa-hunters seeking a valued food source. The traditional cultivated foods that Maori introduced to New Zealand included the root-crops gourd, *kumara* and *taro*, while their other plant foodstuffs included berries from the *nikau* palm and other indigenous trees, along with the roots of fern and *raupo*, a swamp plant. Feathers, and fibres from a range of plants, were used for hand-weaving of clothing, kit bags, mats and nets. Without iron, Maori used bone and stone in tool-making.

The time of pre-European Maori settlement has been depicted as three distinct periods. Initially, the colonial phase, which was known as the *Moa Hunter* period, was characterized by exploration and extended excursions throughout the land in hunter-gathering, and by the decimation and extinction of various species of birds and marine fauna. This was followed by a *transitional* phase in which Maori developed cultivation and food preservation skills, along with the gathering of small game. Establishing permanent tribal settlements, Maori during this phase began to develop arts and crafts. Almost exclusively, land was held collectively, by tribes or *iwi*, rather than in the hands of individuals. The final phase, the *tribal* era, saw various established settlement groups in competition for property, power and prestige, becoming involved in successive periods of conflict and conquest, occupation and displacement.

In 1642 Dutch explorer Abel Tasman sighted and named the country Staten Landt, believing it to be connected to Chile. It was changed to Nova Zeelandia and then later, Captain James Cook, the first European 'beachcrosser', named it New Zealand. Other than missionaries, the first Europeans to have substantial interaction with Maori were the eighteenth-century whalers and sealers, who brought with them muskets and other weapons, later used by Maori for inter-tribal warfare. These early marine wayfarers introduced a style of life and a Western culture and value system that, along with alcohol, were to change the Maori, and Maori culture, for ever.

The colonial haze

While New Zealand has always been known as one of the Antipodes of Britain, as Britain's geographic opposite, it is essentially an English-speaking nation with predominantly English customs and culture among its Pakeha (European) and Maori citizens. The Europeans who arrived in New Zealand in the nineteenth century were mainly from Great Britain and Ireland, and, among these, the English were the largest group to settle, comprising more than 65 per cent who arrived before 1850. Until the 1970s, the English represented more than 40 per cent of foreign-born New Zealanders. Smaller groups from Europe arrived in the nineteenth century: those from Denmark settled around Dannevirke, Norwegians settled at Norsewood, and Germans near Nelson, but these groups adopted the English language. Other groups settling early in defined areas to become engaged in specific occupations were Chinese gold-diggers and Dalmatian kauri-gum-diggers and vintners. They, too, chose English as their language.

In the 1830s the New Zealand Company was established to facilitate the migration of colonists from Great Britain and Europe. This company bought up large tracts of Maori-owned land, often in a dubious fashion, exchanging it for guns and ammunition, blankets, food, tobacco, alcohol and other goods. During the early colonial period, few Maori made ready contact with the new colonists. Those who did were employed to grow new food crops, such as corn and wheat, to help mill native timbers, or harvest kauri gum and *harakeke* or New Zealand flax, all of which were among the first colonial exports.

On 6 February 1840 a treaty between Maori and the British Crown concerning matters of governance and sovereignty was signed. The Treaty of Waitangi, as it is known, became New Zealand's founding document and, being written and signed in both Maori and English, it has been open to competing claims of interpretation. Wars between tribal *iwi*, and between Maori and British, marred the history of the colonial period, and, as this historical period is reinterpreted and rewritten, so have the names of the respective altercations been revised. Originally termed the Maori Wars, the inter-tribal wars are now known as the Musket Wars. The Maori–Pakeha colonist wars were also originally known as the Maori Wars, and later became the Land Wars. Their name in the twenty-first century is the New Zealand Wars.

Described variously since 1835 as God's Own Country[1] (or more succintly *Godzone*), a half-gallon, quarter-acre pavlova paradise,[2] a social and economic laboratory, and a fragile Eden,[3] New Zealand has enjoyed a range of roles and reputations among other players on the world stage. In 1914 Rupert Brooke wrote of New Zealanders: 'They are more civilized than the Canadians and have some good laws'.[4] Nineteenth-century premier Sir Julius Vogel had a steadfast vision of the country as 'Britain of the South Seas' and in 1875 Anthony Trollope claimed 'the New Zealander is more English than any Englishman at home'.[5] Since then, while Australia, its big-brother neighbour, developed a culture that is aligned more to the United States, the more conservative New Zealand has remained more British. As late as the 1960s, Mother England was still described as 'home', even by third-generation New Zealanders.

The nation became a self-governing British colony in 1841. In 1907, it took the identity of a Dominion. At that stage, New Zealand's dependent economy had already been dealt the blows of international depression. It was not until 1947 that Parliament ratified the Statute of Westminster, giving the nation complete autonomy as a fully independent member of the Commonwealth.

A Governor-General is the British Queen's representative in New Zealand and until 1972 was a British person. Since then, a former New Zealand prime minister, a Maori archbishop, two women and several members of the judiciary have occupied Government House in the capital city, Wellington. In April 2006, an Indo-Fijian Catholic and former judge was appointed to the position. Mr Satyanand is the first to occupy this position without the title of Sir, Dame, Earl or Lord. He does, however, have an honour equivalent to a knighthood, being a Distinguished Companion of the New Zealand Order of Merit. (In 2000 knights and dames, long regarded as colonial relics, and a hierarchical irrelevance, were abolished by the Labour government.)

In post-colonial times the country represents a microcosm of twentieth- and twenty-first-century global social, ethnic, economic and political concerns and challenges. Despite the relatively minor trials that have beset the country's short history, the editors of *The Lonely Planet Blue List* of 2006 suggest that 'they don't call this the land of milk and honey for nothing'.

Geography

By definition, New Zealand is a South Pacific Island nation, comprising two large islands, known as the North Island (*Te-Ika-a-maui*) and the South Island (*Te Wai-pounamu*) and a major southern offshore island, Stewart Island (*Rakiura*). The land area of these three islands is 270,500 sq. km or 27 million hectares, which is similar to that of Great Britain or the state of Colorado. Cook Strait, which separates the North and South Islands, is 20 km wide at its narrowest point. The Chathams, the other significant inhabited offshore islands to the east, are made up of the Chatham and Pitt Islands. Both the Chathams and Stewart Islands show evidence of long-term pre-European habitation, in the case of the Chathams from the fourteenth century by Moriori, a pacifist Polynesian people with a distinctive culture and dialect. Other islands, some of which are subantarctic and uninhabited, include Antipodes Islands, Auckland Islands, Bounty Islands, Campbell Islands and the Kermadec Islands. All together, New Zealand is comprised of more than 220 islands larger than 5 hectares in size.

New Zealand has a temperate maritime climate, with a prevailing westerly wind. The bulk of the country is hilly and mountainous. Three-quarters of the total land area is over 200 metres above sea level and is scattered with dormant and active volcanoes, the most recent activity being located at Mts Ruapehu and Ngauruhoe in the North Island, and at White Island and Raoul Island. New Zealand's geological history is complex. Boiling mud, geysers, steam emissions and earthquakes have given rise to the name 'Shaky Isles'. New Zealand sits on two colliding tectonic plates, the Indo-Australian and the Pacific, which push and slide against each other, causing the Southern Alps to rise and causing quakes along fault lines. The highest mountain peak, Mt Cook, known as *Aorere* or *Aoraki*, is located in the Southern Alps among 17 other peaks of more than 3,000 metres, and more than 300 glaciers. Although blessed with picturesque and safe swimming beaches, the coastline of more than 15,134 km is rugged, and features both sounds and fjords.

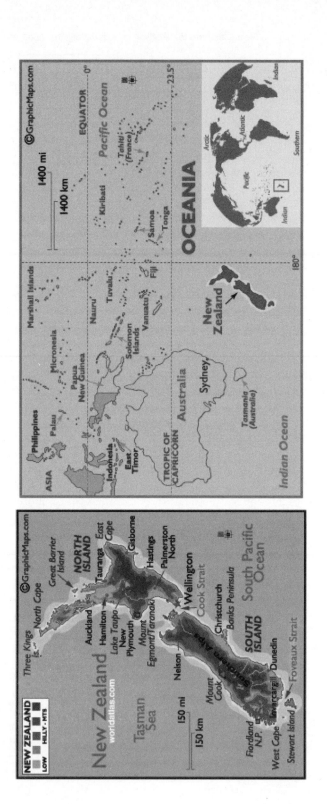

Farming: the backbone of the nation

Farming has occupied a central position in the culture and economy of New Zealand since sheep were first imported by missionary settlers in 1814 to what was then an isolated and predominantly rainforested land. For decades, New Zealand was termed 'Britain's overseas farm', 'the Empire's dairy farm' and Taranaki in particular was dubbed 'the Empire's butterland'. In what has become a cliché since, Sir Robert Stout in 1888 described farming as the 'backbone of the nation' and in a specialist history, McLauchlan (1981: 11) claimed 'The history of New Zealand farming is in a real sense the history of New Zealand. Until the Second World War all life here was powerfully conditioned by what happened in the country'.

The rush for land in New Zealand was a fever that preceded gold fever and, like gold mining, generated its own patterns of settlement, social differentiation, and vocabulary. Barker, an early station holder, reported that 'the paramount anxiety in men's minds seemed to be to secure land and "You must take up more country directly" was the invariable formula of the advice we, comparatively "new chums", received on all sides'.[6] Although the taking-up of large tracts of land was competitive and not always honourable, a globally significant sheep-breeding industry was developed with enthusiasm, for as Fuller (1859: 155) noted, 'sheep farming on the squatting system is the favourite occupation of colonial life at the Antipodes'.

As well as being a broad mix from much of England, the Border Country and Scotland, only a minority of New Zealand's very early pioneer landholders had been practising farmers. Before run-holding, several had been businessmen, doctors, engineers, lawyers, merchants, military men, sailors, tax collectors, tea-tasters and vicars. In one part of the North Island, sheep station labour comprised, in the main, deserters from two or three British army regiments. Despite the lack of experience, absorption in the experimental farming situation was total, with a settler commenting to Kennedy,[7] an early visitor in 1876, that 'the people are sheep-struck'.

New words were required for the vast and diverse new environment and its climatic, geographic and ecological challenges. Just as they arrived from parts widespread, the rural pioneers settled in all parts of the new land, occupying the widely separated valleys, bony ridges and rugged, isolated headlands that characterize the New Zealand topography. The range of landscape and rivers of the South Island was particularly novel to the pioneer pastoralist and farmer. Consequently, terms from the gentle rolling countryside of Britain, such as *rill*, *fen*, *vale*, *spinney*, *rivulet*, *thicket*, *dingle* and *glade* did not flourish within the new land and, as early as 1889, this difference was regaled in verse by a Canterbury 'old chum', G. P. Williams.[8]

What they call a brook or brooklet, or a streamlet, or a rill,
I do only, I confess it, call a *creek* and always will
Then there's what we call a *gully*, which of course we take to mean
Just a small and narrow valley, in which bush is oftimes seen
You perchance, were you a new chum, might describe this as a dell,
Bushy gully suits me better, serves my purpose just as well;
Bush, too, means the *native forest*; you will never, I'm afraid,
Hear a self-respecting *bushman* call a bush a sylvan glade.
Nor a copse, nor shady bower; ev'ry kind of native shrub
Growing rank in wild profusion, he denominates as *scrub*,
I admit the name's not pretty, but it's hard to recognize
Objects that are so familiar under any other guise.

The South Island pastoralists settled in an environment with both advantages and challenges remote from those of the North Island bush districts. Covering 25 per cent, or 5 million hectares, of the South Island area, the extensive southern tussock grasslands had their distinctive landscapes, plant species, soils and rare fauna. Geographic and cultural boundaries were set up between high-country and down-country farmers and this distinction is still evident in the culture and vocabulary of high-country dwellers. In 2002 Ansley[9] made the point that 'the high country is a big part of our legend, like the Australian outback or the Swiss Alps ...'

The early names that were ascribed to animals, property and sections of property reveal something of the background of the newcomers, as well as their attitudes to the new environment. There are several examples of *Isolation, Mount Difficulty, Mount Horrible, Mount Misery, No Man's Land, Siberia* and *Terrible Gully* in the South Island and in the Waioeka area of the North Island, along with the ubiquitous *Blowhard, Breakneck Gully, Deadman's Creek, Devil's Elbow, Gentle Annie, Roaring Meg, Scrubby Gully, Smother Creek, Staircase* and *Starvation Gully*.

The North Island bushman farmer set up his tent and later his bark *whare* or *ponga and daub whare* in a small clearing of thickly forested terrain. His experience was in stark contrast to that of the sheepholder of the South Island; and for many isolated bush settlers, life meant 'mud, mutton and monotony'.

Although the term 'bush' in Australia is widely used for the rural world, its main use in New Zealand is for the rainforest that originally clothed the land. Not only did the bush dominate the lives of settlers, but it also dominated their vocabulary. In Orsman's 1997 *Dictionary of New Zealand English*, 15 A4 pages are dedicated to entries associated with bush and its combinations and collocations.

In isolated areas, the earliest rural exploration and settlement was principally a masculine domain. In the first years of colonial New

Zealand, men outnumbered women, women immigrants being actively recruited in the pastoral age between the years of 1852 and 1888. Men, horses and dogs populated the back country and, in such wild and rugged country, sheepdogs, such as the New Zealand-bred huntaway, were the indispensable farming companion. The world's first sheepdog trials were held in the midst of wild country near Wanaka in 1867, and the opportunities for competition that trials provide are as keenly sought today as they were then.

Much of the land management of the pioneers and those following was injudicious, giving rise to serious and dramatic land erosion. Cumberland (1944: 7) described the land erosion situation following pastoralism as 'of greater significance than that of any other Commonwealth nation, with the problems being distinct and separate in different areas'.

Wool and sheepmeats found favourable international markets until 1982, when more than 70 million sheep were pastured. Markets changed, but adaptation, experimentation and innovation have saved the New Zealand farmer. De-population in outer-lying areas since the 1950s, the change from family-centred farming, the increase in lifestyle blocks and the increasing differentiation of occupations associated with farming have impacted on rural communities. At the close of the nineteenth century, more than 58 per cent of the population was rural-dwelling, but 100 years later, this had reduced to 15 per cent. In the 2001 census, the rural population was found to be older than the urban population, and men outnumbered women.

Twentieth-century diversification of rural land use includes the farming of goats, fitches, alpaca, ostriches and deer, and thousands of acres have been harvested of flax, wheat, barley, oats, maize and corn, sorghum, *poroporo* (a fruit), asparagus, pip and stone fruits, tamarillo, kiwifruit, *kiwano* (a fruit), grapes, sub-tropical and citrus fruits, an increasingly wide range of vegetables in extensive plantings, linseed, pasture seeds and fodder crops. During the last two decades of the twentieth century, ecological concerns had a major impact on farming practices, culminating with the Resource Management Act of 1991. A new awareness of the significance of conservation has led to farmers drawing up protective covenants. Marketing pressures have led to special legislation allowing an almost total amalgamation of the dairying industry and its market. Over time, family farms have been both expanded and contracted, and in the twenty-first century, conversions and corporate holdings, farm forestry and dairying have collectively diminished the national sheep-farming culture and economic dominance. Although the farming way of life, population numbers and farming economy have at times been under threat, the sector's influence remains significant, as it continues to dominate the country's export market.

Social and political history

Despite its conservative reputation, New Zealand's short social history can easily be described as progressive. In many respects, the nation's social history can be divided into two discrete periods: the years preceding the Second World War, and those following the Second World War.

Prior to the Second World War, New Zealand lacked social influence from the outside world, although, in economic terms, world recessions did indeed have an impact. In the late 1800s the nation began to develop a reputation for egalitarianism. Women were granted the right to vote in 1893 and, in the chronology included here, it is easy to see that New Zealand was often at the vanguard of social and educational 'firsts' in the British Empire and later the Commonwealth, particularly in the education of and opportunities for women. Towards the end of the nineteenth century, large land tracts held in the hands of the few and fortunate were broken up for new settlers. Prior to 1905, progressive labour laws and old-age pensions were introduced, along with the provision for state housing. Despite this, a rigorously productive approach to life and work still prevailed, with an emphasis on 'getting on' in life rather than 'getting by'. A sense of duty to the motherland is reflected in the numbers of men enlisting for service in the First World War, with 41 per cent of men between the ages of 19 and 45 in active service.

During the early years of the 1930s depression, New Zealand's exports dropped by 40 per cent, leading to significant unemployment. The Conservative government cut public works by 75 per cent, public servants' wages by 20 per cent, and old-age pensions by 30 per cent, abolishing family allowances. The years of 1929–36 are widely known as 'the sugarbag years', owing to the recycling of sacking sugarbags for use as garments, and bags in which to collect handouts. Following the depression, New Zealand's first Labour government developed innovative social welfare policies under the umbrella of the Social Security Act, which gained for the country the reputation of a *modern welfare state* and *the world's social laboratory*. This legislation meant guaranteed support for the elderly, the sick, the mother-to-be, the poor and the unemployed.

While geographically isolated from the theatres of the Second World War in Europe and Japan, New Zealand's allegiance to Britain was strong, and privations were as commonplace in New Zealand as they were in Britain. The effect of the war was pervasive, with the threat of a Japanese invasion keenly felt. From a population of just over 1.5 million, more than 194,000 men joined the armed forces. New Zealand provided food not only for its own troops and for Britain, but also for American troops fighting in the Pacific. Women were manpowered into a variety of jobs normally occupied by men, as they did in other nations, becoming tram conductors, farm labourers, fruit and vegetable growers and munitions workers. Prisons were set up for the incarceration of German and Italian settlers, regarded during the war as 'aliens', and for Japanese prisoners-of-war.

The post-war period was a time of rebuilding, just as it was elsewhere, with families adjusting to the loss of more than 11,500 servicemen and the maiming of several thousands of others. During the war, New Zealand conscientious objectors encountered ostracism and harsh treatment, which included imprisonment and hard labour for 800 men. On the other hand, returning servicemen were treated well, being provided with bursaries for study, job training and opportunities to settle on and develop farm land. Despite continuing rationing of basic foodstuffs, the immediate post-war years were a period of national rehabilitation, characterized by booming birth rates.

The 1950s are recorded as a decade of moral panic in New Zealand. The social change that occurred in response to new-found prosperity and freedom, and the widening technological expansion following the Second World War, was accompanied by rock culture and international media influences. As a consequence, the flash bodgie, the streetwise widgie, milkbar cowboys, and rock'n'roll took a small conservative population by surprise. Teenagers took to meeting on street corners and in motorcycle gangs, and congregating at dance halls. In 1954, a Special Committee on Moral Delinquency in Children and Young People held hearings in Parliament and in Auckland, Wellington and Christchurch. Known as the Mazengarb Report, the committee's findings argued for rushed new legislation in the form of the Indecent Publications Amendment Bill, the Child Welfare Amendment Bill, and for amendments to the Police Offences Bill, so that it was an offence to sell contraceptives to persons under the age of 16 or to provide instructions on their use. Such law changes meant that young people who showed 'delinquent' behaviour could be dealt with. Another crisis stalked the government, in the form of the 1951 Waterfront Strike, a dispute that lasted 151 days. Related to this was the influence of the Cold War mentality, through which a number of public servants were accused of communist involvement, or were sacked, with reputations in tatters. Suspicion stalked the land, with rumours of the presence of high-level 'reds under the beds', and clandestine meetings with members of the Communist Party. Despite these problems of protest and control, the golden years of the wool boom which started in 1950 cast a golden glow over the land until well into the next decade.

The 1960s were a decade of progress and consolidation. Social legislation continued to be effected. Universities and their rolls expanded. Television transmission was introduced and New Zealanders joined the world of watchers. Regular passenger-jet services began between New Zealand and the motherland. The Beatles visited and the first real display of pop hysteria was seen. Wool prices began to sag, and meat took over as the principal export earner. The late 1960s began a long period of public protest and activism. Collective consciousness and commitment, and the hippie movement, developed, for which the government sponsored communes, known as *ohu*. Regular student protests initiated anti-Vietnam War demonstrations, attracting the weight of both participants and public sympathy. People protested on a range of issues, from environmental defence to racism in sport and nuclear disarmament. In 1969 HART (Halt All Racist Tours), a strong lobbying body against international racially-selected sports teams, was formed.

The feminist movement flourished in the 1970s, as it did elsewhere. New Zealand was a country on the move. In 1972 the New Zealand Values Party was formed, in 1974 18-year-olds were given the vote, and in 1975 one of several *hikoi* or long protest marches, the Maori Land March, took place. The Accident Compensation Corporation (ACC) was established in 1974 as a no-fault national state compensation system for injury caused by accident. In 1977 abortion law was reformed so that abortions became easily, and controversially, available.

In 1981 the nation was rocked with the violence that erupted in opposition to the racially-selected touring Springbok rugby team. People took to the streets and game venues to protest in unprecedented numbers. Special police units were empowered to use force never seen before, and the population was polarized, opening a wound that took decades to heal. In 1985 New Zealand banned visits from nuclear-powered ships and, two years later, the Labour government passed the New Zealand Nuclear Free Zone Disarmament and Arms Control Act. The nation was declared a nuclear-free zone. (The US Congress later passed the Broomfield Act, downgrading New Zealand's status from ally to friend.) Awareness that men dominated positions of power and prestige in society led to the establishment of the Ministry of Women's Affairs in 1986 and, in the same year, the Business Round Table, a powerful right-wing group of CEOs from some of the country's largest business organizations was formed. Its influence on the government's policy development was to be wide-ranging and enduring. In 1987, under the regime of the Labour government's finance minister Roger Douglas, New Zealand underwent considerable economic restructuring, when much of the state sector was privatized and local government was rationalized. Dubbed Rogernomics, this was a controversial period in the country's political history, polarizing groups both within the Labour Party and in the electorate.

New Zealanders voted on the FPP (First Past the Post) system until 1996, when a switch was made to MMP (Mixed Member

Proportional) voting, similar to the German electoral model. Voters have two votes, a party vote and an electorate vote, for the single House of Representatives. The major parties in the New Zealand Parliament in 2006 are centre-left Labour, centre-right National, the Green Party (formed from the Values Party), New Zealand First and the Maori Party. Minor parties that occasionally contest general elections include both the philosophically sublime and the ridiculous with such confidence-shaking names as the McGillicuddy Serious Party, the Pull Yourself Together Party, the 99 MP Party, and the WIN Party. A dreadlocked hemp-suited Rastafarian has been an MP, representing the Green Party, since 1999.

The centre-left Labour Party has dominated politics since the 1990s. Its policies have the approval of those working for social justice. Among its members are the first transexual MP, along with several gay MPs. Under the Labour government, there has been a strengthening of 'pro-social' portfolios such as the Ministries for Disability Issues, for Senior Citizens, and for the Community and Voluntary Sector. Prostitution was legalized in 2003, and the rights for Civil Unions between partners of either sex were introduced in 2004, giving same-sex couples the same rights as married couples.

Not only were New Zealand women able to vote before women from other nations, but they have also been appointed to the highest offices in the land. Towards the close of the twentieth century, the Prime Minister, the Governor-General, the Attorney-General, and the Chief Justice were positions held by women, and since then a woman has been appointed as Speaker of the House.

Although in 2006 women are among the highest paid business executives in New Zealand, and occupy significant roles in central government, they hold less than 17 per cent of professorial positions across all universities.

While New Zealanders have been protected from the extremes of poverty, there are still gaps between the unemployed or poor and needy, and those who can afford several houses, boats and cars. The very wealthy in New Zealand are easily visible in that annual statistics are published which reveal the identity and respective wealth of the wealthiest New Zealanders, along with the salaries of the nation's top-earning employees. In 2006, 13 chief executives each earned more than NZ$1 million. The two highest paid executives in 2006 were paid NZ$3,117,395 and NZ$2,905,000.

From a traditional position of strength, unions were robbed of their power in the 1990s, but in 2000 the unpopular Employment Contracts Act was repealed and a new form of industrial relations based on encouraging relationships of mutual trust between employer and employee developed. OSH (Occupational Safety and Health) is respon-sible for the improvement in working conditions, and for the recognition of the role of stress and its related problems in the workplace. The average wage/salary in New Zealand in 2006 is NZ$20.20 per hour. The GRI (Guaranteed Retirement Income) which pays 65 per cent of the average wage to those over the age of 65, is not means-tested. New Zealanders are keen owners of cars, and statistics for 2006 show that 550 cars are owned for every 1000 of population. Home ownership has always been a cherished Kiwi ideal, so that there has always been a higher level of owner-occupier housing than in many countries. Since 2000, the cost and value of housing has risen, as it has globally, so that the national average cost of a house is more than NZ$340,000. Labour costs and distance from both materials and markets have meant that many New Zealand manufacturers have moved off-shore, often taking workers with them. New Zealanders are enthusiastic users of credit cards which, for some, means a debt that easily becomes out of control.

Demography and the Kiwi cultural mix

Following the Second World War, Pakeha (European/non-Maori) began to move to urban areas from small and scattered rural settlements, preceding Maori urbanization by at least a decade. In the 1950s and 1960s, integration and assimilation policies pioneered a 'pepper-pot' housing development, which saw Maori and Pasifika (Pacific Island peoples) pepper-potted in Pakeha-dominant suburbs. The ethnocentrism and conformity that formerly characterized New Zealand cities and city life has been replaced with an overarching diversity of cultures, ethnic groups and lifestyles. At the same time, the country regards itself as a traditional bicultural nation, of indigenous Maori and colonial settlers.

Whereas Australia's immigration has had a Mediterranean component, New Zealand's has been mainly from the Pacific Islands and Asia. The demography of the Pacific Islands has changed since the 1950s, so that greater numbers from some Pacific Island nations live in New Zealand rather than in their homeland islands. It could well be argued that there is no single New Zealand culture but several cultures, with the various peoples who now call New Zealand home contributing extended traditional histories of their own from their respective cultures and homelands.

Auckland, the world's largest Polynesian city, is considered to have a culture of its own, with the widest demonstrable gap between wealthy and poor, and the greatest number of ethnic groups is represented here. It is the home of the 200,000-strong Pasifika festivals, and of groups with a strong sporting culture of team sports, including dragon-boat racing.

Although the 2006 census figures are unavailable, this table of figures from the 2001 census shows twenty-first-century cultural trends.

Table 6.1 New Zealand population, 2001 census

Total population	3,586,731
European	2,868,009
Maori	526,281
Asian	237,459
Pacific Island	231,801
Mid-East, African, etc.	24,924

In order of numbers, Samoans, Cook Island Maori, Tongans, Niueans, Fijians, Tokelauans, Tuvalu Islanders, Rarotongan and Society Islanders make up the Pacific Islands' resident population by census measure. In addition, however, significant numbers of migrants from French Polynesia, Kiribati, Papua New Guinea and the Solomon Islands have entered the country. Of Cook Islands and Niuean residents, seven of every ten were born in New Zealand. To add to these numbers, New Zealand customarily has 20,000 overstayers per annum, made up of Samoan, Tongan, Chinese, Thai and Indian visitors whose permits have expired. The Kiwi cultural mix is influenced further by refugees from parts of the northern hemisphere (see below, 'New Zealand's place in the world').

Today there is an expectation rather than a tolerance of multi-ethnic involvement in power and prestige, and this is reflected in both national and local government participation. Since 1968, there have been three Chinese mayors, two of whom have been leaders of cities. For several years, Dunedin's mayor was an Indian female. A Maori, Sir Paul Reeves, has been both an Anglican archbishop and governor-general, and in April 2006 an Indian governor-general was appointed. Race relations conciliators (now commissioners) have been from a range of cultural and ethnic backgrounds, including those of Dutch, Jewish, Indian and African/Afrikaner descent. In 1996 the first Asian Member of Parliament, a Chinese woman, was elected, and in 2002 the first Muslim MP was sworn in. The Minister of Youth Affairs and Minister of Customs in the current Labour government is a woman of Rarotongan and Maori descent. In addition to a Minister of Maori Affairs, there are Ministers for Pacific Island Affairs and Ethnic Affairs, respectively. The Minister for the Community and Voluntary Sector is a Pacific Islands woman. Maori can choose whether to vote on the Maori roll or the general roll, for, among the 121 seats in Parliament since 2005, there are seven seats for which Maori have the option to vote. In the 48th Parliament of

2005, 39 women and 82 men made up the 121 seats; of these, 21 are occupied by Maori MPs.

Since the 2001 census, the population has risen to stand at 4,133,679 in April 2006, with a population density of 14 per sq. km, considered low by world standards. The 'four main centres' were the four most significant of New Zealand's early settlements, being built at or near safe ports and serving as early provincial capitals. Although together they are no longer the four largest of New Zealand's urban centres, they have retained the status and are still regarded as the four principal cities. In the north, Auckland, known as the Queen City or the City of Sails, is the largest city. Wellington, named for the Duke of Wellington, is the world's southernmost capital city, and is regarded as the cultural capital. Christchurch, the most English of New Zealand settlements, and known as the 'garden city', is the largest South Island city, while southernmost Dunedin, founded by Presbyterian Scots, is strongly associated with early tertiary education in New Zealand.

New Zealand's place in the world

As Britain entered the Second World War, Labour Prime Minister Michael Joseph Savage announced: 'With gratitude for the past and confidence in the future, we range ourselves without fear beside Britain. Where she goes, we go; where she stands, we stand.' And so it followed that New Zealand troops were sent to the Middle East, Europe, the Pacific and the East, to assist other Allied servicemen and women. Casualties were heavy.

In 1965 more than 50 per cent of New Zealand's exports went to Britain, but 20 years later, it was less than 10 per cent. When Britain entered the European Union, New Zealand was forced to find new markets. Ties with 'the motherland' were weakened as New Zealand had to find its own place in the world. Alliances have been formed most closely with Australia, with the ANZAC connection since 1914, and the Trans-Tasman Agreement signed in 1983 to facilitate Closer Economic Relations (known as CER). Citizens can move across the Tasman without visas. A well-established Trans-Tasman rivalry that evolved from the sporting domain has done little to damage political and economic ties (Australians are commonly referred to as Aussies or Ockers, and the country itself as the Big Frisbee). The idea of a republican status has been floated in the last 20 years, with little general support shown.

New Zealand has had a special historical and constitutional relationship with several smaller Pacific Islands nations, being a former colonial administrator for Samoa, the Cook Islands and Niue, and having administrative power over Tokelau. Since 1923 it has had sovereignty over the Ross Dependency, an extensive area of the Antarctic.

Relationships with France faltered with the continuation of French nuclear tests in the Pacific during the 1970s, and New Zealand and Australia took France to the International Court of Justice. In 1973 the navy's warship HMNZS *Otago*, with a Member of Parliament on board, was sent to Mururoa Atoll to protest against the continuing testing. In 1985 French secret service agents bombed and sank the Greenpeace flagship the *Rainbow Warrior* in Auckland Harbour. There was unprecedented outrage.

New Zealand troops served in the South African (Boer) War, in both World Wars, the Korean War and the war in Vietnam, but did not participate in the invasion of Iraq with its traditional allies Great Britain, United States and Australia. Since the 1980s and the breach in relationships with Australia and the United States through the opposition to nuclear-powered ships in New Zealand waters, New Zealand has become increasingly involved in United Nations-sponsored peacekeeping activities in Africa, Asia, the Balkans, the Middle East, Malaysia and the Pacific. It provided non-combat support during the Falklands War and has engineering and reconstruction teams in Afghanistan.

New Zealand has always been a dependent economy. In 2006, products from agriculture and horticulture still make up more than half of the nation's exports. Of beef, dairy and lamb production, 90 per cent is exported. New Zealand exports cut flowers,[10] plants and bulbs worth more than $120 million, mostly to Japan. Interestingly, children's scholastic books and wine are among the products which have found a ready world market since the 1960s.

During the Second World War, 733 Polish children and 108 Polish adult people were resettled in New Zealand, beginning a commitment to enable those from other nations who need protection to settle permanently. In fulfilling its responsibilities as a signatory of various United Nations conventions and protocols, the government resettles 750 refugees each year. In 2003 and 2004, the largest numbers of refugees came from Afghanistan, Kuwait, Iran, Zimbabwe, Sri Lanka, Iraq and Somalia. The country has not always been as welcoming. Chinese were designated 'undesirable aliens' in the nineteenth century and subject from 1881 to a poll tax of ten pounds, later raised to a hundred pounds.

Languages

Along with New Zealand English, two languages have become official languages of New Zealand: *te reo Maori* (1987) and New Zealand Sign Language (2006).

Te reo Maori

New Zealand Maori is a Polynesian language closely related to Cook Islands Maori, Tahitian and Hawaiian. The first written records of *te reo Maori* were made by explorer James Cook and other early adventurers who compiled short lists of words, followed by the Church Missionary Society's publication of a vocabulary of 100 pages in 1820.[11] In preparation for six years, a comprehensive work, *A Dictionary of the New Zealand Language, and a Concise Grammar*, by missionary Archdeacon William Williams, was published in 1844; and between 1848 and 1861, *The Maori Messenger*, a newspaper in *te reo Maori*, was published. From that time, there was a decline in the use of *te reo*, and in 1867 Maori became disadvantaged by the banning of the use of *te reo* in schools. Eurocentric laws and customs further marginalized Maori people, who then, in the main, lived in rural areas where their natural customs and culture were submerged for almost a hundred years. It was not until the urbanization of the Maori in the 1950s and 1960s that the danger of the loss of the language was recognized. In the 1980s, *kohanga reo* (total immersion pre-schools or language nests) and *kura kaupapa Maori* (total immersion schools) opened and in state schools since the 1980s, the use of Maori is widely encouraged, being a language elective in most secondary schools.

Since that time, several policies and practices to preserve the language have been successful. Numerous Maori dictionaries, including monolingual Maori dictionaries and Maori–English and English–Maori dictionaries have been published and in 2005 the Microsoft XP and Office Maori version became available. The first indigenous language free-to-air television channel, Maori Television, was established in March 2004. Earlier, in 2002, a major production of *The Merchant of Venice* in Maori toured the country.

The alphabet in *te reo* has fifteen letters: the vowels *a, e, i, o, u,* and the consonants *h, k, m, n, ng, p, r, t, w* and *wh*. Typical examples of transliterations of English words and traditional English names into Maori include: Jack = Haki; Joseph = Hōhepa; Matthew = Matiu; Victoria = Wikitoria; Latin = Rātine; London = Rānana; January = Hānuere; curtain = *kātene*; million = *mirione*; and mortgage = *mō kete*. Personal names, such as Ngaio, Rewa, Pita and Hemi are commonly used to name Pakeha children.

Occasionally, English speakers use the definite article 'te' instead of 'the', or 'nga' which is the definite article in its plural form, for emphasis, in keeping with a context, or to be facetious, so that you might read of 'te gang', or 'nga heavies'. Increasingly, blends of English and Maori, such as *cyberhui* (a meeting to discuss the use of electronic communications) and *kaumatua flat* (granny flat) are used.

New Zealand English

Standard New Zealand English differs from Standard British English chiefly in its pronunciation and vocabulary; in grammar, the two varieties are basically the same. The distinctive vocabulary of New Zealand English clearly reflects the bicultural population of New Zealand, whose two cultures have travelled far from their origins. The first Pakeha settlers adopted Maori words for indigenous plants, birds and fish, such as *totara* (a coniferous tree), *tui* (a songbird) and *hapuku* (a groper fish), and for other features of the environment, such as *pakihi* and *tomo*. They also borrowed words associated with Maori culture and society, such as *marae, mokihi* and *pa*. In the twenty-first century, New Zealand English includes an even greater variety of terms from *te reo*, all of which make the culture and language distinctive. Today, terms like *hapu, hui, mana, taonga* and *turanga-waewae* are used widely and meaningfully. Corruptions of words from *te reo*, such as puckeroo (broken) from *pakaru*, are also common.

New Zealand English is also influenced by other Polynesian languages through Pacific Islands immigration. Terms such as *afakasi, aiga, lava lava* and *Palagi* are now in common usage and new cultural terms, such as *White Sunday*, have also come into New Zealand English.

New words and usages have been generated by a variety of means. Compounding is a notable characteristic, so that terms like *achievement standard* (a school qualification level), *sharemilking* (the sharing of profit by a landowner and a dairy herd owner), *state house* (a house provided by the government at a low rental), *woolshed* (a sheep shearing shed) and *All Black* are commonplace. Prefixes and suffixes are added to existing terms, such as *Maoridom* and *Rogernomics* (an economic strategy developed by Finance Minister Roger Douglas). Acronyms are increasingly formed from initials, such as *WINZ* (Work and Income New Zealand) and *DOC* (Department of Conservation), while other words are formed from abbreviations, such as *Nat* (National Party), and initials such as *DPB* (Domestic Purposes Benefit, for single parents). New Zealanders have also taken words in use in British and other varieties of English and given them new senses or meanings. Examples are *berm* (a strip of grass between footpath and road), *paddock* (a fenced area of land) and *unit* (a suburban train, and a small semi-detached house).

Much of the slang and informal vocabulary of New Zealand is shared with Australian English, such as *rattle your dags* and *she'll be right*, while terms such as *howlybag* (cry baby), *munted* (broken), *poozle* (fossick), and *savs and pavs* (saveloys and pavlovas) are limited to New Zealand use. Other terms, such as *tiki tour* (a sightseeing drive), are taken from proper nouns and used in a new colloquial sense. Inclusion of names from a place of invention, discovery or event, such as *Onehunga weed*, *Tukidale* sheep and *Castlepoint daisy*, has been common since colonial days. Words have also been generated from the names of people who have discovered, bred, invented or had a special relationship with an article, product or event, such as *Chewings fescue*, *Coopworth* and *Perendale* sheep, and *Hamilton jet*.

A characteristic shared with Australian English is the generation of new words by using diminutive or shortened forms, and/or pet names. Well-known examples of these are *possie* (position), *Swannie* (a Swanndri woollen coat) and names of places, such as *Kune* for Ohakune, *Gissy* for Gisborne and *Palmy* for Palmerston. Familiar landmarks have taken the definite article to become *the Mount*, *the Basin*, *the Brook* and *the Park*, while pet names have also been given to specific buildings and structures, such as the parliamentary *Beehive*, *Cake Tin* for the Wellington Stadium, and *Nippon Clipon* for additional lanes on the Auckland Harbour Bridge.

The rural world has been dominant in generating new home-grown terms, and as well as having its own meanings for *office* (a ledge on a steep cliff face), *straight black* (a pure Aberdeen Angus cattle beast) and *tight stocking* (a form of pasture management), none of which would be heard in a city, it has been responsible for much of New Zealand's unique lexicon. More than 150 terms have been generated for sheep, and the same number for sheepdogs. The rural domain is where terms like *cobber* (friend) and *offsider* (assistant) live on, terms that have been superseded in the urban environment.

The principal word-generating domains of recent times have included politics, sport, crime and the environment. Reflecting as they do our changing society and attitudes, words come from domains that are undergoing change. In the case of the environment, new terms such as *open space covenant* (a restricted use of land without bush), *insurance population* (a secondary population kept in case of disease in the primary colony), *kawenta* (a Maori protective covenant) and *paunch dump* (a waste collection area for animal entrails) reflect an increasing concern for conservation of the natural world. Other words and phrases, such as *No 8* and *on the sheep's back*, have taken on an 'iconic' identity, and New Zealanders are slow to leave behind colloquial usages that have been around for 'donkey's years', such as 'She's a tough ask …'[12] and 'having a bob each way'.[13]

The New Zealand English lexicon continues to be influenced by terms from other languages, particularly in food and sports, such as *pétanque*, *bocce* and *boules*. Surprisingly, there has been little adoption of words from the United States, despite over 50 years of American television. New Zealanders use duvets, not comforters, use chilly bins, not eskies, use kitchen benches, not counters, hang clothes in wardrobes, not closets, and wear jandals, not thongs. They follow

British spelling conventions – for example, they vote for an organization called the *Labour* (not Labor) Party.

Changes in pronunciation and grammar are not always greeted with approval. There is a large and conservative 'language police' operating in New Zealand, who comment particularly on mispronunciations, such as the use of 'woman' for the plural 'wimmen', 'Priminister' for 'Prime Minister', and 'Mary Christmas' rather than 'Merry Christmas'. It is possible to hear men rage against policies of the 'Gummint' (Government) and the country itself is often pronounced as 'New Zilin'. 'The three bears', as it is known in linguistic circles, represents the increasing merging of beer, bear and bare. The high rising terminal and the rhotic burr of the Southlanders are further characteristics of Kiwi pronunciation, together with the introduction of the schwa vowel in terms like 'grown' ('growen'), with young people increasingly pronouncing 'hour' as 'ower'.

Since the rise in status of *te reo Maori* and the increase of borrowing into New Zealand English, mispronunciations have diminished. For years, New Zealand radio announcers were untutored in the pronunciation of placenames, pronouncing, as an example, *Paraparaumu* as 'Parapram'.

New Zealanders have a keen interest in words and word change, particularly in the use of slang, which is reflected in the number of slang dictionaries published since the 1970s.

New Zealand Sign Language received recognition as an official language of New Zealand in April 2006, eight years after the *Dictionary of New Zealand Sign Language* was published.

Casual conversation

New Zealand males will probably greet you with 'G'day', whereas women will almost always say 'Hello'. When you are introduced to somebody, it is most usual to say 'Pleased to meet you'. The positive response to 'How are you?' will often be: 'a box of birds', 'a box of fluffy ducks', 'okey doke', '*kapai*' (fine), '*tino pai*' (excellent), 'pretty good, considering' or, more recently, 'sweet as'. When things are 'just OK', you will hear terms like 'fair to middling' or 'half-pai'. Many older Maori will say that they are '*kei te pai*' (kay teh pie), meaning fine.

New Zealand males are the masters of litotes – they express positive messages in a negative way. They will say 'not bad', when they mean 'really good', or will give non-commital answers. When things are fine, you will never hear terms like 'wonderful' or 'excellent', but rather 'could be better', or even 'could be worse'.

A response to a story that is hard to believe will be 'Fair go?', 'Dinkum?', 'You're kidding?', 'You're joking?', 'Blimey, charlie', 'Well, bugger me', 'I'm gobsmacked', 'Yeah, right', 'Holy moley' or the traditional 'That'll be the day'. In less polite company, it might be 'Bullshit' or 'What crap'. 'You could have knocked my socks off' is also a common way to describe a surprise.

New Zealanders can be lazy conversationalists and will often end a statement with 'et cetera', 'you know' or 'and all that'. Young people often use 'and stuff' in place of 'et cetera'. Sentence tags such as 'eh' and 'you know' are still features of New Zealand conversation.

When New Zealanders are very busy, they will say that they are 'flat out', 'flat to the boards', 'flat stick', 'flat tack', or things are 'full on'. You could be asked to 'rattle your dags', which means that you are expected to hurry, the term taken from the rattling sound of a dag-ridden sheep as it runs.

In informal situations New Zealanders, especially male, will often use the third-person feminine *she* in place of the third-person neuter *it* as the subject of a sentence, e.g., 'She's a hard road',[14] 'She's a tough one, that new regulation', 'She was a real beauty, that storm' and 'She's a big ask ...' (if something seems difficult or daunting, it is described as a 'big ask'). A common expression, 'She'll be right' means 'It's acceptable', or 'That's fine'. Often you will hear 'She's right, mate', when you thank somebody.

Negative emotion is expressed with a variety of slang terms. When somebody becomes angry, they 'chuck/pack/throw a mental/spaz/wobbly', 'do their nana' or 'do their scone', 'drop their bundle', 'have a blue/pink fit', 'pack a sad', or 'spit tacks'. New Zealanders often use casual euphemistic terms to say that somebody has died. They might say that somebody has 'carked', 'kicked the bucket', 'snuffed it' or 'croaked'.

A typical farewell will simply be 'See you later' or '*Ka kite ano*' (kah kee-the ar-noh), 'Catch you soon', 'Hooray' or 'Cheerio'.

What is *tapu* (taboo) in conversation? Older New Zealanders are unlikely to discuss openly their income, health, financial situation or investment practice, their religious and political affiliation or their contraceptive practice. Many will be reticent about telling you that a family member is involved in a same-sex relationship, is on a welfare benefit or has been in trouble with the law. Young people tend to be more open, and are often keen to talk about personal income and investing, sexual and spending practices or their plans for the future. New Zealand men and women do not call each other 'darl', and are somewhat circumspect about showing affection in public.

In shops and services

Diffidence and formality were left behind in New Zealand in the 1980s. You might find that approaches to strangers are more casual and friendly than you have been used to. When you approach a shop counter or place of business, an assistant will normally ask 'Can I help you?', or 'Yes?', or 'Have you been served?'[15] When somebody interrupts or needs attention in New Zealand, 'Excuse me' is used, but it is used less often for an apology. An apology is simply 'I'm sorry', so if an assistant appears to be involved in recording details on a computer, or preparing an item for display, you would normally interrupt by saying 'Excuse me'. If you bump into somebody on the street, it is more usual to say 'I'm sorry' than 'Excuse me'. You will hear 'That's OK', 'No worries' or 'Never mind' in response. Recently, the multi-purpose term 'sweet as' is a young person's response that means 'fine', 'excellent', 'never mind' and even 'I apologise'!

When you thank a person in a shop or restaurant, you might hear a very casual 'No problem', 'Not a problem', 'No probs', 'No worries', a more polite 'It's a pleasure' or, more recently, the use of the American term 'You're welcome' or 'You're very welcome' in reply. Increasingly in New Zealand it is common to be addressed by your first or Christian name by strangers. When you telephone a bank to ask about opening an account, you will usually introduce yourself by saying ' My name is Kim Smith', or 'It's Kim Smith speaking', not 'Mr Kim Smith'. In the response, you will usually be addressed as 'Kim' and not 'Mr Smith'. Modals are commonly used – for example, 'Could you ring after 4 p.m.?' or 'Would you prefer to wait for a customer adviser?' New Zealanders would be offended if the imperative 'Ring back after 4 p.m.' or 'Wait for a customer adviser' were used. Sometimes the anachronistic 'Hold on, please' and 'Please don't hang up' will be used by a telephone operator, but increasingly you will find that unpopular automatic answering machines are installed on 'customer service lines' in New Zealand businesses. With these, customers have to make choices about who they want to speak to immediately, and such practices are considered impersonal and less helpful than a person answering.

Once you have been introduced to somebody at a social event in New Zealand, your first name will usually be used, so that your new neighbours and colleagues will call you by your first name. Do not be surprised if they ask you personal questions about your arrival and background. This is not so much to enquire into private or personal matters, but is regarded as a friendly way of making you feel comfortable and at home, and to reassure you that people are interested in you. It is polite in New Zealand to ask questions, such as where you were born, how long you have been in New Zealand, if you have a family or what your occupation is. You will not be asked questions about your financial position, your religion or your sexual preference.

New Zealanders use a variety of names for their gatherings, the least formal being noun conversions from verbs, such as 'bash', 'do', 'get together', 'leer up' or 'stir'. From *te reo Maori* comes *hui* (a general term for a variety of gatherings including meetings) and *hakari* (a feast or meal). 'Aftermatch function' is a term derived from sports events, and has been extended to cover all types of social gatherings, from seminars to weddings and funerals. During December, workplaces and groups of all types from babysitting and book clubs to government departments hold their 'end-of-year' and Christmas functions, usually consisting of drinks and dinner or barbecues. The country tends to 'close down' for 10 to 14 days over Christmas, when government departments and offices are closed, only some restaurants are operating, and everybody has 'headed for the beach'.

The domestic world

New Zealanders like to provide hospitality to visitors, and you will become very familiar with the exhortation 'Come for dinner', which means the main evening meal. It is not common for people to be asked for 'tea' or 'supper'. (Tea is a break in the mid-morning and mid-afternoon, and is just as likely to be for coffee as tea. Supper usually refers to a warm drink of tea or chocolate that is taken in the late evening or before bed.) During the week, family dinner is usually served between 6 p.m. and 7.30 p.m., so that children have time for homework before bed. At weekends, you are likely to be invited to a person's home for dinner from 7 p.m., when you will have drinks, with dinner served around 8 p.m. Evening meals tend to be served later in the summer and, increasingly, out-of-doors. Since the 1980s, New Zealand housing has increasingly included what is known as 'indoor–outdoor flow', involving the use of decks and courtyards next to cooking and living spaces. Increasingly, too, it is common for New Zealanders to ask friends to 'Sunday lunch' or to elevenses, and these are often eaten out-of-doors.

Continental or light breakfasts consisting of tea and toast, yoghurt and muesli, porridge or other cereals with fruits are common in New Zealand homes during the week. At weekends, people often have a late cooked breakfast or, in cities, go out for breakfast, which is usually a variation of egg dishes, perhaps with bacon, smoked salmon, mushrooms, hash browns and tomatoes.

When a person answers a telephone at home in New Zealand, he or she usually says 'Leanne Brown speaking' or 'Leanne Brown here', 'Hello', or will give the telephone number without identifying himself or herself. Some older people might still use 'Are you there?' or simply 'Yes?' You will be asked to 'Call in on us' not 'Visit with us'.

New Zealanders wear singlets, not vests or undershirts, and dressing gowns, not bathrobes. They hang their clothes on clothes lines with pegs, not pins, and their babies are pushed in prams and pushchairs. Living with a 'host family' is the easiest way to become familiar with New Zealand. A night in a bed-and-breakfast accommodation, a farmstay or a homestay will teach you far more about New Zealand life than a night in a hotel with an atlas and a guide book.

Eating and drinking

Although New Zealand has some dated food customs, and some interesting terms that relate to food, a food revolution has hit the nation in the form of 'lifestyle' and food fashions. It was not until 1961 that the first restaurants were licensed to serve alcohol. The term 'café' in New Zealand is used loosely. Cafés might serve all-day breakfast, brunch, lunch, coffee or tea, light meals, tapas and alcohol, just as bars and pubs might. Many bars and pubs have a theme, such as a sports bar, where snooker is played, where sport is watched on large screens and where bets are laid. Cities sport 'international' bars, such as Irish bars and Belgian bars. In most bars, cafés and restaurants, you pay for your meal after you have eaten it. When a meal is placed in front of you at a café, you will be told 'Enjoy', elliptic for 'Enjoy your meal', but at some city restaurants 'Bon appetit' is still used. In private homes, you will be told 'Please start', and it is customary for guests to start eating before the hosts begin their meal.

What are New Zealanders' quaint food customs? They are ambivalent about Christmas cuisine, many families still attempting to cook a hot roast turkey dinner complete with trimmings, and a Christmas plum pudding, to eat in the middle of the day in the heat of an Antipodean summer. Others have picnics, taking the regulation Christmas ham and the pavlova with whipped cream. Rich fruit cakes and fruit mincemeat pies are regular Christmas fare, accompanied by Christmas crackers, gifts and traditional trees. Christmas is often spent at the family *bach* or *crib*, known in other parts of the world as holiday home or summer house. Revellers congregate at particular beach locations, lakes or tourist towns to celebrate New Year.

Traditional Kiwi food includes Anzac biscuits (made from oats and golden syrup), afghans (iced chocolate biscuits made with cornflakes), Marmite, custard squares (squares of pastry, filled with custard and topped with jam), hokey-pokey (a brittle toffee, often served in ice cream), Moro bars, fairy bread, lamingtons (sponge pieces dipped in chocolate icing and coconut), pavlova (cream-topped meringue cakes), Jelly Tip ice creams and Jaffa chocolate sweets, flavoured with orange. Fish and chips, also known as 'greasies' or 'shark and taties', constituted the main takeaway meal prior to the 1960s.

Sausages are known as 'snarlers', and 'savs and pavs' is the name given to 'ordinary' dance-hall suppers and children's birthdays (savs, or saveloys, are pre-cooked sausages wth bright pink skins, while pav is an abbreviation of pavlova.) Cervena (venison) is increasingly found on restaurant menus.

Kiwifruit, *kumara*, *kumikumi* and *kiwano* make up some of the country's signature fruit and vegetables that are used in 'Pacific rim' cuisine, a seafood-and-fresh-produce fusion style of cooking.

Native foods, known as wild foods, are avant-garde. The Hokitika Wildfoods Festival, sometimes attracting around 20,000 festival-goers annually since its 1990 inception, celebrates indigenous foods and the popular West Coast beers. Among the delicacies, you might find *huhu* bugs, traditionally considered a delicacy for Maori, *paua* (abalone), *toheroa* and *tuatua* (shellfish), crayfish (lobster), indigenous whitebait, *weta* (large cricket-like insects), Bluff oysters, and muttonbirds (sooty shearwaters). *Karengo* and *parengo*, seaweeds, are also prized native fare.

Sauvignon Blanc is the most frequently grown grape variety, but Chardonnay, Riesling, Cabernet Sauvignon, Merlot, Pinot Noir, Pinot Gris and Syrah are widely grown in the seven main wine-growing areas. If you want to buy drinks for somebody, the casual style is to offer to 'shout' them. You will say, 'This is my shout', because 'I will buy the drinks this time' is regarded as too formal. At many gatherings, you will be asked to 'bring a plate' or 'bring a *koha*', a custom that is also known as 'pot luck'. A plate simply means a plate of food, whereas a *koha* is a donation, in the form of either food or money. Maori society is by tradition communally based and colleagues and visitors can be expected to share in costs and contributions. It is wise to ask what would be preferred, if you are asked to contribute. You could be invited to a *hangi*, which is a traditional Maori meal of meat and vegetables, steamed in an underground oven 'fired' with hot stones. Other traditional Maori meals include 'boil-up', which is a thin stew, usually containing both meat and vegetables, and 'pork and *puha*', a native sow thistle blend with fatty pork. Rural people in particular speak of 'tucker' for food. (The term 'dog tucker' has been transferred from its use for aged sheep to mean any person who is worn out, defeated or bankrupt.)

On the streets

There are no tips or gratuities required for service in New Zealand hotels, restaurants, taxis, and so on. Because of this, many New Zealanders find tipping somewhat alien when they travel overseas. Identity cards are not required, although you will now be asked to show a driver's licence or passport when checking in at an airport. New Zealanders do not have freeways or drugstores, they have motorways and chemist shops; they have car boots, not trunks, and car bonnets, not hoods. They walk on footpaths, not sidewalks, and park in car parks, not parking lots. Their cars require warrants of fitness, not inspection certificates. They gamble in pokie bars and sports bars, not gaming rooms. While there is considerable disquiet about the proliferation of large shopping malls, estates and barns, and fast food outlet chains, the large retail estates found in the United States are beginning to be found adjacent to some cities. In small towns, Red Sheds, occupied by the large chain The Warehouse, have forced small and locally-owned retail outlets out of business, and this is not considered 'the Kiwi way of doing things'.

Men and women commonly walk hand-in-hand on the street, but it is less likely that you will see same-sex couples doing so, particularly in small towns. New Zealanders expect to drive their cars right to the door of a venue, and have not yet adopted the 'park and ride' method of organizing public transport. Consequently, you might encounter traffic jams, particularly in Auckland, where the 'City of Sails' is known as the 'City of Snails'.

The *Haka, Hongi* and *Hakari* of *Tikanga Maori*: culture, protocols and traditions

Tikanga, the collective term for Maori customs and traditions, includes Maori arts, craft and dance, speeches, welcomes, funerals, farewells and family structures. It is essential for visitors to observe Maori protocol, as an unwillingness to do so is considered offensive. At ceremonial gatherings, you could be expected to *hongi* (rub noses) while standing in a reception line. You will see the *haka* (a traditional war dance) performed at sports matches and at a variety of events. And you will be invited to join a *hakari* (traditionally a feast, but more often nowadays a sharing of food after an event). In modern New Zealand it is as common to be greeted with 'Kia ora' as it is with 'Hello', by both Maori and Pakeha. Pronounced keeyau-ra, rolling the r, this telephone and personal greeting is widely used in government departments and offices, on the street, and in academic circles to begin speeches and lectures. *Haere mai* (welcome) and *haera ra* (goodbye) are also common in everyday conversation. A *mihi* is a welcome speech, and a *karakia* is a prayer with which Maori begin most meetings. Many ceremonies and meetings are also begun with a *powhiri*, which is a welcome and essential exchange of background, conducted in *te reo*. Carvings of bone, wood, shell and stone, particularly greenstone (*pounamu*), are among the traditional arts given as gifts to visitors.

Celebrations and holidays

Agricultural and pastoral (A & P) shows, first held in the mid-1800s, take place throughout the country, with more than 100 A&P

associations still hosting shows. A 'show day' was once a rare chance for all citizens of a community to dress in finery and enjoy themselves. In the past, shops would close for the event, which still consists of fairground activities, horse and pony sports (showjumping), exhibits of farm stock and produce, and retail stands and exhibits. Apart from shows and gala days (which you may know as fairs) and the Blossom Festivals held in Alexandra in the South Island and in Hastings in the North Island, there is little evidence to suggest that New Zealanders were interested in celebration and ritual before the 1970s. Since that time, a variety of events have proliferated: Golden Shears, Sweetwaters, Big Day Out, Battle of the Bands, World of Wearable Art, and Mystery Creek 'Fieldays'. Ethnic food fairs, wine and food festivals, and medieval fairs with jousting, apple bobbing and stocks feature alongside the celebration of *Matariki*, the Maori New Year, the Chinese New Year, and the festivals of Diwali and Holi. St Patrick's Day, the only Saints Day that is openly celebrated, is signified by hospitality staff in bars, sports clubs and restaurants dressing in green, serving green food and paying homage to Irish traditions. Halloween has also recently sneaked into the Kiwi calendar, but 5 November is still celebrated as Guy Fawkes Day, with community fireworks.

The two most significant national holidays are Waitangi (or New Zealand) Day on 6 February and Anzac Day on 25 April. These are the two days on which New Zealanders reflect upon the nation's culture and heritage, and which are accompanied by ceremony. In some years, Waitangi Day, signifying the day that the treaty between the British Crown and Maori was signed, has been a day of disunity and protest in which Maori have sought recognition of land rights. It is celebrated nowadays by a variety of ethnic festivals. On the other hand, Anzac Day has been one of unity of different age, ethnic and philosophical groups within the country, with occasional protest against external events such as the Vietnam War, nuclear armament, and the occupation of Iraq. Anzac (an acronym for Australia–New Zealand Army Corps) was formed in 1914 with the merger of the Australian Imperial Force and New Zealand Expeditionary Force in Egypt, and the Anzacs made their first appearance at Gallipoli in 1915. Anzac Day has been celebrated with a public holiday since 1921 and, unlike other Commonwealth countries where red poppies are worn on Armistice Day, it is the day for the wearing of red poppies to honour the dead in wars. On ceremonial occasions, such as Anzac Day commemoration or graduation, one or both of the country's national anthems, *God Defend New Zealand* and *God Save the Queen* are sung.

New Zealanders do not have bank holidays but each province has a separate Anniversary Day, signifying the day it was founded. The other day that provides a holiday for workers is Labour Day, held at the end of October. The typical New Zealand family holiday during summer, to a seaside or lakeside *bach* or *crib* (holiday cottage). As shops and businesses close for Christmas and Easter, roads are clogged with holiday-makers. During the winter, families make for the ski-fields. You can spend your holiday accommodated at motels, B&Bs, DoC (Department of Conservation) huts, ecobaches and ecolodges, farmstays, homestays, serviced apartments, lodges, tourist flats, cabins, youth hostels, backpackers and flashpackers.

Arts and the media

National radio has iconic status in New Zealand. When a proposal was made to discontinue the morning native bird calls to signify the hours between 6 and 9 a.m., the nation rose in protest, and the proposal failed. There are four main television channels, including a Maori television channel. Sky and Discovery channels are available as 'pay TV'. Since the late 1990s, life in New Zealand has been represented in films of Maori provenance in particular, and in the first months of 2006, two dramatic films of Polynesian life in New Zealand were released: *Sione's Wedding* and *No. 2*.

New Zealanders have a high rate of literacy, and reading is nominated as one of the most favoured adult pastimes. Book publication thrives, with the largest genre of published material being educational books, followed, in order, by general non-fiction, professional and technical books, children's books, general fiction, history, reference and trade, and biography. Women writers are the most successful, in terms of an international profile. Katherine Mansfield was an eminent short-story writer; Keri Hulme won the Booker Prize with *the bone people* in 1985; Margaret Mahy, prolific writer for children, has won the Carnegie Medal twice, the Hans Christian Andersen Award, and a host of other international awards. New Zealand writers are well supported by scholarships, awards and writers-in-residence schemes, including the annual Prime Minister's Literary Awards which provide $60,000 for each of three recipients. The prestigious Montana Book of the Year contest covers prizes in several categories, while the Art Foundation rewards living icons of the arts. Maori writers have always had a strong following in New Zealand. The publication of multiple novels from Maori authors Alan Duff, Witi Ihimaera and Patricia Grace, in particular, have found broad international markets.

In a small island nation at the base of the southern hemisphere, isolation was keenly felt by newly settled Europeans and the first newspaper was published before the land was officially declared a British colony. Even the smallest of towns, including Eketahuna, regarded somewhat pejoratively as one of the smallest of New Zealand's small towns, boasted several newspapers. There were 16 newspapers in the colony by 1851; and between 1860 and 1879, 181 newspapers were founded. By 1900 most small clearings and settlements had their own newspaper, and often more than one. Newspaper founders, known as rag-planters, were just as enthusiastic to find readers, Scholefield[16] noting that at the end of the nineteenth century 'the rag-planters waged a picturesque struggle in the back-blocks, vying with each other for the favour of bush farmers and "cow cockies" '.

In fact in 1911, when the total population of the country was 1,058,313, there were 193 newspapers.[17] Per capita, New Zealand still has a large number of newspaper publications, with community and suburban newspapers having a favoured place in both cities and provincial areas.

It was not until the mid-twentieth century, in the surge of post-war national reconstruction, that some of the nation's artistic and cultural bodies were established. In 1947 the New Zealand National Orchestra, now known as the New Zealand Symphony Orchestra, was formed, following the establishment of the State Literary Fund, which serves to support writing and publishing. In 1953 the New Zealand Ballet Company was formed, followed by the New Zealand Opera Company in 1954. Earlier, during the Second World War in 1941, the National Film Unit was formed, which functioned for many years to record and publicize people, places and events. Music, art and drama bursaries and awards are rich in number and worth, particularly for Maori and Pasifika. Professional live theatre can be found in most cities, while repertory societies and amateur drama groups have remained a popular tradition.

Religion

Church-going has decreased since the 1970s, so that religious affiliation for most New Zealanders is basically nominal. The state educational system is secular, but several independent schools are sponsored by religious groups or have traditional ties with a particular denomination without being 'church schools'. *Ratana* is a Maori Christian religion with a large following. In 2004 a new evangelical religious movement, known as the Destiny Church and of particular appeal to Maori and Pasifika, marched on Parliament to oppose the Civil Unions Bill, polarizing opinion and giving rise to counter-marches. Under 'Quick facts', below, the major religions are listed in order. Although of a minor religion, Muslim students are provided with prayer rooms at tertiary institutions and in several secondary schools. In the 2001 Census the number of New Zealand residents declaring Islam as their religion was 23,637, a rise of 4 per cent from the 1996 census, and this is expected to have risen significantly when the results of 2006 are analysed. Church leaders are often regarded as the social and political conscience of New Zealand, speaking out with significant involvement in social issues and debate about racism, national and international poverty, discriminatory government policy, and the environment. As an example, in April 2006, 18 New Zealand and Pacific Islands bishops called on the New Zealand government to take action concerning the threats associated with climate change.

Education

Kiwi pre-schoolers attend play centres, kindergartens and *kohanga reo* (language nests) before entering primary schools at the age of 5, where they remain until the age of 12. Secondary schools, known as high schools or colleges, cater for students from the ages of 13 to 17. There is an alternative to the state system in the form of private and independent schools, some of which are based on Montessori and Steiner, while others are historically church-sponsored. Today, most schools are integrated with the state system, which means that they enjoy a reasonable level of state funding, usually in the form of teacher salaries. New Zealand is well served with polytechnics and universities, including Maori *wananga* (tertiary institutes).

Stereotypes, attitudes and popular views

Isolation and a small population base have had a significant influence on what is popularly called the Kiwi national psyche. Nineteenth-century colonists and the settlers who followed established a reputation for 'Kiwi ingenuity', a characteristic that has remained, and is valued, to this day. With little choice for the individual but to develop independence and confidence to 'do it yourself' or 'have a go', New Zealanders have earned a robust reputation for being practical and 'jacks of all trades'.

Ingenuity is basic to another national psychic image, the 'No. 8 wire mentality'. A term from the rural domain, where farmers are renowned for fixing anything from gates to generators and plumbing with No. 8 gauge fencing wire, this image has sustained over time and technology. Citizens with initiative are described as 'No. 8 wire persons' or are simply 'No. 8 wired'.

Since 1900, the term 'wowser' has been widely used, originally to describe a teetotaller, and one disapproving of the consumption of alcohol. The term is said to be an acronym of the prohibitionists' catch cry, 'We only want social evils reformed', but its use has been extended to cover killjoys, puritans and spoilsports in all contexts. Being a spoilsport in itself is highly disapproved of in New Zealand! Better it is to be regarded as a *dag*. While to be described as a dag in

Australia is not a compliment, New Zealand dags are good-humoured, entertaining, semi-eccentric folk.

The New Zealand 'She's right, mate' or 'She'll be right' attitude is an assumed casual expression of acceptance, of dismissal of potentially troublesome situations or expectations, or of nonchalance, and is gradually being replaced among young people by expressions such as 'Sweet as' or 'No worries'. 'Mate' is still used as a form of address between males, particularly in sporting contexts and in casual work encounters.

For decades, New Zealand had the reputation of a frontier nation committed to 'rugby, racing and beer'. That motif, and that of the 'lone man', commonly conveyed in literature, has been laid to rest, although some rural men and sportsmen still align themselves with a strong macho retrosexual image, that of 'Southern man'. 'WASP' (white Anglo-Saxon Protestant) city men are more likely to subscribe to the metrosexual image, as they do internationally. For females, 'solo parent' or 'solo mum' was a negative stereotype that has also had its time in the sun. The Americanism 'white trash' has only entered the New Zealand vocabulary in the twenty-first century, and is not well regarded. 'Hoodies' and gangs are seen as a threat to many citizens, in part due to menacing gang patches and their relationship with drug dealing. With changing ethnic diversity in urban areas, there is an imagined threat to security of persons and property among the very wealthy; and in isolated suburbs, small gated communities can be found.

Friendly antipathies and rivalries between cities and areas are common. In particular, Auckland is seen as separate from 'the rest of New Zealand', which is known by Aucklanders as 'RONZ'. Outside of Auckland, the retaliatory acronym JAFA is used for 'Just another f-ing Aucklander' while, within Auckland, the 'Westies' are regarded as an underclass. Rural localities are known as the 'Wop-Wops', a somewhat derogatory term. Both North and South Islanders refer to their island as 'the mainland'. British people in the nineteenth and twentieth centuries were not unfondly known as 'homies' and 'Poms'.

'The great Kiwi clobbering machine' is the term used to express the egalitarian attitude in which no individual should shine, be more high achieving, or be more privileged than others: 'Jack is as good as his master'. The attitude is similar to Australia's 'tall poppy syndrome', which Kiwis adapted to 'tall *ponga* syndrome', and which historians refer to as 'negalitarianism'. So ingrained is the attitude that New Zealanders are only as good as each other, that several pejorative terms have been coined to describe the bright stars who are brought down by repute to an earthly orbit, including '*Ngati Aorere*' (cloud-piercers or high-fliers), 'stilt people' and 'high heelers'. At the same time, the Maori concept of *mana* (respect, prestige, honour) has helped

Pakeha New Zealanders to recognize the worth of their exemplary fellows, so that certain high performers on the world stage, particularly in science and sport, are treated with pride and possessiveness. Sir Edmund Hillary, the first person to reach the peak of Mt Everest, Nobel Prize winners Lord Rutherford and Alan MacDiarmid, and those who have established or broken world records and demonstrated great sporting achievements, are regarded with warmth and pride. War heroes, among them Victoria Cross double-award-winner Captain Charles Upham of the Second World War, remain national heroes or *taonga* (treasure). Kate Sheppard, who worked tirelessly for women's franchise, is regarded with a quieter admiration, as are other females of renown, such as writers Katherine Mansfield and Janet Frame. There is an inverted pride in many New Zealanders, and you will often hear the comment 'Not bad for a New Zealander'.

People and passions

New Zealanders are no strangers to protests, demonstrations and marches, where lobby groups and activists represent all cultural, socio-economic, religious and ethnic groups. Not long after colonial settlement, strikes and rallies were commonplace, as everybody clamoured about how the country should be administered; and from the 1830s, many of the protests centred around alcohol, 'the demon drink'. When Kiwis become passionate, they are extremely focused, and inevitably form groups to strengthen and express their passion.

The demon drink and other of society's ills

New Zealanders' attitude to alcohol has been, and continues to be, one of ambivalence. The isolation encountered by colonist farmers and boundary shepherds led to succour with alcohol, and 'runholders' disease' was an early name for alcoholism. At the same time, itinerant sealers and whalers introduced alcohol to the Maori, to the detriment of many, and the first temperance society was formed in the Bay of Islands in 1836. In 1847 an ordinance prohibited sales of alcohol to Maori. The first bill passed by the New Zealand Parliament in 1854 was actually the 'Bellamy's Bill', the Licensing Amendment Act that permitted sales of alcohol on the premises of Parliament. The Women's Christian Temperance Union, formed in 1885, was one of New Zealand's longest-serving lobby groups. Sunday closing of public houses became law in 1881, and by 1910, 12 of 76 districts prohibited the sales of alcohol. Women, at the time, were barred from employment in bars. New Zealand prohibition literature is voluminous; temperance songs date from the 1860s, and several temperance novels with a strong moral stand were published, while throughout the nation, anti-temperance cartoons were rife. Following the Second World War, there was a swing away from prohibition, but New Zealand voters voted for national continuance, national prohibition or State purchase and control every three years during parliamentary elections until 1987. New Zealand bars and pubs closed at 6 p.m. until 1967, when closing was extended until 10 p.m. Since then, hours have been extended further and the 'drinking age', allowing individuals to drink in public bars and to buy liquor, has become a permissive 18 years. Following concerns about 'binge drinking' of minors, the drinking age has been the subject of wide community debate and the Sale of Liquor (Youth Alcohol Harm Reduction) Amendment Bill, seeking to raise the minimum purchase age from 18 to 20 years, is under consideration in 2006.

Despite decades of calls to legalize cannabis, the possession and supply of cannabis remains illegal in New Zealand, as is the case with all Class A and other Class B drugs. The penalties for manufacturing, importing or supplying Class A drugs (cocaine, heroin, methamphe-tamine, and so on) are harsh and extend to a maximum term of life imprisonment. Cannabis is, however, grown in New Zealand and dedicated police squads make regular raids by helicopter and other means. Non-addictive party pills, which are, controversially, legal, are popular with young people.

Among the strongest lobbying groups in society are two which have had long histories. SPUC, or the Society for the Protection of the Unborn Child, with many adherents from the Catholic faith, has continued to fight for the rights of the foetus, even after relatively liberal abortion law reform in 1977. The Society for the Promotion of Community Standards was a self-appointed film and book censoring group established in 1970 and led for many years by a former nun, the late Patricia Bartlett, who disapproved of masturbation, regarded homosexuals as sick and depraved, and supported corporal punish-ment. Despite such concern, gay television shows such as *Kiwifruit* and *The Outhouse*, along with a range of gay periodicals, have become part of media offerings.

Sport and recreation

The sports team with the highest profile internationally is the All Black rugby team. The first team to be ascribed the 'All Black' label was thought to be the national rugby union team of 1901, the first team to wear both black shorts and black jersey. Maori and Pacific players have had a long history of national rugby participation, with a player of Samoan descent appointed as captain in 2004. The passion for and emphasis on rugby is in part media-driven. In reality, New Zealand schoolchildren participate in a wide range of sports. Like Australian sportspeople, New Zealanders use pet names or hypocoristics for players and places, 'the Blacks' being a substitute for 'the All Blacks'. 'Let's go and watch Cairnsy deal to the Windies at the Cake Tin' will be heard far more often than 'Let's go and watch Chris Cairns play against the West Indian cricket team at the Wellington Stadium'. The black and white team colours and the silver fern motif have been carried over from rugby into other codes, so that the cricket team is the Black Caps, the basketballers are the Tall Blacks, and the hockey players are known as the Black Sticks. Netball is represented by the Silver Ferns, and soccer by the All Whites.

Not surprisingly, New Zealand is a nation of 'boaties', with a high level of ownership of boats of all types. In general use for recreation and fishing, there is also a strong interest in competitive yachting and jet-boating. The gaining of the America's Cup in 1995 and the winning of the Whitbread round-the-world race in the same year provided a broad profile for local yacht designers and builders.

The country has a reputation for the pioneering of extreme and adventure sports along with endurance events, such as the gruelling Coast to Coast Ironman triathlon. Whitewater and blackwater rafting and jetboating, caving, wild water surfing and a variety of marathon events provide opportunities for adventurers to pit their courage and fitness against that of others. Surfing, scuba diving and *waka ama* (outrigger canoeing) are some popular summer pastimes, while in winter, five main ski areas host snowboarders and cross-country and downhill skiers.

It is more difficult to buy weapons in New Zealand than it is in the United States, for example. Gun licenses are available under relatively restricted conditions for recreational sports and competition, although there remains a strong anti-gun lobby.

In New Zealand, tramps do not go tramping, trampers do! Known elsewhere as hiking or mountain walking, tramping is one of the nation's most popular all-year pastimes. With mountain chains running through both of the main islands, tramping tracks are easily accessible and most national parks and conservation parks provide trampers' huts which are maintained by Department of Conservation staff. Since the 1980s, 'boutique' tramps over private farmland have proliferated, where packs are transported and meals are provided by farming families.

In general, New Zealanders are passionate gardeners, being blessed with outdoor space, even in quite central city areas, where they retain the traditional quarter-acre section. Lifestyle blocks, on which owners indulge in animal or plant breeding, pepper the outskirts of most towns and cities. Interestingly, Highland dancing, known as Scottish country dancing, still retains a strong following in New Zealand.

The natural environment

The recognition of a need to conserve the country's material and physical culture did not surface until the 1960s and 1970s in New Zealand, but since then it has developed a force of its own. New Zealanders are fiercely proud of their indigenous forests, birds and fish, and timbers from indigenous trees that were used to make furniture and floors of houses are now highly treasured – the *kauri*, *rimu*, *totara* and *matai* being the principal furniture or building timbers. New Zealanders are also strongly aware of the problems of pollution, of finite resources and of balancing preservation and protection with recreation, adventure tourism and economic development. Mining and the logging of indigenous forests have been sources of continuing controversy.

The nation's first national park, Tongariro National Park, was gifted by a Maori leader, Te Heuheu Tukino IV, in 1887. Since that time, 13 other national parks and 23 conservation parks have been established, totalling more than 4,534,842 hectares of the nation's area. Since 1975, more than 28 marine reserves have been established in New Zealand waters, including the offshore Auckland and Kermadec Island groups, protecting almost 8 per cent of New Zealand's territorial sea.

A range of new terms and usages has been required in the conservation domain. Hearteningly, new species are still being discovered and named, while new colonies of species thought to have been extinct for almost a century have been discovered. Trusts and ecogroups have proliferated since the 1970s, with ECO (Environment and Conservation Organisations of Aotearoa New Zealand Inc.), an umbrella network of 70 environment and conservation organizations in New Zealand, acting as a central education, lobbying and campaign voice for a range of environmental concerns. The Ministry for the Environment was established in 1986, and the Department of Conservation, with extensive powers, has operated since 1987. While the restrictive and somewhat controversial Resource Management Act requires permission for buildings, fences, dams or driveways to be erected and certain trees to be removed, the general public appreciates the rationale. The 2005 example of an Auckland businessman being fined $100,000 for removing a protected native tree found favour with all ecogroups and the general populace.

Travel

New Zealanders are frequent overseas travellers. 'OE' is the common initialism for overseas experience, essentially an overseas trip. Used widely since the early 1960s, the expression is in general use for an overseas holiday, whereas a working holiday or extended time out of the country is usually known as 'the big OE'. People are described as being 'on their OE' or 'doing their OE'. Generally, one does not *have* an 'OE', but can 'get a bit of OE'. People living in Europe where travel outside the borders is easily accomplished, and often of little consequence, are no doubt surprised that this expression is used in many contexts, both formal and informal, including banking, Parliament, literature, and newspaper journalism. But in New Zealand, apart from travel to the closest Pacific neighbours, and to Australia, across 'the ditch', as the Tasman Sea is called, overseas journeys are extended and expensive.

Kiwis and Kiwiana

The kiwi, a flightless bird, is a common emblem for New Zealand and the informal name given to a New Zealand citizen. The New Zealand dollar is also known as the kiwi. 'Kiwiana' is the collective name given to representations of valued but often rather crass cultural emblems and 'icons', including *paua* shell, plastic tiki pendants, pavlova meringue cake, gumboots, corrugated iron sheds, *baches* (holiday homes) and sculptures. 'Kiwiese' or 'Kiwese' is often used to describe New Zealand English. Another common emblem is the curled *koru* motif, a pattern derived from the new shoots of the *ponga* fern which represent a new beginning. The silver fern leaf, adopted by the All Blacks representative rugby team as their official emblem in 1893, has been further adopted by sports teams and other groups, and, like the kiwi and the *koru*, is incorporated into logos in a variety of domains. The remaining pattern that you are likely to see depicted is that of the *tuatara*, a primitive 'living fossil' which is in fact a rare reptile with the appearance of a small dinosaur, and which can live up to 100 years. Protected by law since 1895, the *tuatara* is the only existing member of the order *Sphenodontia* and, being highly valued, it has been developed as a motif by many groups.

Conclusion

In 1972 when Mitchell (p. 18) commented, 'New Zealand is what it is because it has been conditioned by isolation, by the need to make the best of what it has not got, and by smallness', the image of the nation and its culture was quite different from what we see today. Mitchell went on to say that minorities were too small to stand out. Modernization has impacted more on New Zealand than it has done on most other nations, due to the bridging of isolation, to its new independence in global relations, and to immigration. From years of a profound strain to monoculturalism and conformity, New Zealanders are not only embracing, but more significantly are also celebrating, diversity.

A Brief Chronology

Circa 1200	First settlements were established in New Zealand
1642	Dutch explorer Abel Tasman sighted the South Island of New Zealand
1769	Captain James Cook, first European 'beach-crosser', arrived in New Zealand
1806	The first European women arrived in New Zealand
1814	The first mission station was established
1840	New Zealand's first newspaper was published
1840	New Zealand's founding document, the Treaty of Waitangi, was signed
1841	New Zealand was declared a British Crown Colony
1850	British imperial coins became the official currency
1851	Census recorded a population of 9,000 European males and 6,000 females
1852	New Zealand Parliament was established, with six provincial governments
1858	The census recorded an outnumbering of Maori by Europeans
1865	Wellington became the new capital of New Zealand (formerly located at Auckland)
1867	The use of Maori language in schools was banned
1869	New Zealand's first university was established at Otago
1877	The first time that a woman in New Zealand and the British Empire was awarded a Bachelor of Arts degree
1877	An Education Act established a national system of primary education
1881	The first time that a woman in New Zealand and the British Empire was awarded a Master of Arts degree
1893	New Zealand became the first self-governing country in the world to give women the vote
1893	The first time that a Maori scholar gained a degree
1893	The first woman Mayor in the British Empire was elected at Onehunga
1896	The first New Zealand female doctor graduated
1899	The first Maori doctor graduated
1902	The New Zealand flag, featuring the Union Jack and four stars of the Southern Cross, was introduced
1907	New Zealand became a self-governing dominion
1908	The New Zealand population reached 1 million
1919	New Zealand women were given the right to stand for Parliament
1933	The first woman Member of Parliament was elected
1947	The first woman Cabinet Minister was appointed
1949	The first Maori woman Member of Parliament was elected

1952	The New Zealand population reached 2 million
1961	Capital punishment was abolished (excluding treason)
1967	Decimal currency, weights and measures were introduced
1973	The New Zealand population reached 3 million
1974	The New Zealand voting age was lowered to 18
1980	The first Maori head of the Anglican church was appointed
1982	*Kohanga Reo* (total immersion Maori pre-school centres) opened
1985	*Kura Kaupapa Maori* (total immersion school) opened
1985	The first Maori Governor-General was appointed
1986	GST (goods and services tax) was introduced at 10 per cent (in 1989 raised to 12.5 per cent)
1987	*Te reo* Maori was recognized as a national language of New Zealand
1989	The first woman Finance Minister was appointed
1990	The first woman Governor-General was appointed
1990	The first woman Anglican Bishop and the world's first diocesan woman bishop was appointed
1993	The first woman high court judge was appointed
1997	The first time a woman became prime minister in a leadership ousting
1999	The first woman Prime Minister was elected
2000	Knighthoods and damehoods were abolished from the Honours system
2003	The New Zealand population reached 4 million
2003	Prostitution was made legal
2004	A dedicated Maori television channel was launched
2005	Microsoft Windows XP and Microsoft Office systems became available in *te reo* Maori
2005	The Civil Union Act established civil unions for same-sex couples

Quick facts

Land area: 268,680 square kilometres
Population (April 2006): 4,133,679
Capital city: Wellington
Largest city: Auckland, the world's largest Polynesian city
Official languages: English, Māori, New Zealand Sign Language
Religions: (in order of numbers) Anglican, Roman Catholic, Presbyterian, Methodist, Baptist, Mormon, Pentecostal, *Ratana*, Buddhist, Hindu
Unemployment: less than 4 per cent (2006)
Natural resources: coal, oil, natural gas, forestry
Exports: dairy products, meat, wool, wood and wood products, fish, wine, manufactured goods

Head of State: Queen Elizabeth II
Open road speed limit: 100 km/hr
Legal age for drinking alcohol: 18 years
Legal age for driving: 15 years
Legal age for marriage: 16 years
Currency: New Zealand dollar (the 'Kiwi'). New Zealand has had decimal currency, weights and measures since 1967
International calling code: +64

Glossary of Maori and Pasifika loan words

afakasi: a person of mixed ethnicity (Pasifika)
aiga: a family (Pasifika)
hapu: a family
hikoi: a long protest march
huhu bug: the edible larva of a flying beetle
hui: a meeting
iwi: a tribe
kiwano: a melon
kumara: a sweet potato
lava lava: a wraparound skirt (Pasifika)
mana: respect, honour, prestige
marae: a communal meeting place
mokihi: a raft
pa: a village, originally a fortified village
pakihi: a bush clearing; a swamp
Palagi: a European (Pasifika)
ponga: a tree fern
poroporo: a type of flowering shrub
taonga: a treasure
taro: a root vegetable
tomo: an underground tunnel
turangawaewae: homeland
whare: a house or hut

Tasks and exercises

1. For many years, New Zealand had a reputation for its dominant male 'rugby, racing and beer' culture. How well do you think this stereotype is supported in the brief chronology and the notes on social legislation provided in Chapter 6? At the same time, the term 'wowser' was prominent in New Zealand. How much evidence is there to suggest that wowsers are less of a feature in New Zealand now?

2. What do you think are the prerequisites for becoming a dinkum (real) Kiwi?

3. How much influence would the post-1950s global mass media have had on the culture of a country in a geographically isolated situation? What resources would you use and how would you go about assessing such an influence?

4. New Zealanders use two terms for a holiday cottage: *bach* and *crib*. Crib is more commonly used in the South Island. In your homeland, what terms do you normally use for holiday cottage?

5. The New Zealand term for homeland is *turangawaewae*, the place of belonging. What is the equivalent term used in your country?

6. Consider and explain the emphasis that New Zealanders place on conservation of the natural environment. Compare this with the situation in your home country.

7. 'Kiwiana' is the name for trinkets and icons that characterize the country and its inhabitants. What word is used in your home culture?

8. Compare the type and history of national holidays in your home nation with those of New Zealand.

9. In New Zealand, the cultural and spiritual values and protocols of the indigenous Maori are considered in land and resource development. To what extent does this happen in your homeland?

10. You have been invited to a *hui* (meeting), and have been asked to take a *koha* (plate). How would you find out what you should wear and what you should take?

11. You will notice that New Zealanders have many slang words for becoming angry – in fact, more than 45. The terms associated with feeling joyful are much fewer in number and are less informal. What words are used for becoming angry in your culture? Are as many slang terms used?

12. Most cultures have taboo subjects of conversation. What subjects are taboo in your culture? Research the taboo subjects in other cultures and compare and contrast these with your own.

13. Many New Zealand myths and legends are centred around the natural environment, in particular trees, birds and fish. Explain how this focus is similar or different from that of your own culture.

14. Some of New Zealand's best-loved icons and citizens are represented on coins and notes: 5 cents: *tuatara*; 10 cents: a Maori carved head; 20 cents: a *kiwi* or a Maori *pukaki* design; 50 cents: Cook's ship *The Endeavour*; $1: kiwi; $2: *kotuku* (white heron); $5: Sir Edmund Hillary; $10: suffragist Kate Sheppard; $20: Queen Elizabeth II; $50: politician Sir Apirana Ngata; $100: Lord Rutherford of Nelson. [You might like to look at www.rbnz.govt.nz/currency/money/0060617-02.html for images of these coins and notes.] How do these contrast with the subjects on the front of coins and notes in the currency of your home country?

Notes

1. This description was popularized by Richard John Seddon, a popular Premier of 1893–1906, known widely and affectionately as 'King Dick'.
2. See Mitchell, 1972.
3. See Hanbury-Tenison, 1990.
4. Letter cited in Eisen and Smith, 1991, p. 164.
5. From *Australia and New Zealand*, cited in Elsen and Smith, 1991, p. 135.
6. Barker, 1879, p. 89.
7. Kennedy, 1873, p. 295.
8. Williams, 1889, p. 19.
9. *NZ Listener*, 2 March 2002, p. 18.
10. Orchids make up the largest selling floricultural export, followed by zantedeschia (calla), hydrangea and peonies.
11. *A Grammar and Vocabulary of the Language of New Zealand*, London, 1820.
12. For example, 'She's a tough ask, selecting a national soccer team', *Sunday Star Times*, 29 January 2006: B4.
13. For example, 'He [the Governor of the Reserve Bank] had a bob each way: We are at the top of the cycle – unless we have to go one more'. *NZ Herald*, 27 January 2006: C1.
14. This is actually a corrupted form of 'She's a hard row to hoe'.
15. For some years, the standard offer for assistance in New Zealand shops was 'Have you been fixed up?'
16. G. H. Scholefield, *Newspapers in New Zealand*, 1958, p. 18.

17. Of the 193 newspapers of that time, 67 were dailies, 32 were tri-weeklies, 26 were bi-weeklies and 68 were weeklies.

Further reading and research

Culture and identity

Bell, Claudia. (1996) *Inventing New Zealand: everyday myths of Pakeha identity*. Auckland: Penguin.

Liu, James H *et al*. (eds) (2005) *New Zealand Identities: Departures and Destinations*. Wellington: Victoria University Press.

History

Dalley, B. and McLean, G. (2005) *Frontier of Dreams: The Story of New Zealand*. Auckland: Hodder Moa.

King, M. (2003) *The Penguin History of New Zealand*. Auckland: Penguin.

New Zealand English

Bardsley, D. (2005) *The Oxford New Zealand Mini Thesaurus*. Auckland: Oxford University Press [provides specific synonyms in New Zealand English].

Bardsley, D. (2006) *The Oxford New Zealand School Dictionary*. Auckland: Oxford University Press [refer specifically to appendices and study pages].

Bell, A. and Kuiper, K. (2000) *New Zealand English*. Wellington: VUP.

Bell, Allan *et al*. (eds) (2005) *Languages of New Zealand*. Wellington: VUP.

Grant, L.E. and Devlin, G.A. (1999) *In Other Words! a dictionary of expressions used in New Zealand*. Palmerston North: Dunmore Press.

Macalister, J. (2005) *A Dictionary of Maori Words in English*. Auckland: Oxford University Press.

Orsman, H.O. (1997) *The Dictionary of New Zealand English*. Auckland: Oxford University Press.

Websites

Remember that some websites contain unedited material and the reliability of information can not always be assured. The websites listed below are useful and authoritative sources for clarification and confirmation of information that is sometimes compiled from impression.

www.teara.govt.nz
a government website, hosted by the Ministry for Culture and Heritage, this is the site for Te Ara Encyclopedia of New Zealand, a treasure house of social, cultural and historical facts.

www.stats.govt.nz
a government website of Statistics New Zealand containing social, economic and environmental statistics.

http://paperspast.natlib.govt.nz
Nineteeenth-century newspapers and periodicals on-line.

www.stuff.co.nz
Up-to-the-minute news of New Zealand and global concerns.

www.vuw.ac.nz/lals/research/nzdc/index.htm
The New Zealand Dictionary Centre site dedicated to New Zealand words and usages, including word games and research activities.

References

Barker, Lady M. (1873) *Station Amusements in New Zealand*. London: William Hunt.

Cumberland, K.B. (1944) *Soil Erosion in New Zealand*. Wellington: Soil Conservation and Rivers Control Council.

Eggers, S and Sellers, S. (eds) (2006) *Lonely Planet Blue List 06–07*. London: Lonely Planet.

Eisen, J. and Smith, K.J. (1991) *Strangers in Paradise*. Auckland: Vintage.

Fuller, F. (1859) *Five Years' Residence in New Zealand*. London: Williams & Norgate.

Hanbury-Tenison, R. (1990) *Fragile Eden: A Ride Through New Zealand*. London: Arrow Books.

Kennedy, D. (1876) *Kennedy's Colonial Travel*. Edinburgh: Edinburgh Publishing Co.

King, M. (2003) *The Penguin History of New Zealand*. Auckland: Penguin.

McLauchlan, G. (1981) *The Farming of New Zealand*. Auckland: Australia & New Zealand Book Co.

Mitchell, A. (1972) *Half-Gallon, Quarter-Acre Pavlova Paradise*. Christchurch: Whitcombe & Tombs.

Scholefield, G.H. (1958) *Newspapers in New Zealand*. Wellington: AH & AW Reed.

Williams, George P. and Reeves, W.P. (1889) *Colonial Couplets: Poems in Partnership*. Christchurch: Simpson & Williams.

7 The United States of America – The Land of Opportunity

Sherry Ash

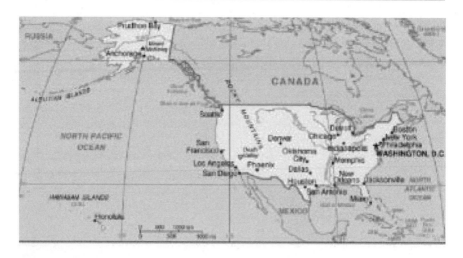

Background information on social and cultural history

Introduction

The United States is on the whole a nation of immigrants. The first immigrant settlers were Spaniards who arrived in what is now Florida in the sixteenth century. Early in the seventeenth century came the English, Dutch, Germans and others, as will be described below. Colonization and development of the resources offered by the new land were largely turned over to private corporations, such as the Massachusetts Bay Company, and to private individuals, such as William Penn (founder of Pennsylvania) and James Oglethorpe (founder of Georgia), through large land grants from the English Crown. By this means, 13 English colonies were established with a population that was predominantly English. By the middle of the eighteenth century, the colonies had large cities, universities, cultural centres and a well-educated middle class. The rule of a distant monarch, the burdens of taxation without representation and other injustices, as well as limitations on personal freedom, gradually drove the colonists to declare their independence from England, as stated in some of the most stirring prose that has ever flowed from a pen. The new nation was founded on the premises that '... all men are created equal, that they are endowed by their creator with certain unalienable rights, that among these are life, liberty, and the pursuit of happiness'. This is what Thomas Jefferson wrote in the Declaration of Independence in 1776, and it is memorized by every schoolchild in the country.

Every word of this phrase, indeed of the entire document, carries weight and the ideas expressed here are the central core of the national ideology. 'All men are created equal' means that no one has special rights or privileges derived from an accident of birth, every individual may strive to achieve his or her wildest dreams. 'Certain unalienable rights' means that the rights are inherent in the human person, not granted by an authority that also has the power to withdraw those rights. 'That among these [rights] are ... liberty ...' refers to many aspects of freedom: freedom of religion, freedom of the press, freedom of peaceable assembly and freedom of speech, among others. These ideas and these words set the stage for the fledgling United States to survive and to grow as a land of opportunity. The land itself offers abundant resources, and the guarantees of 'life, liberty, and the pursuit of happiness' continue to draw people to US shores in search of a better life.

Yet the heartening words of the Declaration of Independence, the Constitution and the Bill of Rights sound hollow indeed in light of many episodes in US history. What happened to the rights of the Native Americans, who husbanded the lands long before the Europeans arrived? Initially they helped the Europeans, teaching them to plant corn, introducing them to tobacco, co-operating in the fur trade and serving as guides to settlers. In return, the Europeans gave them alcohol and smallpox, decimated their game populations, cleared the lands they used for hunting, violated a long succession of treaties and met objections with gunfire. It is a national disgrace.

What were the rights of the Africans, who were brought to the United States against their will, kept as slaves until 1863 and exploited mercilessly for as long as possible after that? Discrimination against African Americans continued to be painfully blatant for another century after the Emancipation Proclamation. The seeds of the Civil Rights movement of the 1960s are found in the Supreme Court case of *Brown* v. *The Board of Education*, decided in 1954. The Court declared that 'separate is not equal'; that is, it is unconstitutional to have separate facilities – schools, in this instance – for blacks and whites, because separateness is intrinsically contrary to the principle of equality. That was a beginning, but real equality for blacks and whites still had a long way to go, as it does to this day.

The disadvantages of other excluded groups could be cited, such as those of women and homosexuals, for example. Furthermore,

221

'freedom' includes the freedom to be poor, to fail, to be homeless, to be hungry, to be unemployed, to lack health care or health insurance. Both the design and funding of programmes to deal with such social problems are woefully inadequate; improvements are made or lost with fluctuations in the political climate. But Americans do cling proudly and tenaciously to the principles of freedom, liberty and justice for all. These are the ideals of the national ethos and they are at the crux of explaining what America means to an American.

Settlement

Beginnings

Christopher Columbus of Genoa initiated the permanent European settlement of the New World in 1492 with the first of a series of four expeditions of discovery and exploration financed by Ferdinand V and Isabella I of Spain. As a result of his voyages and those of succeeding explorers, Spain claimed the southernmost part of what is now the United States, as well as Mexico, Central America and beyond. The North American claim included all of present-day Florida and the southern parts of the present states further west, all the way to the Pacific Ocean. The little town of St Augustine on the Atlantic coast in northern Florida was the first permanent European settlement in North America, founded by the Spanish conquistador Pedro Menendez de Aviles in 1565.

John Cabot was an Italian (born Giovanni Caboto), but he settled in England and sailed to the New World on behalf of his adopted country. In 1497 he landed in the area of Newfoundland and in 1498 he explored the Atlantic coast from Labrador to Hatteras. These voyages were the basis for England's later claims to land in North America.

Jamestown, in south-eastern Virginia, was the first permanent English settlement in America, established in 1607. Its inhabitants nearly perished from disease, starvation and Indian attacks in its earliest years and the original colonists prepared to return home. However, new settlers and supplies arrived and the colony survived. It was here that John Smith gained renown as a leader; Pocahontas married the Englishman John Rolfe, thereby bringing peace with the natives; and the cultivation of tobacco by Europeans began.

Plymouth Rock or the Plymouth Colony on Cape Cod in present-day Massachusetts was established by Pilgrims from England who arrived in December 1620. The Pilgrims were English Puritan separatists. The Puritans opposed the ecclesiastical establishment and demanded 'purification' of the church, which gave them their name. They constituted the predominant group of early settlers in New England and they also advanced the idea of congregational democratic government. The Pilgrims who landed at Plymouth Rock are especially noted for the Mayflower Compact (named for the ship that carried the group), an agreement that provided for the temporary government of the colony by the will of the majority of colonists, rather than by that of the Crown. The settlement nearly perished during the first winter, but it was saved in part by the generosity of the natives, who shared maize (corn) with the colonists. The settlement grew and was incorporated into the royal colony of Massachusetts in 1691.

New York was established by the Dutch in 1624 with the name Nieuw Amsterdam. Peter Minuit, the first director general of the colony of New Netherland, is said to have bought the island of Manhattan from the natives who lived there for $24 worth of trinkets in 1626. This was the capital of the colony, which included the Hudson and lower Delaware river valleys, from 1626 until 1664, when it (and all of New Netherland) was seized by the English and renamed New York in honour of the king's brother, the Duke of York.

Like the settlement at Plymouth, Boston was founded by Puritans in 1630 as a refuge for political and religious dissidents in the Massachusetts Bay Colony.

The colony of Virginia flourished on profits from the exportation of tobacco. Seaport towns such as Williamsburg (founded 1632), Richmond (on the James River, founded 1637) and Norfolk (founded 1682) became thriving market centres. Other important late seventeenth-century towns were founded at Charleston, South Carolina (1680) by Puritans from the Bermudas and Philadelphia (1681), founded by William Penn in his colony of Pennsylvania as a refuge from religious persecution for Quakers.

Westward movement

The settlement of the vast reaches of the continent is a complicated story with at least four major subplots: the migrations of people from one part of the country to another; the waves of new immigration from Europe in consonance with the tides of political strife and economic distress there; exploration of the land and the making of roads and trails; and hostilities exchanged with the original possessors of the land, the American Indians.

Until the industrial development of the nineteenth and twentieth centuries, the Atlantic coast had the relatively even population distribution of agricultural land, but with concentrations of population in the seaports. These cities were entry points for new immigrants, centres of cultural life and high society and conduits to the west. Until 1720, the population of the Atlantic seaboard (north of Florida) was almost entirely English, except for the Dutch in the Hudson Valley.

During the half-century before the Revolution, large numbers of

Pennsylvanians and new immigrants moved to farmlands along the Shenandoah and across the Blue Ridge into the piedmont of the Carolinas. The new immigrants were Scotch-Irish and Palatine Germans, large numbers of whom started arriving in 1720. A little later, the coastal settlements of Virginia and the Carolinas also expanded into these areas.

After the Revolution, which lasted from 1775 until 1783, westward migration accelerated. People from western New England relocated to central and western New York State, northern Pennsylvania, and the Western Reserve of Connecticut on Lake Erie. Daniel Boone blazed the Wilderness Road in 1775, from Virginia, through the Cumberland Gap, to the Ohio River and it was a principal route of westward migration from about 1790 to 1840. Southern uplanders went west across the Appalachians to central Kentucky and Tennessee, and then on to southern Ohio, Indiana and Illinois during the first decades of the nineteenth century.

Settlements on the upper Ohio River in the area of Pittsburgh and Wheeling expanded along the rivers into West Virginia, up to Lake Erie and further down the Ohio. These settlers came from eastern Pennsylvania, western New Jersey and Europe. By 1810, the streams of those coming from Pittsburgh and those from Kentucky met and mixed in Cincinnati and Louisville.

Expansion from southern settlements went west in search of new cotton fields. By 1830, cotton was being grown throughout the Gulf States as far as the Mississippi River by settlers from the cotton plantations of Virginia and the Carolinas.

The 1830s marked the beginning of the great migrations from Germany and Ireland, which increased to dramatic proportions in the following decades. National Road, from Cumberland, Maryland, to St Louis, Missouri, was completed in 1833 and supplanted the Wilderness Road as the main westward artery. As early as 1830, German farmers were arriving in Illinois, Wisconsin and Missouri, where land was selling at $1.30 an acre. Following political upheaval in Germany in the early 1840s, thousands of German people, many of them well educated, fled to the United States. Many of these immigrants settled in cities, particularly Chicago, Milwaukee, Cincinnati and St Louis. The Irish famine of the 1840s brought immigrants to New York and Boston. At the same time, Norwegian and Swedish farmers were settling in Minnesota, the Dakotas and Wisconsin.

The upper Midwest was important in the fur trade as early as the late 1600s, but real settlement only began in 1833, when the government opened part of the land following the end of the Black Hawk Wars. There were two principal movements of settlers from the East to this area. One was of Northerners from western New England and New York State coming across the land just south of the Great

Lakes (northern Indiana and Illinois) to the Mississippi River. The second consisted of Midlanders from New Jersey, Pennsylvania and northern Virginia moving west across Ohio, Indiana and central Illinois. Additional settlers came from the Carolinas, Virginia and Tennessee across Kentucky and into southern Indiana and Illinois. These South Midlanders first settled in south-eastern Iowa; as former Indian lands were opened, Midlanders continued across the southern two-thirds of Iowa and into Nebraska.

Continuing the westward surge, the Santa Fe Trail, from Independence, Missouri, to Santa Fe, New Mexico, took settlers about 1,250 kilometres (780 miles) to open land in the south-west from 1822 to about 1880. The discovery of gold at Sutter's Mill in 1849 precipitated the mad dash of 7000 'Forty-Niners', prospectors seeking the precious metal. They did not search in vain: $450 million in gold came out of the earth, while the population of California jumped from 15,000 to nearly 300,000 in seven years.

Migration was still going on in the Upper Midwest at this time, as the Far West was being settled. Lumbermen from Vermont and Maine had already settled along the St Croix River in eastern Minnesota, and subsequently, in the 1850s, more settlers came from New England, New York, Michigan and Ohio to southern Minnesota and northern Iowa. The Mississippi River served as a route to the area of St Paul, Minnesota, both for northerners from northern Illinois and for midlanders from St Louis and southern Iowa.

The Homestead Act of 1862 offered 160 acres of unoccupied public land (a quarter of a square mile, 65 hectares) to any citizen or alien intending to become a citizen upon payment of a ten-dollar registration fee and on condition of residing on the property for five years and making certain improvements. This Act brought settlers to the Midwest from New York, Wisconsin, Illinois, Ohio and New England.

Nebraska was settled by the Union Pacific Railroad. By 1866 it had already established two towns and by 1873 it had settled over 2,000 families. These settlers were mostly newly immigrated Scandinavians or transplants from the previously settled Great Lakes states, namely Illinois, Indiana, Ohio, Pennsylvania and New York.

The Great Lakes area, along with Minnesota and New England, was also the principal source of settlers of present-day North and South Dakota, again under the Homestead Act of 1862. South Dakota was settled earlier, between 1868 and 1873, and North Dakota was opened up by the Northern Pacific Railroad when it reached Moorhead, Minnesota, in 1870. The last major battle of the Indian wars, the Battle of Wounded Knee, took place in 1890 in South Dakota; 200 Sioux Indians were killed by US troops. After that, with the restriction of the Sioux Indians to reservations, the land west of the Missouri River was opened to settlement.

225

Some of the European countries which supplied settlers to the newly opened lands during this period have been mentioned already, but there were others as well. In order of descending numbers, the largest groups came from Germany, Sweden, Norway, Denmark, Russia, Canada, Czechoslovakia, the Netherlands, England, Ireland, Finland and Poland. During the Civil War (1861–5), immigration decreased. Following the war, immigrants were again actively recruited, both to replenish a labour force that had been reduced by war casualties and to settle unpopulated areas.

Beginning about 1841, the offer of free land in the Oregon Territory, the far north-west, brought more than 300,000 settlers west in covered wagons along the 3,500 kilometre (2,170 mile) Oregon Trail. It began at Kansas City or Independence in Missouri and led over the Rocky Mountains to Oregon City, near the Columbia River in present-day Oregon. These pioneers came from Missouri, Kentucky, Tennessee and other states where disease and economic depressions in 1837 and 1841 gave both farmers and city folk a reason to look elsewhere for a better life. Branching off the Oregon Trail were the Mormon Trail, leading to the Great Salt Lake, and the California Trail to San Francisco. The Santa Fe Trail was extended from Santa Fe to San Diego in 1847. These were all important routes for hopeful pioneers seeking a new life in the West. In 1869, the transcontinental railroad was completed, and migration by covered wagon receded. Exploration of the West was complete by 1872 and the frontier was declared closed.

In the 1880s, crop failures in Europe again brought waves of farmers from Northern and Western Europe to the Mississippi Valley and westward. Also at this time, immigrants from Southern and Eastern Europe began to increase in number. From 1851 to 1860, only 1 per cent of all immigrants were from this region. By the 1880s, this had increased to almost 20 per cent and in the first decade of the twentieth century the proportion topped 70 per cent. These people, Italians, Portuguese, Spanish, Greek, Russian, Polish and others, came in large numbers until the First World War. They mostly settled in large cities, where they worked in hard, low-paying jobs. Many had little education. They tended to congregate in ethnic communities, some of which degenerated into slums. While some assimilated quickly, Americanization was delayed for many.

In the 30 years preceding 1924, 16 million immigrants came to the United States and the ends of the two World Wars brought further surges of immigration from war-stricken countries. Immigration continues to this day. The most recent waves, beginning in the 1960s, come from Asia, Mexico and Central and South America, and from the West Indies, with a surge from Cuba in 1968. According to the 2000 census, the foreign-born population in the United States is 11.1 per cent of the total of 281,421,906.

Settlement, social class and the American ethos

Most colonists were middle-class or poor. The middle-class immigrants worked as farmers or tradesmen, while the poor worked as indentured servants. However, each colony also had some well-educated and learned men. This produced a measure of social stratification in the oldest cities on the East Coast although, as mentioned above, the Puritan founders of the New England colonies believed in a democratic society as part of their theology. Plantation culture, established in the eighteenth century in the south, was the most socially stratified region of the new land. The essence of the plantation system consisted of the large landowner, the white overseers and slaves. There was little room for the small farmer, and the white craftsman was subservient to the landowner. With the economy based on the cultivation of cotton, rice and tobacco, this system thrived until the Civil War. After that social differences were gradually reduced by greater access to schooling for all social classes.

In general, however, the strenuous demands of making a life in the New World tended to result in a levelling of social classes, particularly in the backwoods and on the frontier. As has been described above, much of the story of the settlement of the United States is one of pushing back the frontier. Frontier life, the pioneer spirit and the idea of setting out for a new land and building a new life are very much a part of the American heritage. Yet frontier life is harsh; there is little room for a privileged class but democracy thrives. A person who makes a sincere effort has the opportunity to succeed, at least as much as any of his or her neighbours has, so there is not an identifiable lower class. These conditions, which prevailed wherever the land was being settled, fostered the spirit of democracy, independence and ingenuity which have contributed to the success of the United States.

Economic success is enthusiastically embraced in the United States; Americans rejoice in their consumerism. They voraciously acquire material goods and modesty is not part of the national perspective. In general, bigger is better. Americans drive big cars, build big houses, have a lot of clothes and buy big-screen television sets. It is the national ideal to own one's own home. Houses built today normally have more bathrooms than bedrooms. There is expected to be a separate bedroom for each child in the family and also a 'master bedroom', which might be larger than an old-fashioned apartment. A nice new suburban home would be expected to have a den, a family room, a breakfast room (connected to the kitchen) and perhaps a TV room. The family should own at least two cars; if there are children old enough to drive, there might be more. There would be several telephones in the house, often with two telephone lines, and there would be several television sets, not to mention audio equipment and computers. Of course, middle- and working-class people and residents of older cities where such housing stock does not exist do not enjoy such conspicuous attributes of affluence; but this is the picture portrayed in the magazines, newspapers and TV shows about modern living. A wide choice of products of every sort is expected as a matter of course, whether it be fast food, laundry detergent, computers, cars, whiskey or underwear. There exists the stereotype of people trying to 'keep up with the Joneses', always trying to be able to show off material possessions at least as impressive as those of one's neighbours.

The general attitude of consumerism and showing off is also a characteristic of people's representations of themselves to the rest of society. Again, modesty does not have much of a place in the American mentality. It is normal for people to present themselves as being as accomplished, successful, capable and knowledgeable as possible, the only limit being what one thinks one can get away with. This does not come from a universally inflated ego; it is just the way things are done. A person who wants to advance in a job, in politics or in any sort of public undertaking will suffer from seeming to be a 'shrinking violet' and benefit by 'blowing his/her own horn'.

Social issues

This section addresses several aspects of American life that are objects of public and political controversy in the United States today. The set of topics is by no means exhaustive, but it attempts to be representative. The most glaring omission is racism and race relations, but this subject is touched on elsewhere in this chapter.

Homosexuality

With its legacy of Puritanism, the United States is only gradually coming to grips with the fact that homosexuality is an attribute of perhaps 5 per cent of the population. In 1993, President Clinton introduced to the US military the policy of 'Don't ask, don't tell', with the idea that no knowledge of a person's sexual orientation is more equitable than excluding gay men and women from military service. This works well enough when it is practised, but when a gay person's sexual orientation does become public for some reason, it causes considerable difficulty. Much of the general population is gradually increasing its acceptance of homosexuality, and more gay people are open about their sexual orientation. Gays tend to migrate to the cities, where the greater diversity of the population promotes greater tolerance of alternative lifestyles and they are often prominently represented among the well-educated, cultured and successful segments of society. This gives the gay community a strong voice in lobbying for fair treatment and changes are slowly being made in such areas as providing family health and insurance benefits for same-sex domestic partners, allowing same-sex marriage and permitting same-sex couples to adopt children. On the other hand, President Bill Clinton's nomination of James C. Hormel for the position of ambassador to Luxembourg brought about an uphill struggle for Senate confirmation. Hormel is gay and he is also a highly respected businessman, lawyer and philanthropist with an impressive record of 30 years of community service to his credit; yet three conservative Republicans managed to put a hold on his nomination, which they say they did because they were concerned that he would use the post of Ambassador to promote a 'gay agenda'. Nonetheless, Hormel's nomination was approved, and he served as ambassador to Luxembourg from June 1999 until December 2000. The latest flashpoint in this area concerns gay marriage.

AIDS

Since its appearance, diagnosis and rapid spread in the early 1980s, AIDS has been a highly charged and politicized public health issue. In the United States, as in other Western countries, its victims are predominantly members of stigmatized groups: homosexual men and drug addicts. The allocation of funds for research and treatment meets with strong resistance from conservative religious groups, which claim that homosexuality is a voluntary and sinful deviation from moral behaviour and should be punished. Most of the general public does not subscribe to this view, however, and after strenuous lobbying by the gay community, with the support of the medical community, AIDS is now treated as a general public health problem and receives considerable public funding.

Women's rights

The Nineteenth Amendment to the Constitution gave American women the right to vote in 1920, but women continued to be second-class citizens with respect to education, employment and women's medical issues, among other things. The most recent women's rights movement started in the 1960s, spearheaded by women such as Betty Friedan and the founding of the National Organization for Women. The movement snowballed throughout the 1970s, forcing the admission of women to professional schools and attempting, with modest success, to force the hiring of women in positions that had previously been closed to them and at salaries equal to those of men. Related issues followed, such as realistic maternity leave policies, flexible work schedules and the development of daytime childcare options for working mothers. The most recent women's issue to come into sharp focus is sexual harassment in the workplace.

Abortion

The Supreme Court of the United States decided the case of *Roe* v. *Wade* in 1973. This landmark decision for the first time allowed American women to have a legal abortion on demand during the first trimester of pregnancy. It also stipulated that the states could restrict but not prohibit abortion during the second trimester and that the states could regulate or prohibit abortion during the third trimester. It made abortion far more accessible than it ever had been before, but the battles of the Pro-Choice group (in favour of making abortion available to every woman who wishes it) and the Pro-Life side (in favour of prohibiting abortion on the grounds that the foetus has the right to be born and live its life) go on with unabated intensity. While most Americans favour a woman's right to decide whether to carry a pregnancy to term, conservative religious groups continue to have a loud voice on the issue and many restrictive laws have been passed at the state level. The debate over abortion also now involves important secondary issues, such as parental consent, insurance coverage for federal employees, funding for family planning services and contraception, and rules for protesters who attempt to interfere with the operations of abortion clinics.

Gun control

The Second Amendment to the Constitution is one of the most obscure. It says: 'A well regulated militia being necessary to the security of a free state, the right of the people to keep and bear arms shall not be infringed.' The National Rifle Association (NRA) and its supporters interpret this to mean that there should be no restrictions placed on gun ownership in the United States. Polls indicate that this position is opposed by the majority of Americans, but because the NRA forms a powerful political lobby, gun control remains a major social issue.

In the 1981 assassination attempt on then-president Ronald Reagan, Reagan's press secretary, James Brady, was crippled and suffered permanent brain damage from handgun fire. In the aftermath of this tragedy, a modest gun-control bill, known as the Brady Bill, was proposed in Congress and it was signed into law in 1993. It requires a five-day waiting period for the purchase of any handgun. During the waiting period, local law enforcement agents are required to conduct a background check on the would-be purchaser. The Brady Bill continues to be attacked by opponents of gun control, who hope to have it declared unconstitutional. When former Beatle John Lennon was murdered outside his New York City apartment building in 1980, there were an average of 29 handgun killings in the United States every day and 55 million handguns were believed to be in circulation.

It has long been the case that 911 (nine-one-one *or* nine-eleven) was the phone number you would dial in a dire emergency – if, for example, your house was on fire, or someone in the house was having a heart attack, or a robber had broken into your house. The phone number 911 still serves that purpose. However, since September 11, 2001, the term '9/11', said 'nine-eleven', has taken on a new meaning, referring to the terrorist attacks in which two hijacked airplanes were crashed into the World Trade Center in New York City and a third hijacked plane was crashed into the Pentagon building in Washington, D.C. In a fourth hijacked plane, the passengers apparently managed to prevent the hijackers from reaching their intended target (which was possibly the Capitol Building in Washington, D.C., where the US Congress meets) and the plane crashed in a field in a rural area of Pennsylvania. There were no survivors from any of the four flights. This day serves as a defining moment for many people in the United States. It burst the bubble of a sense of security, since it marked the first time there were terrorist attacks on US targets that originated outside the country. It has changed the American way of life in innumerable small and large ways. It has also changed the way the US relates to other countries.

Preservation of the environment

All of North America is rich in natural resources, but the burgeoning of the population, massive industrialization and the ruthless exploitation of those natural resources began threatening the health of the natural world at least by the middle of the nineteenth century. There continues today fierce competition between commercial interests and the concerns of Americans to preserve the land's natural heritage and to conserve non-renewable resources. Agencies of the government such as the Environmental Protection Agency, the US Fish Wildlife Service and the National Park Service, as well as private organizations such as Greenpeace, the National Wildlife Federation, the Audubon Society, the World Wildlife Fund, the Sierra Club, the Cousteau Society and the Nature Conservancy Council, are among the groups that seek to preserve the ecological health and the environmental beauty and diversity of the country and the planet.

Drugs

The use of illegal drugs in the United States is, as elsewhere, a serious social problem as much because it is illegal as because it is harmful to the individual user. Illegality keeps drug prices high so people commit crimes in order to get the money to buy them. It also contributes dramatically to the spread of blood-borne diseases such as AIDS, because it makes it difficult to obtain sterile needles, so drug addicts re-use and share them. The US has never come close to developing a policy that would reduce the demand, the supply or the social damage of illegal drug use. Some communities have decriminalized the possession of marijuana in small quantities, but efforts to make marijuana available for medical use as a pain reliever have met with strong resistance from conservative groups. Recreational drug use continues to be widely practised by college students and other adults, however, as well as by high-school students, younger children and citizens from all classes of society.

Health care

The United States is the only Western nation with no comprehensive national health insurance plan. President Bill Clinton's strenuous efforts to develop a programme that would provide coverage for the general population have been opposed repeatedly. The prospects for the passage of any such programme in this generation are dismal.

There are two tax-supported programmes, established in 1965, which provide partial medical coverage for specific groups: Medicare, which covers people over the age of 65, and Medicaid, which applies to the poor. Under these plans, as well as under private plans, coverage is partial. For example, during a calendar-year period, Medicare will pay 80 per cent of a doctor's charges, with an annual deductible of $100. Therefore, the subscriber has to pay the first $100 and then 20 per cent of the doctor's charges for the rest of the year, unless he/she has supplementary insurance. Employers with more than a certain number of employees are required to offer medical care plans with private insurers to their employees. The employer's contract with the insurance company typically provides lower rates than an individual can get by him/herself and the employer pays part or all of the premium.

However it is obtained, medical insurance is a major expense for Americans. Since it is an elective expense rather than a tax obligation (except for the costs of Medicare and Medicaid, which generally do not benefit those who are paying the taxes), many Americans simply do not have any health insurance or at least not adequate health insurance. When a serious medical problem arises, they either cannot have appropriate care or they incur huge debts. It is hard to understand how a society that considers itself civilized can permit this situation to persist.

System of government

A detailed description of the American system of government would fill a library, but a minimal outline should be useful in explaining how many aspects of society work in the United States.

The Founding Fathers met in Philadelphia in 1787 to write the Constitution of the United States and they voted to adopt this document on 17 September 1787. The Constitution sets up the system of government, but it does not explicitly include the enumeration of certain rights. These rights were listed in ten Amendments to the Constitution, which collectively are known as the Bill of Rights. This will be discussed briefly below.

The government established by the Constitution provides a system of checks and balances: the power of each branch is constrained by the powers of the other branches. There are three branches of the federal government. They are the executive, headed by the President, who appoints a cabinet of officers as his highest level of assistants; the legislature, consisting of the House of Representatives and the Senate, together referred to as Congress; and the judiciary, which consists of the system of federal (US, as opposed to state-level) courts, with the Supreme Court being the highest court in the land.

A few examples will illustrate the system of checks and balances. Congress has the sole power to pass laws. However, the President proposes programmes and asks Congress to pass legislation to implement them. Bills must be passed by both the House and the Senate, and then they must be signed by the President. If the President vetoes a bill, it can still become law if the House and Senate vote on it again and both houses pass it by a two-thirds majority. Even if a law is passed by the override of a presidential veto, it can be struck down later if it is challenged as being contrary to the Constitution. This matter would go through the court system. Thus all three branches of government have a say in what a law is, but no one branch has exclusive control.

Another simple example of the system is the appointment of federal judges. The President selects the prospective new judge, but his nomination is subject to approval by the Senate. Senate confirmation hearings can be hostile indeed and many a presidential nominee has not attained the office. Once confirmed, federal judges serve for life (on condition of good behaviour), freeing them from any obligation to either the appointing President or the confirming Senators.

The two houses of Congress have somewhat different structures. There are 435 members of the House of Representatives. They are elected for terms of two years and their numbers and distribution are determined by the population of their respective states. Each state is divided into Congressional districts, which are all about the same size in population, and the voters in each district elect one representative. Redistricting is carried out periodically, as the distribution of the population changes. As examples, populous New York presently has 31 representatives, while little Connecticut has 6. Both Representatives and Senators can be re-elected any number of times, unlike the President, who is limited to two terms. Senators are elected for a term of six years, and there are two for each state. The powers of the two bodies are similar, but not identical. The House has the sole right to introduce legislation having to do with revenue, while the Senate has the power to ratify treaties and confirm presidential appointments.

The Constitution establishes the structure of the government. It also establishes a mechanism for change, which is the passage of Amendments. A proposed Amendment must be approved by both houses of Congress, and then it must be ratified by the legislatures of three-quarters of the states before it becomes part of the Constitution. As mentioned above, the first ten Amendments constitute the Bill of Rights, which enumerates the most basic and cherished rights of Americans: freedom of speech, freedom of the press, freedom of religion, the right not to bear witness against oneself, the right against unreasonable search and seizure, the right to a jury trial, the right to confront one's accusers and others. These rights are truly an integral part of the fabric of American society. Many of them are household words; any ordinary citizen can talk about his Fifth Amendment rights, the right to bear arms or the due process clause.

The Tenth Amendment declares that powers not assigned to the federal government by the Constitution are reserved to the states or to the people. Much of the law that governs American life therefore is state law. Most crimes are defined by the state; murder, for example, is not a federal offence – you may only be tried, convicted, imprisoned or executed for this by a state's courts. The driving age and drinking age are also set by each state. The state government usually mimics that of the federal government in structure, with a constitution, a governor as the chief executive officer, a house and senate and a parallel court system.

Since the ratification of the Constitution and the Bill of Rights, 17 additional amendments have been passed, making a total of 27. Many of them have a profound impact on daily life. These include the amendments that prohibit slavery, forbid denial of the right to vote on account of 'race, color, or previous condition of servitude', allow Congress the power to impose and collect income taxes, give women the right to vote and limit the President to two terms of office. Undoubtedly the bleakest moment in Constitutional history was the passage of the Eighteenth Amendment, which prohibited the manufacture, sale and use of alcoholic beverages. This absurdity was fortunately ended by the passage of the Twenty-first Amendment,

Section 1 of which simply states: 'The eighteenth article of amendment to the Constitution of the United States is hereby repealed.'

Holidays

Much of American culture is trumpeted around the world by film and the mass media. US contributions to film, sports, literature, the arts, politics and so forth are beamed around the world the instant they come into existence. However, American holidays and holiday practices, while very much a part of the core culture, are not so well known outside the country. Only the most important and most specifically American holidays will be discussed here.

New Year's Eve is a time for parties with friends. People get together and wear party hats, blow on noisemakers, drink a lot and kiss everybody in sight when midnight strikes. Millions of people have their televisions tuned to watch the ball drop in Times Square at the exact moment of the beginning of the new year. The next day is universally a holiday from work, as people sleep off their hangovers and clean up after their parties.

President's Day is held on a Monday between 12 February and 22 February, which are the birthdays of Abraham Lincoln and George Washington respectively. Government offices and some businesses close for the occasion. People might hang the American flag outside their houses, but otherwise it is a low-key observance. Martin Luther King Day, observed on the third Monday of January, is treated the same way. It honours the birthday (on 15 January 1929) of this great African American civil rights leader who was assassinated in 1968.

The Bill of Rights begins by stating: 'Congress shall make no law respecting an establishment of religion, or prohibiting the free exercise thereof ...'. Thus, Easter, Christmas, Yom Kippur, Ramadan, and other religious occasions have no government-mandated observance. However, businesses may close if they choose to do so on Good Friday, Easter Sunday, Easter Monday, or at any other time, and some do. Most employers make allowances for employees to take vacation days in order to observe the religious practices of their private choice.

Memorial Day was originally termed Decoration Day. It was established to honour the soldiers who died in the Civil War, and it was set for 30 May. Its intent was later extended to honour Americans who died in combat at any time or in any place, and, along with many other holidays, it is now observed on a Monday, the last Monday in May. It is celebrated with community parades and backyard barbecues, as friends and families get together to mark the beginning of the summer season.

The Fourth of July, also called Independence Day, commemorates the adoption of the Declaration of Independence on 4 July 1776. Almost every community has a parade of community groups, veterans' groups, Boy Scouts and Girl Scouts, bands and anything else that belongs to a joyful and festive occasion. Typically, people get together with their families or groups of friends and have a barbecue, preparing hot dogs, hamburgers and other all-American fare and eating outdoors. At night there are displays of fireworks throughout the land.

Labor Day in the United States is observed on the first Monday in September. There is really no conscious connection between Labor Day and any aspect of the Labor Movement. It is universally a holiday from work, celebrated much the same way as the Fourth of July, except without fireworks, and vastly fewer communities are likely to have a Labor Day parade. The main thrust of this holiday is to mark the end of the summer vacation period. Children go back to school, typically sometime during the week following Labor Day, and fall seems to be in the air.

Halloween, on 31 October, is centred around children. It is not a holiday from work or school, but it is a festive time. Children dress up in costumes and go from house to house to get candy, or sweets. The most traditional costume is that of a ghost or a witch, but the awareness of the source and original meaning of the occasion ('hallowed evening', the night before All Saints' Day) is totally absent for many people. There are costumes that portray everything from the current US President to Humpty-Dumpty. Children usually go from house to house in small groups. If they are quite young, they will be accompanied by a parent who will wait a few metres away while the children ring the doorbell. When someone answers the door, the children shout: 'Trick or treat!' The homeowner feigns surprise and anxiety (over the non-existent trick that he/she is being threatened with) and admires the costumes, while dropping a couple of pieces of candy in the bag that each child is carrying. Then the children go off to the next house to continue their evening of trick-or-treating (as it is called) until their bags are full, it is past their bedtime and they have completed the rounds of their neighbourhood. All Saints' Day, on 1 November, is virtually unknown in the United States.

Thanksgiving is a stand-out among American holidays. One reason is that it occurs on a Thursday, which leads to a four-day weekend for many people. Schools are closed both on Thanksgiving and on the following day, and some offices and businesses are also closed all or part of the Friday. Thanksgiving is set for the fourth Thursday in November. It is a harvest festival, commemorating the first Thanksgiving, a feast held in 1621 by the Pilgrims who settled the Plymouth Bay colony. As described above, they had arrived in Massachusetts the year before and barely survived the first winter. The natives helped them, teaching them to plant corn and trading other foods and goods. Supposedly, the Pilgrims shared the celebration of their first harvest with their Native American benefactors and they gave thanks to God for the bounty of the earth. While many people do have religious associations as part of the meaning of Thanksgiving for them, it is not a religious holiday, and it is not an occasion for attending church services.

Thanksgiving is primarily a family holiday. Family members often travel long distances to be together and the day before Thanksgiving is one of the busiest travel days of the year. Friends may attend a Thanksgiving dinner, but the guests would be whole families, not just parents leaving their children at home with a babysitter. (It would be impossible to get a babysitter on Thanksgiving anyway; all the babysitters would be having Thanksgiving dinner with their own families!) The celebration is nothing more than having dinner, but it is a long, leisurely meal and people spend most of the day socializing. The centrepiece of the feast is a whole turkey, most often filled with stuffing (also called 'dressing'), which has been roasted in the oven. For a sizeable bird, this takes several hours, during which time the house becomes filled with its delicious aroma. Root vegetables, such as potatoes and squash, are usual accompaniments, along with gravy made from the turkey juices. There is usually pie for dessert, pumpkin pie being the most traditional. After more than 350 years, the composition of the meal follows rather closely what the original celebrants would have eaten.

The Friday after Thanksgiving is the 'official' beginning of the Christmas shopping season, although merchants nowadays seem to start advertising for Christmas around the time of Halloween. In any case, Black Friday is the biggest shopping day of the year, as people who are off from school or work fill the shops and malls, searching for Christmas gifts and enjoying the holiday decorations that have sprung up all over every town. The next four weeks are a veritable frenzy of shopping, buying and decorating. As Christmas nears, there are also Christmas parties in every office, in schools and in homes; eating and drinking are added to the list of seasonal over-indulgences. (The most frequently heard – and broken – New Year's resolution is to go on a diet.)

Christmas is more commercialized and more secularized than any other religious holiday. Schools have vacation and virtually all offices and businesses are closed for Christmas itself. The observance of Christmas is different in different families. The religious aspect of the holiday varies in accordance with one's beliefs. On the secular side, people buy a Christmas tree and decorate it with lights, tinsel and ornaments. Christmas gifts may be put under the tree ahead of time for all to admire. Some families open gifts on Christmas Eve; others on Christmas morning. Usually the children hang Christmas stockings on the fireplace mantel (or a substitute) with the expectation that Santa

Claus will come down the chimney during the night before Christmas and fill the stockings with candycanes, nuts and small gifts. Depending on a family's own traditions, Santa Claus may also bring gifts for the children that are put under the tree.

Christmas dinner is also part of the family celebration. A whole roasted turkey, identical to that of Thanksgiving, is a staple of the Christmas dinner menu, but many families substitute ham or have something else entirely. The celebration of Christmas ends on 25 December. The following days see people rushing back to the malls to exchange unwanted Christmas gifts, to take advantage of the post-Christmas sales and simply to enjoy the festive air of the holiday season. Christmas decorations, both in public and in homes, may stay in place for days or weeks. Christmas trees may be found waiting for the trash truck throughout January as life gradually returns to normal and people get down to the business of the new year.

Characteristic features of American English

Some of the features of American English have already been discussed in Chapter 2. This section will describe in more detail the phonological features that set American English apart from British English and outline the dialect areas of the United States on the basis of phonological data. There will follow some comments on other levels of linguistic structure and their distribution in the dialect areas.

Only two features are needed to account for the bulk of the differences that give American English its vast difference in flavour from British English. First, most dialects of American English are r-pronouncing. Second, the 'starting point' for a short *a* in American English is in low front position, and in many dialects, some or all of the allophones of short *a* have been raised and tensed as well. These points will be explained in detail below.

R-pronouncing

The vocalization of r has been discussed elsewhere, so only the briefest review is needed here. As a linguistic variable in English, r-vocalization (or r-lessness) refers both to r preceding a consonant, with or without a following syllable boundary, and to r preceding a word boundary. Thus *card*, *person*, and *her* are all candidates for r -vocalization in English. On the other hand *raven*, *break* and *merry*, all with a vowel following the r, never show r-vocalization in standard English, not in the US or anywhere else. Thus the r that is of interest in distinguishing varieties of English should properly be termed 'pre-consonantal and pre-pausal r'.

R-lessness was not an indigenous feature of English in North America. It developed in Britain in the late eighteenth century and was subsequently adopted as a prestigious import from London in all the major seaports of the United States, with the exception of Philadelphia. (The City of Brotherly Love was founded and dominated by Quakers, with few social ties to England and with a less numerous and less prominent population of Loyalists. The influence of London was much weaker there than in Boston, New York, Baltimore, Richmond, Charleston and Savannah.)

Since the Second World War, constricted (that is, unvocalized) r has emerged as a prestige feature in areas that have traditionally been r-less. In Boston, for example, in three generations of an upper-middle-class family observed 20 years ago, the grandparents were entirely r-less, the parents were mostly r-less, and the children, in their mid-20s, were r-pronouncing in almost all words, with a few exceptions such as 'drawer'. The r-pronouncing variety is now typical of the younger generations of the upper middle class in Boston, but it has not advanced so far among groups with lower social status. It remains to be seen whether constricted r will eventually become generalized throughout the New England speech community.

The case of New York City is one that has been examined systematically. Labov's (1966) well-known study of three department stores in New York showed that r was a strongly socially stratified variable, with significantly more constricted r produced by sales people and other staff in Saks Fifth Avenue, the most prestigious store, than by those in Macy's, a middle-level store. The staff in Macy's, in turn, consistently produced more constricted r than those in S. Klein, a discount store.

Labov's fieldwork was conducted in 1962. In 1986, Joy Fowler completed a detailed replication of Labov's study (reported in Labov, 1994), with results that strongly confirmed the intricate pattern of effects of age, social class and stylistic variation (casual emphatic) found by Labov. She also found that the use of constricted r had increased in the 24 years that had elapsed. The increase was small, only 10 per cent or less. These findings corroborate every casual listener's impression of New York, that it is still strongly r-vocalizing, although, clearly, change is taking place.

Changes are found to be taking place in the south, too. Feagin (1990) has reported a rapid increase in constricted r in Anniston, Alabama. There, r-vocalization has always been stratified along class lines, as is suggested above. The large landowners were of the original English stock of settlers, and they had maintained close ties to England. The working class had a heavy concentration of the less affluent Ulster Scots immigrants, who settled the Piedmont and gradually moved into the cities, and they had brought constricted 'r' with them from their homelands. Upper-middle-class Anniston speakers have been r-less for generations, but this is now changing. Younger speakers in Anniston use constricted *r* much of the time, joining their working-class peers.

One may ask: 'What difference does it make if you do or don't vocalize *r*?' The answer is that it makes a huge difference. The *r* that follows a vowel has a powerful effect on the acoustics of the vowel. When the *r* is pronounced, it conditions many and varied alterations of the preceding vowel. In Philadelphia, for instance, it is an old, established characteristic that *a* before *r* moves in the direction of *o*, so people joke that Philadelphians *pork their cores* on the street. If *r* is vocalized, vast numbers of homonyms can be generated, such as *sauce* and *source*, *card* and *cod*, *fared* and *fed*. The list clearly could go on for a long time, since *r* is a very frequently occurring phoneme. Intervocalic *r* can also be involved in the merger of preceding vowels. In Philadelphia, most native speakers have a merger or a near-merger of the vowels in *merry* and *Murray*, so you might hear someone talking about going on a *furry* boat ride. In the Midwest and West, speakers merge *Mary*, *merry* and *marry*. These mergers are a rich source of misunderstandings among speakers of different dialects.

Raising and tensing of short *a*

The other phonological variable that helps set the tone of American English is short *a*, the vowel of *cat*, *bag* and *laugh*. British RP divides these into two classes, the short *a* of *cat* and *bag* and the broad *a* of 'laugh'. Some dialects of British English do not distinguish these two classes and then all of short *a* is low and front, though not as front as in the US, and, more importantly, it is not a candidate for raising. In the United States, short *a* may be low, but it is definitely a front vowel. There is no broad *a* class at all, except for some older speakers in Eastern New England.

In many US dialects, some or all of the allophones of short *a* undergo what linguists call 'tensing'. This term is somewhat difficult to define. It is said that tense vowels are actually produced with more muscle tension, or more force of articulation, but it is perhaps clearer to say that tense front vowels are more front than their lax counterparts, and they tend to have off glides in the direction of 'schwa'.

Short *a*, if tense, can also be raised in the direction of short *e*, even as high as short *i*. It has been recounted that a New York family named their new baby daughter Ann, and they were criticized for giving their child a boy's name, because in New York *Ann* sounds like *Ian*. Similarly, in experiments on cross-dialectal comprehension, listeners from Birmingham, Alabama, and Philadelphia, Pennsylvania, mis-interpreted a Chicago girl's production of 'that' as 'the act' about half the time in three conditions: when they heard the single word 'that' in isolation, in the phrase 'scared of that', and even in the full sentence, 'And so, nobody really got scared of that.' Listeners from Chicago had about as much difficulty as listeners from other areas when they heard only the isolated word, but they were moderately successful in understanding the full sentence correctly.

The preceding detailed description of a phonetic process is important because it accounts for the short *a* that characterizes many American dialects and it is especially important because this vowel is one that speakers are aware of: they use it to label themselves and others and they disapprove of it. The stigmatization of this vowel varies from mild to powerful. A generation ago in Philadelphia, schoolteachers tried to change the speech of their pupils to reduce the use of extreme forms of tense short *a*. Many Philadelphians will declare that they never say *bee-id* for *bad*, but in fact all native Philadelphians say something along these lines, though not always to such an extreme. In the Midwest, people apologize for the 'awful' sound of their 'flat' *a*s. Phonetically, the Midwestern tense and raised short *a* is about the same as tense short *a* in Philadelphia and New York. This vowel is also described by non-linguists as 'nasal'. It is generally agreed that it is an 'ugly' sound, but speakers are generally resigned to accepting that nothing can be done about it.

The dialect areas of the United States

If asked about dialect differences in the US, most lay people would probably first distinguish the North from the South, then perhaps mention New England (Boston) and New York City. This is a first approximation, but there are additional important dialect differences which also reflect historical and cultural dividing lines and therefore should be outlined. The dialect areas of the United States, as determined by current studies of differences in pronunciation, are shown in Figure 7.1, which the reader might want to use as reference while reading the following text.

This and following maps have been constructed in the course of two research projects carried out at the Linguistics Laboratory of the University of Pennsylvania: 'A Telephone Survey of Sound Change in Progress', funded by the National Science Foundation and Bell-Northern Research Inc. (BNR), and 'A Phonological Atlas of North American English', funded by the National Endowment for the Humanities and BNR/Nortel Inc. These and subsequent projects have culminated in the publication of the first atlas of the sound systems of all of English-speaking North America (Labov, Ash and Boberg, 2006).

We begin this discussion of dialects in the middle of the country. **The Inland North** includes the highly industrialized area rimming the Great Lakes, with urban sprawl spreading out from Chicago, Detroit, Cleveland, Buffalo, Rochester and Syracuse. It is most clearly defined by the Northern Cities (Chain) Shift.

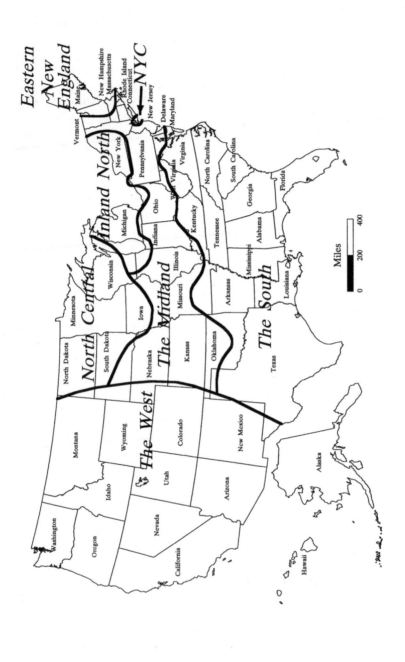

Figure 7.1 Dialect areas of the United States (after Labov, Ash and Boberg, 1997)

The Northern Cities Shift is a rotation of the short vowels affecting a large part of the lexicon and it produces the distinctive sound of this variety of northern speech. The tensing and raising of short *a*, mentioned above, is the first and most advanced step in this process and it affects all short *a* words. Thus, for an extreme speaker, *tack* can sound like *tee-ek*. Short *e* moves towards the back, out of the way of short *a*, so *tech* can sound like *tuck*. Short /u/ moves back and down, so *tuck* can sound like *talk*. The vowel of *talk* moves down and front towards the vowel of *tock*, and, finally, the short *o* of *tock* moves front so that it sounds like the *tack* of speakers from other dialect areas. All of these features were examined in the studies of cross-dialectal comprehension mentioned above, in which natives of other areas (Philadelphia and Birmingham, Alabama) listened to Chicago speakers' productions of such words uttered in spontaneous speech and then isolated by digital means. The listeners regularly interpreted *steady* as *study*, *busses* as *bosses*, *talks* as *tocks*, and *socks* as *sacks*. With the addition of a phrasal context, listeners' comprehension improved in some cases but not in others. With the context of an entire sentence, more listeners were able to correct their interpretations, but some of the items remained opaque to many listeners even then. In general, Americans believe that they can understand their fellow speakers from different parts of the country, and indeed they can, but the dialect differences are great enough to interfere with comprehension when the context is reduced.

The North Central region includes most of Wisconsin, the northern half of Iowa, the north-eastern part of South Dakota, essentially all of North Dakota and Minnesota. This is the area where the Scandinavian influence is greatest and it also received large numbers of German settlers. It is characterized phonologically by conservative long high and mid vowels; the stereotype is in words such as *Minnesooota*, where the *o* is a long, back monophthong. While speakers in much of the rest of the country are moving this vowel to the front, as in British speech (*We're gewing he-om* for *We're going home*), the North Central region remains a stronghold of vowels that sound distinctly Scandinavian.

Moving back to the East Coast, a small but prominent dialect area is **Eastern New England**, centred on Boston and also including eastern Massachusetts, New Hampshire and Maine. The speech of this area has already been discussed insofar as it concerns *r*-vocalization. Another important characteristic of the area is the merger of the vowels in *cot* and *caught*. The merger means that these two words – and all other such pairs with these vowels – are pronounced the same, with a low, rounded vowel that is articulated far back in the mouth. It affects a large number of words, such as *odd* and *awed*, *stock* and *stalk*, *Don* and *Dawn*, *pond* and *pawned*. Theoretically, such mergers, resulting in many homonyms, could produce frequent opportunities for confusion. However, research shows that members of a speech community who share such a feature apparently learn to attend to disambiguating information provided in the context. In a large collection of naturally occurring misunderstandings gathered by members of the linguistics department at the University of Pennsylvania for a project headed by William Labov, it has been found that confusion occurs primarily on the part of a listener from a place where the merger does not exist when speaking with someone from a place where the merger does exist. For example, I was once asked by a Boston native, 'How did the coffee machine work out?', referring to a coffee machine loaned to the department for a small conference. I am a linguistic native of the Chicago area and I make a clear distinction in my own speech between *cot* (front and unrounded) and *caught* (back and rounded). I understood *coffee machine* as *copy machine* and launched into a long-winded story about difficulties in getting the photocopier to work properly in the preparation of my handout for the conference. Labov (1994) cites many other examples of confusion between *copy* and *coffee* by academics at conferences (where, as he points out, both items are prominent fixtures), but it is virtually always the person who makes a distinction between *cot* and *caught* in her/his own speech who is misled.

It should be noted that mergers typically are not stigmatized by the population that produces them. People are conservative about the norms of their language, so that Philadelphians berate each other for the sound of their *bad*, New Yorkers do likewise for their *coffee* and everybody scorns those who say *dis and dat* for *this and that*. However, the mergers of *cot* and *caught*, of *Mary, merry* and *marry* in the Midwest and West and of *which* and *witch* by practically everybody attract no public notice.

New York City is a dialect area all by itself. While the characteristics of the speech of other large cities spread beyond the city proper to the surrounding suburbs and nearby towns, New York City speech is severely limited nearly to the city limits. It is believed that this is because it is a strongly stigmatized dialect. I once casually remarked to a highly cultivated gentleman I met at a dinner party that he must have come from New York originally, and he reacted with horror. 'How did you know I come from New York?' he demanded. 'I've been trying to lose my accent for thirty years! No one can tell I'm from New York!'

Distinctiveness has another side as well. Most people feel affection and loyalty towards their home cities and neighbourhoods and New Yorkers may feel especially entitled to hold this attitude, as their hometown is undeniably the business and cultural capital of the country (if not of the Western world, or perhaps of the universe, as many New Yorkers might assert). The recognition value of the New York dialect can outweigh whatever negative prestige it holds, at least for speakers who are secure in their place in society. One woman, a lawyer from Brooklyn, told me that she was very pleased to be recognized all over the world as being a New Yorker by her speech.

New York City speech is a mixed bag of features, like other Midland cities, as will be discussed further below. Some of the linguistic variables that are distinctive in New York have already been mentioned: r-lessness, the tensing and raising of short *a* (but only in certain sets of words, not in all, as in the Inland North) and the substitution of stops for interdental fricatives reported by Labov (1966), that is, *dis* for *this* and *tink* for *think*. Another characteristic of New York speech is a high back, rounded production of the vowel in *coffee, caught, talk* and so forth. This pronunciation is stigmatized by middle-class speakers, while the working class seems to be indifferent to it (Labov, 1966). Another infamous, universally stigmatized stereotype of New York City speech is *oi* for *er*; any reference to this variable usually evokes the expression *Toity-Toid Street* for *Thirty-Third Street*.

The South is by no means uniform, but the broad outlines of Southern speech are found throughout a grand sweep of a geographical area. The Mason-Dixon Line, the border between Pennsylvania and Maryland, is the traditional dividing line between North and South, between the Union and the Confederacy during the Civil War of 1861 to 1865. Linguistically, we draw the dialect boundary of the South a little to the south of the Mason-Dixon Line at its eastern end. It passes through the bottom of Delaware, the middle of Maryland and the top of West Virginia, then more or less follows the Ohio river along the southern boundaries of Ohio, Indiana and Illinois. From there, it passes through the southern part of Missouri and the middle of Oklahoma, and it also includes Texas. This is a large and populous area, which history, culture and speech have set apart from the rest of the United States in innumerable ways.

Southern speech could be defined by just one linguistic variable, the monophthongization of the vowel in 'I' and *ride*. This is a feature that everyone throughout the entire country is aware of; the youngest child in Alaska probably knows that he/she can sound like a Southerner by saying: *Ah'm takin' mah tahm (I'm taking my time).* There is a long-standing social division over one aspect of this straightforward situation though. The monophthongization is considered perfectly acceptable in the words mentioned so far; however, it is NOT acceptable when a voiceless consonant follows the vowel. A voiceless consonant is one for which there is no voicing accompanying the consonant itself, as for *s, p, t, k*, among others, as opposed to *z, b, d, g* and others which are voiced. Therefore, if a person says *Ah lahk whaht rahs* for *I like white rice*, he/she is not only Southern, but may also be labelled as a hillbilly, hick, redneck or some other pejorative term. However, the weight of this social stigma seems to be lessening in recent years.

The first phrase transcribed above as an example of Southern speech illustrates another characteristic of Southern speech that deserves mention. In all dialects of English, there is alternation between two variants of the suffix '-ing'. This is a frequently occurring form that is found in the progressive forms of verbs, as in 'walking', and also in nouns that are derived from verbs, such as 'wedding'; in a few nouns that are not transparently derived from verbs, such as 'ceiling', and in the indefinite forms 'something', 'nothing', 'anything', and 'everything'. The Standard English form is '-ing'. The principal alternant is pronounced as 'in' and is commonly written '-in'' to show 'dialect' speech or informal speech. All speakers use both forms (though many would deny it), but in most of the United States the '-in'' form is unquestionably marked as informal; the self-styled guardians of purity in language call it 'sloppy' or 'lazy'. However, in the South, the '-in'' form is the norm. The most proper, affluent and well-educated southern belle will be dancin' the night away at Cousin Tillie's weddin'.

In addition to these features of Southern speech, of which people are consciously aware, Southerners exhibit the Southern Shift, which moves some vowels in directions opposite those of the Northern Cities Shift discussed above. The basic elements of the Southern Shift are that the long front vowels move to a lower position and the short front vowels rise and may be lengthened. This means that the vowel called long *e* sounds like long *a*, and the vowel called long *a* moves in the direction of long *i*. As part of the experiment described above, in which listeners tried to understand words taken out of context, a Birmingham, Alabama, woman's pronunciation of 'beatin'', taken from the sentence, 'No, he started beatin' me and then he said, "I let you win!"' was heard as 'baitin'' by about 85 per cent of the listeners from Chicago and Philadelphia. Similarly, her pronunciation of 'weight' taken from the sentence 'She's on a Weight Watcher's diet now, so she eats a lot of cottage cheese' was heard as *white* or something similar by more than half of the listeners from other areas. Thus the opening line of the national anthem, 'O say can you see', so pronounced amid the skyscrapers, forests, steel towns, cornfields and deserts of the North and West can be transcribed as 'O sigh can you say' in Dixie.

The South is also famous for the Southern drawl. This is a lengthening and diphthongization which can affect any vowel. With the short front vowels, which tend to rise to a higher position, it results in, for example, 'set' being heard as 'say it' (in the sentence 'Yes, and everybody's so upSET') and 'tram' being heard as 'train' (in the sentence 'Last time I went to Albuquerque it was in March, and there was snow, and we rode the TRAM.')

The West, according to the distribution of linguistic features, begins a short distance to the east of the Rocky Mountains. It includes Montana, Wyoming, Colorado, New Mexico and the states further west, as well as the westernmost parts of the Dakotas, Nebraska and Texas. It is an even greater area than the South, but it is very different terrain. There are a few very densely populated urban centres, but there are also vast deserts and rugged mountains. These result in large areas that are relatively empty of people, making any dialect map based on representative sampling look rather sparse. Nonetheless, the West exhibits some defining linguistic features. One is the merger of the vowels in *cot* and *caught*, which was discussed above. In the West, the vowel that results from the merger can be pronounced either with or without rounding; the distinction in rounding has been neutralized along with the distinction in vowel quality.

Linguists notice a number of other features of Western speech, but they are miscellaneous in character and need not be enumerated here. In general, Western speakers do not notice anything remarkable about their speech, either fine or ugly, and they are apt to say that they 'don't have an accent'.

This discussion has so far covered the North, the South and the West, but there remains a stretch of land in the middle, with at least ten major cities, stretching more than halfway across the continent. This is the **Midland**, which spreads west from Philadelphia on the East Coast. It includes most of Pennsylvania, with Pittsburgh in the western part of the state. It includes most of Ohio, with Columbus and Cincinnati, and continues west through Indiana, with Indianapolis in its centre. It takes in most of Illinois and the parts of Missouri and Iowa that are south of the North and north of the South. Missouri is girded by two very important population centres, St Louis and Kansas City, and Iowa has a major population centre in Des Moines. Finally, the Midland meets the West after covering part of Oklahoma, with Oklahoma City, all of Kansas and most of Nebraska, including Omaha.

The Midland is characterized linguistically by its diversity. Each city seems to be going its own way, making interesting and unique changes in its vowel system. A catalogue of the features that have been remarked has no place in this general discussion, but a few of the unique characteristics of Philadelphia have already been mentioned, such as the merger of *merry* and *Murray*. To offer just one other simple example, it is found in Pittsburgh that speakers monophthongize the vowel of 'eye', as is done in the South; the result sounds like the vowel of 'hot'. They also monophthongize the vowel of 'house', and it sounds the same as the monophthongized vowel of 'eye'. Thus 'mice' and 'mouse' are homonyms, as are 'file' and 'fowl', and 'down' and 'Don'. 'Pines', 'ponds' and 'pounds' can all sound alike. One begins to wonder how people can communicate at all!

There has not been extensive research on the Midland as a whole, but it seems that in each city there is some Northern influence and some Southern influence. Mere geography would dictate this, and it is plausible that the unique character of each population centre in the Midland results from the particular mixture of influences that are at work in each place and from the unique solution to the problem of resolving conflicting pressures on the linguistic system into a coherent phonological structure that is arrived at in each place.

Lexical features

Traditional dialectology in the United States has focused mainly on the distribution of words, rather than sounds. Attention has been concentrated on specialized vocabulary in rural areas, connected with activities such as farming and cooking and with items such as horse-drawn carriages that have changed in recent times, with many of the words now forgotten. Despite the difference in focus, the research on lexical variation produces dialect maps that agree very well with the description above based on pronunciation.

In a larger perspective, the subject of lexical variation in the United States seems minor in the context of English worldwide. The differences within the United States are absurdly few in comparison to the differences in lexicon between the United States and, for example, Britain. There is no obvious relationship between the members of the American/British pairs elevator/lift, truck/lorry, sweater/jumper, thumbtack/drawing pin, mail/post, I'll call you/I'll give you a ring and innumerable others. There are, indeed, some examples of different terms for the same thing in different places within the US, but they seem insignificant next to the massive differences between British and American lexicons. Many of the examples that come to mind have to do with food, such as the term for a sandwich on a long roll, containing cold cuts, sliced tomatoes, shredded lettuce and oil and vinegar. In different parts of the US this may be called a submarine (sandwich), a hero, a hoagie or a poor boy.

Another universally known food item is the sweetened, non-alcoholic carbonated beverage. There are a number of generic terms for this, as can be seen from Figure 7.2. 'Soda' is solid in the East, including all of New England, most of New York State and Eastern Pennsylvania. 'Pop' predominates throughout the Midland, the Inland North, the North Central region and the West, although California and other states of the Southwest seem to be subject to considerable influence from the East on this point, with a predominance of 'soda'

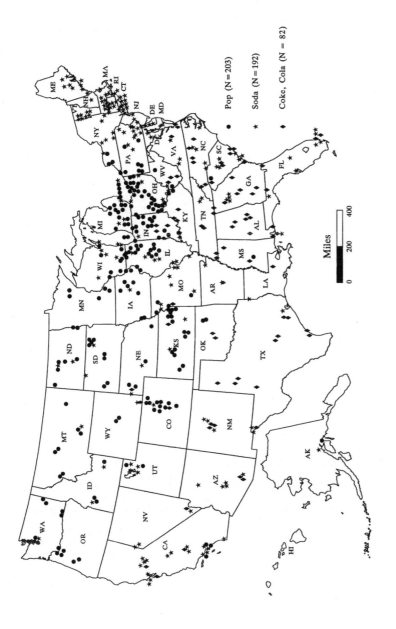

Figure 7.2 Generic terms for a carbonated beverage

speakers. (In the Midwest, where 'pop' is the usual term, an alternative is 'soda pop'. This clearly relates to the 'soda' of the East, although Easterners do not seem to view 'soda pop' as a viable alternative to 'soda'.) The South is distinct in using the term 'coke' or 'cola' as a generic term. To northern ears it sounds strange indeed to hear 'You want a coke?'; 'Yeah, how about a Sprite?'

Grammatical features

There also exists regional differentiation at the level of grammatical features with marginal status. These are constructions which are not discussed in any grammar books, either for native speakers or for second language learners of English. They are rarely noticed or commented on. One example is referred to by linguists as 'positive ANYMORE'. It is a generalization of the domain of the word 'anymore', which indicates a contrast between present and past situations. Standard American English allows 'John doesn't like Susie anymore', which means that John previously liked Susie but that has changed, and now he does not like her. A sentence with 'positive anymore' is 'Cars sure are expensive anymore', which means that cars previously did not seem to be very expensive, but now they do. The regional distribution of this form is shown in Figure 7.3, which clearly shows positive 'anymore' to be primarily a Midland feature that has made some inroads in the West and South.

These findings parallel the acceptability of another marginal grammatical form, 'needs Xed', that is, 'needs' followed by a past participle. This construction is an alternative to the standard form of 'needs' followed by an infinitive, as in 'This job needs to be done' or by a gerund, as in 'This job needs doing'. Figure 7.4 shows that it is also a Midland feature to be able to say 'The car needs washed', or 'Your hair needs cut'.

Marginal grammatical features are by no means limited to the Midland. The South is well known for double (or multiple) modal verb constructions: 'I might could do it', or 'I thought you might would like that.' The Northeast allows the expression 'So don't I', denoting agreement with a negative proposition. The list could go on and on. These features are not judged as 'bad English'; like the vocabulary items that are often the study of dialectologists, they are regionally distributed, not socially stratified.

Regional differences at the lexical level are the heart and soul of traditional dialectology. Two further examples deserve mention, one of long standing and one quite new. As any learner of English knows, there is no way to differentiate between singular and plural 'you' in English; at least, there is none built into the standard language. This lack is keenly felt by speakers at times, and different speech

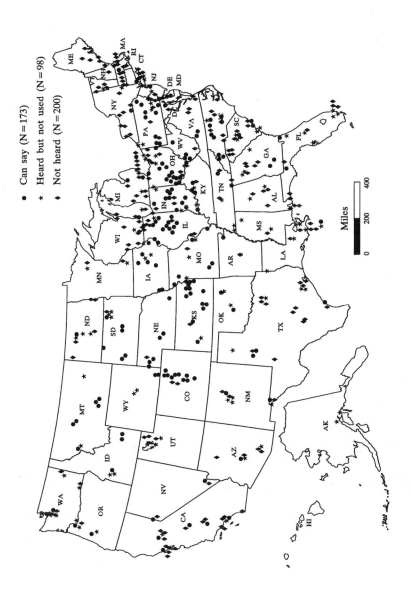

- • Can say (N=173)
- ★ Heard but not used (N=98)
- ◆ Not heard (N=200)

Figure 7.3 Distribution of 'positive ANYMORE'

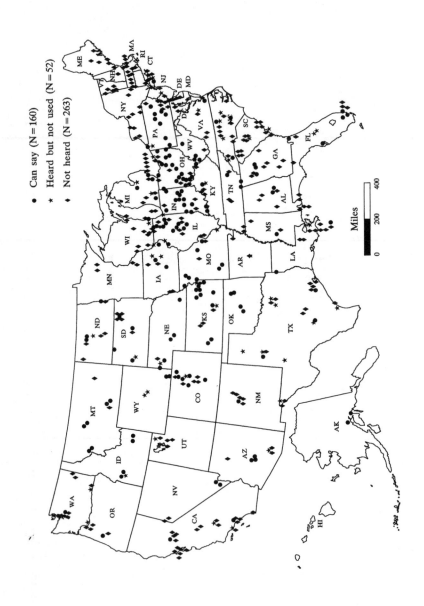

Figure 7.4 Acceptability of 'needs Xed'

communities have adopted different means of compensating for the absence of differing pronouns. The plural 'y'all' is a stereotypical Southernism, though the full form, 'you all', may occasionally be heard anywhere in the country. 'You guys' is common most everywhere else, though it is markedly informal, probably used predominantly among children and young people. Adults have to manage with 'you people', 'you folks', and 'you all'. In some urban centres, such as Philadelphia, a regular plural is made simply by adding '-s' to the pronoun, producing a form pronounced 'youz', usually spelled 'youse' when it appears in print.

A final example of marginal lexical variation is the remarkable appearance within the last couple of decades of three new synonyms for 'say/says' as verbs of quotation. In reporting the speech of someone else, a person speaking ordinary standard English can say, for example: 'John said, "Hey, it's time to get going!" ' In reporting a past event as part of a narrative, the present tense is used with great frequency once the story is underway, so this example could just as well be 'And John says, "Hey, it's time…" ' The innovative forms 'go', 'be like' and, most recently (and least frequently), 'be all' are now heard all across the country, most often among high-school- and college-age young people, as in:

> He's like, 'Mmm, this is good – what's in it?'
> And they go, 'We don't have one.'
> She's all, 'Wow, that's cool.'

African American Vernacular English

As of the 2000 census, the proportion of African Americans in the United States stood at about 12.9 per cent. The speech of this ethnic community covers a broad range of varieties, from slightly to extremely differentiated from Standard American English. Before the Second World War, there were comparatively few African Americans in the North, and those who were established there rubbed shoulders with Euro-Americans to a great extent. The pre-war African American Northerners spoke a variety of English that was rather close to that of their Euro-American neighbours. After the war, the demographics changed. Vast numbers of African American Southerners moved north, looking for better jobs and less racial discrimination than they found at home. The abrupt immigration of massive numbers of members of one ethnic group, particularly of one that was the object of bigotry, resulted in sharp residential segregation in the Northern cities to which Southern African Americans migrated. This has resulted in the development of large urban ghettos of African Americans all across the industrialized North, from New York City to Los Angeles, taking in such cities as Rochester, Syracuse, Buffalo, Cleveland,

Detroit, Chicago, St Louis, Kansas City and San Francisco. The most remarkable finding of linguists concerning this migration and resettlement is that the grammar of urban African Americans across this vast area is essentially uniform. The degree of marking with features of AAVE (African American Vernacular English, previously referred to as BEV, Black English Vernacular) is variable for different groups of speakers and individuals within those groups, but the system itself is one, unlike the many that have been described above for the white vernaculars of different regions of the country. African American vernacular speakers in New York, Chicago and Los Angeles will be found to be using the same grammar, though they may differ in the degree to which they exhibit features marked as AAVE. The variation is determined by social or personal considerations, not by geographic ones.

Even the most rudimentary description of AAVE is beyond the scope of this chapter; a few salient points will have to serve to give the flavour of this important variety of American English. On the lexical level, African American English has been abundantly productive, with new words – inevitably viewed as slang, but some ultimately entering the standard lexicon – arising on a daily basis and gaining wide exposure through certain channels, especially popular music. Many words of African American origin have moved into general currency, and this process continues today. Such words as 'jive', 'banjo', 'banana', 'voodoo', 'shades' (for sunglasses), 'jazz', 'hip', 'hustle' and 'hustler', 'dig' (meaning understand), 'chill (out)', 'copasetic' and the ubiquitous 'cool' all come from the African American community. So do innumerable expressions, including 'jerk someone around', 'high five', 'from the get-go', 'be on somebody's case' or 'get off my case', 'lay it on me', 'nickel 'n' dime' (as an adjective or a verb) and 'catch you later' (Smitherman, 1994).

On the level of syntax and morphology, AAVE is characterized by major differences in the verbal system, a different development of tense and aspect from Standard American English. Sentences such as 'He be steady coming' and 'I be done smack that dude upside the head' are generated by the rules of AAVE, although they are completely outside the grammar of Standard English. Deletion of the copula is common, yielding 'He a doctor' or 'She my mother'. Final -s on the third person singular of the present tense verb is absent, producing 'He come home at 5:00'. (Third singular -s seems to be used variably as a marker of narrative, rather than for grammatical agreement.) Possessive -s is absent when a modifier occurs before the modified noun, as in 'His wife name was Louise', but final -s is added to the first person singular possessive pronoun, presumably by analogy to the other possessive pronouns: 'Those gloves are mines', alongside 'Those gloves are yours/his', etc.

254

In phonology, one of the most noticeable features of AAVE is the weakening of final consonants. This produces innumerable sets of homonyms, such as *told* and *toll* both sounding the same as *toe*. There are some sound substitutions, such as *f* and *v* for *th* in the middle or at the ends of words, resulting in *muvver* for *mother* and *baf* for *bath*. Some features of Southern speech are included, such as the monophthongization of the vowel in 'I' discussed above. Another Southern feature that is found in AAVB is the merger of *pin* and *pen*, *tin* and *ten*, *him* and *hem*, and so forth. The e- preceding -m or -n is pronounced as *i* by Southerners in general and by AAVB speakers everywhere.

The ramifications of this massive body of differences between black and white speech are many and they work to the detriment of AAVB speakers in a white-dominated world. The grammar of AAVB is not understood to be systematic by most non-linguists; it is seen simply as 'bad grammar'. The deletion of final consonants is typically viewed as 'lazy' or 'sloppy', and features such as the merger of *pin* and *pen* have caused AAVB children in the North to be labelled 'learning disabled' by school personnel who do not realize that children of all ethnic groups and social classes in the South share the same absence of a distinction between those two words. Furthermore, the developments in AAVB have carried it further away from the writing system of English, making it more difficult for AAVB children to learn to read and write. These problems feed into the complex of racism in the United States by posing greater barriers to the success of AAVB children in mastering the standard language, and simultaneously providing fodder for people who are inclined to blame these problems on the children themselves. It is one of the great challenges to America today to advance the teaching of the basic skills of reading and writing so that all children will be able to derive the fullest value from their education and thus to work towards erasing the most painful and pernicious divisions in American society.

Everyday communication

Social status

Social differentiation is evident in generous supply in the United States, but an overriding component of the national ethos is that social boundaries are not fixed from birth. An individual can come from the humblest beginnings and rise to the highest levels of society. This comes about in large part because social status and economic circumstances are intimately interdependent. Scientists who use measures of social standing in grouping people for purposes of research do not speak of social status separately from economic status;

rather, subjects are grouped according to 'socio-economic status'. This aspect of American culture frequently gives rise to the criticism that Americans are money-hungry creatures who do not value more abstract virtues but rather spend all their time and energy simply trying to make another buck. On the positive side, if money – or its frequent correlates, power and fame – are the main determinants of social rank, then the field is open for anyone and everyone to become successful. You do not have to come from the 'right' family to go to the 'right' schools, and you do not have to go to the 'right' schools to get a good job or to be successful in business. The American story is rife with people from poor families who, through hard work and natural intelligence, became skilled, accomplished, visible and highly success-ful. President Bill Clinton is one of the most conspicuous examples of this kind of upward mobility today. He was born in the small town of Hope, Arkansas, three months after his father was killed in an automobile accident. He lived with his grandparents while his mother went to nursing school in another city so that she would be able to support herself and her son. After she finished her training, she married a car salesman. These are respectable but modest occupations, not the beginnings that would inspire the conviction that the son was on his way to the White House.

That said, it must be allowed that it is certainly easier for people who come from affluent families to make their way in the world. Public school education is free. It comprises kindergarten, begun at age five, through five grades (years) of elementary school, followed by three years of junior high school (sometimes called middle school), and then four years of high school. There are variants on this allocation of years to the three levels of school, but it is universal that public school is 'K through 12', and a high-school diploma is the most basic qualification for entry to the job market.

The problem with this is that many public schools offer a very poor level of education. Public school education is funded in part by local property taxes, so in a poor area there is little tax revenue to support a high-quality education. Urban schools are badly hurt by this state of affairs, so middle-class families in large cities often send their children to parochial or private schools. Working-class families do the same, if they can afford it.

Inner-city schools are beset with problems of not enough staff, inadequate and insufficient educational materials, poorly maintained buildings and all the social problems of the poor. An inferior education through high school obviously provides inadequate preparation for higher education, thereby closing the biggest door to opportunities for good jobs, successful careers and upward social mobility.

In addition, college and other varieties of higher education cost money, varying from little enough so that most students can pay their way by working at the same time to well over $30,000 per year at the most prestigious institutions. Scholarship support is available virtually everywhere, but there is never enough to support all qualified candidates. Therefore, affluent families are more easily able to send their children to better schools, and graduates of better schools are more easily able to get better jobs.

However, the individual who comes from a poor family who *is* able to get into a good school – whether by scholarship support, loans, working while in school, having saved his/her pennies for a long time or with a surprise inheritance from Great-Aunt Ida – will not find him/herself excluded in any way from circles of friends who are much better fixed financially. People tend to cluster with others of similar socio-economic backgrounds, but that is because they tend to have similar interests. If young Joe Blow from the 'wrong side of the tracks' meets Reginald Morgan Moneybags III at school, and they discover shared passions for building small rockets, military history and Beatles music, then the differences in clothing, amount of spending money, home address, and parents' occupations will not keep them apart. Young Reginald – or his mother – might be loath to go to young Joe's home neighbourhood, considering it to be unsavoury or dangerous, but Joe would most likely be welcome in Reginald's home.

There is actually a tiny segment of the population that claims high social status by exclusive virtue of family background. Philadelphia is one example of an old East Coast city which has a Social Register, a listing of the 'old' families, the nearest equivalent in the United States to an aristocracy – and woe unto the member of such a family who rashly marries outside that select group! Banishment from the in-group follows as a matter of course. The influence of these few people – in their capacity as members of the social elite – is, however, virtually non-existent. Those who are wealthy, who are prominent in the community because of their work, public service or support of charitable causes, will be known for those contributions. No one in the city would defer to them because their names are in the Social Register.

In sum, the United States offers everyone the opportunity to become a self-made person, and a person who achieves wealth or fame is accorded respect regardless of his/her family background. This is not to say that all people are regarded equally; it is only to say that the criterion for high status is money and achievement, not bloodlines.

Perhaps it is a corollary to this quantitative view of a person's inherent worth that everyday face-to-face communication in the United States carries a heavy dose of informality. Your waitress or waiter in a restaurant will walk up to your table and say: 'Hi, I'm Lisa [or Larry], and I'll be serving you this evening.' In some schools, ten-year-old children address teachers by their first names. Strangers engage in conversation at bus stops, in elevators, waiting in line at the bank or post office and in other impersonal but public situations. Since the notion of social class depends mainly on occupation and income and not at all on family background, it is possible for any two people, however disparate in their social situation, to fraternize when they find themselves in the same circumstances.

Terms of address, introductions

One aspect of everyday communication that is no simpler in American English than it is in any other variety of English or, indeed, in any other language, is terms of address. English speakers are spared the problem of deciding between levels of formality or familiarity in pronoun usage, since 'you' is the same for all numbers, genders and levels of formality. There remains the issue of how to address someone by name. When people meet as peers, the question of whether to use first names or honorifics plus last names is most likely to be resolved in favour of first names. By 'peers', I mean people meeting in circumstances in which both have the same role: parents of children in the same school who meet at a Parent–Teacher Association meeting, students in the same class or school, employees with the same job in a company, people meeting at a party or other purely social gathering, or even passengers on a train who strike up a conversation and reach the point of exchanging names. Age and status outside the peer group setting have little effect on this convention. One of the parents at a PTA meeting might be the president of a large company and another might be a shop clerk, but they meet on equal footing as parents of children in the school.

Among people who work together, first names are routine, but there is a good deal of variation, depending on the personalities of the individuals, the frequency with which they interact, and the nature of their relationship to each other. A 35-year-old lawyer earning $150,000 a year will most likely be addressed by her secretary by her first name in private; however, in taking phone calls the secretary will say: 'Ms. Johnson is on the phone just now; may I take a message?' The client may or may not be on a first-name basis with the lawyer, again depending on the level of friendliness that they have established.

Exceptions to the rule of first-naming colleagues with whom one associates closely in the workplace apply to those in the most exalted professions, such as judges, members of Congress and other high government officials. In the ordinary case, however, a teenager picking up extra money as a sales clerk during the Christmas season will be on a first-name basis with the 50-year-old long-term employee who is his/her co-worker for the time being.

Beyond the general rule that informality tends to prevail, there is a great grey area in which people do not know how to address each other and therefore use the option of 'no-naming'. This can always be resolved by the person with higher status – at a higher occupational level, older or female – either inviting the other person to use first names or using an honorific plus last name. If the person of higher status uses the other's first name without inviting reciprocity, the other person is left in limbo and must decide whether to reciprocate the first name, risking offence, or whether to use the more formal form of honorific plus last name, thereby establishing the maximum social distance. A third option is to continue using 'no-naming', perhaps hoping to clarify the relationship at a future date. A sensible alternative is to confront the subject directly and ask: 'May I call you Mary?' Oddly, people are often very reluctant to ask such a question, but it is really much friendlier to resolve the issue than to go on for years without using names.

The academic environment is one in which many different possibilities can be realized. It is common, but not universal, for graduate students and most of the faculty to address each other reciprocally by first names. At the same time, there are often faculty members who would never be addressed so informally by students. They are not necessarily the oldest or the most eminent, but they are those who simply are formal in demeanour. Undergraduate students are likely to be on more distant terms with faculty, using 'Professor' or 'Doctor' with the last name as terms of address and being addressed either by honorific plus last name or by first name.

Impersonal service encounters may elicit either formal or informal terms of address. Of course, in most such encounters, the service person (sales clerk, waiter/waitress, etc.) does not know the client's name. However when I pay for something with a credit card, the person receiving payment has my name in front of him/her. In that case, I may be subsequently addressed by any of the alternatives: 'you', 'Sherry', 'Ms./Mrs./Miss Ash'.

More personal service encounters, which are not anonymous and in which the client has more contact with the service provider, can work in almost any way. Often, initial contacts with a plumber, electrician, auto mechanic, banker, insurance agent or nurse in a doctor's office are carried out with honorifics plus last names, but in subsequent encounters, the same participants switch to first names without ceremony. The best approach is to recognize that the person with higher status – the client in a service encounter of any sort – has priority in deciding on the level of formality and otherwise not to worry too much about how to address and be addressed.

The honorifics used in the United States are Mr., Mrs., Ms., Miss, and Dr., and they are written as shown here, with periods following all but Miss. Miss has no period because it is not an abbreviation. Mr., Mrs. and Dr. are abbreviations for Mister, Missus (derived from

Mistress) and Doctor, respectively. Ms. is pronounced 'Miz', and it is written with a following period on the analogy of Mr. and Mrs., though it is a recently invented form, not an abbreviation of an older pre-existing form. Ms. arose as the feminine of Mr., an honorific for women that is neutral with respect to marital status. It has become widely used and accepted, as sexism in all its manifestations is increasingly being taken seriously as a social (and linguistic) issue which must be corrected. On the barrage of forms which ask for name, address, and other information that Americans are faced with filling out every day (it seems), Ms. is very often given as one of the options of a title to be circled or checked, along with Mr., Mrs. and Miss.

Ms. is a particularly appropriate honorific for a woman who is married but who uses her maiden name as her surname, either only professionally or both socially and professionally. The numbers of such women are increasing and since they are typically those who are well educated, affluent and vocal, their presence and views are prominent, even if they are a minority of married women overall. 'Mrs. Krantz' traditionally means 'the wife of Mr. Krantz', while 'Miss Wyatt' traditionally means 'an unmarried woman whose father's surname was Wyatt'. This corresponds to the use of these honorifics with first names in addition to last names. 'Mrs. Krantz' is 'Mrs. Joseph Krantz', not 'Mrs. Alice Krantz'. When a woman uses the latter, with her own first name, it traditionally means that she is divorced from Mr. Krantz. However, most Americans do not seem to have maintained an awareness of this subtlety of usage and many happily married women give their names in the format of 'Mrs. Alice Krantz'. Miss Janice Wyatt naturally would never use any first name other than her own in this phrase. 'Ms. Wyatt' means 'a woman whose surname is Wyatt, who may be married or not, but if she is, there is no indication of what her husband's surname might be; it could be Wyatt, or it could be something else entirely'. For a married woman with her own business or career, who wishes to be known to her colleagues and clients by her own first name, it provides the option of using either her husband's surname or her maiden name.

No reader will be surprised to learn that the considerations of formality in the use of terms of address do not begin at birth; young people are addressed by first names until the end of secondary school, around the age of 18. At that point, they begin to induce uncertainty in others as to terms of address.

A further set of terms of address are polite forms that can be used without a name: Sir, Ma'am (for Madam, which is almost never used) and Miss. It is common to hear expressions such as the following:

Can I help you, Sir?
Excuse me, Miss, can you tell me how to get to Walnut Street?
Yes, Ma'am, what can I do for you?

Miss and Ma'am are distinguished by the perceived age of the addressee, perhaps adjusted by a measure of flattery on the part of the speaker. The plurals of these forms are Gentlemen and Ladies. For example:

> Yes, Ladies, your table is ready. Right this way, please.
> Excuse me, Gentlemen, let us begin the meeting.
> Ladies and Gentlemen, it is my pleasure to introduce our speaker, who needs no introduction ...

The existence of the polite plural 'Ladies' does not imply that 'Lady' is a polite singular. On the contrary, it is rather rude, most likely to be heard in an utterance such as the following:

> Hey, Lady, why don't you watch where you're going?

'Mister', as a stand-alone term of direct address, fills the same slot.

There is little difference between formal and informal introductions; the expected alternants of terms of address constitute the most noticeable one. At a party you might hear:

> Jennifer, I'd like you to meet my friend Dick Johnson. Dick, this is Jennifer Randolph.
> Dick: Pleased to meet you, Jennifer.
> Jennifer: Pleased to meet you.

In a business or formal setting, the encounter might be as follows:

> Sam, this is Ralph Hammond. He's the consultant I told you about. Mr. Hammond, this is my colleague Sam Kolb.
> Kolb: Nice to meet you. I've heard a lot about you.
> Hammond: I'm pleased to meet you, Mr. Kolb.

Telephone calls

The beginning of a typical telephone conversation in the United States goes like this:

> Ring!
> Hello?
> Hi, this is Susie. Is Jamie there?
> Yes, just a minute, please. [Aside] Jamie! Telephone!
> Jamie: Hello?
> Susie: Hi, it's Susie. You called?
> Or   How are you?
> Or   Guess what?
> Or   innumerable other scripts.

This is obviously a phone call between friends or acquaintances. There are two noteworthy features of this conversation. First, the person answering the phone simply says 'Hello'. This is all that is necessary, although some people answer the phone by giving their own names or telephone numbers:

> Ring!
> This is the Clyde residence.
> Or
> (This is) (Bruce) Greenberg speaking.
> Or
> 727-4470.

The rationale for the three alternatives above is that the caller is informed as to whether he/she has dialled the number he/she intended to dial. However, people are also (justifiably) concerned about revealing their identities to strangers who may have nefarious ends in mind and so many people prefer not to provide any personal information in answering the telephone.

The second noteworthy feature about the exchange between Susie and Jamie given above is that the caller identifies herself immediately when the phone is answered. This is not a universal practice, but it is the most polite one. It would also be quite normal for the above conversation to go like this:

> Ring!
> Hello?
> Hi, is Jamie there?
> Yes, just a minute, please. [Aside] Jamie! Telephone!
> Jamie: Hello?
> Susie: Hi, it's Susie.

OR

> Ring!
> Hello?
> Hi, is Jamie there?
> Who is calling?
> It's Susie/This is Susie Jones.
> Just a minute, please. [Aside] Jamie! Telephone!/Jamie! Susie's on the phone for you!
> Jamie: Hello?
> Susie: Hi, it's Susie.

These scripts illustrate two options of the person answering the telephone: either to hand over the phone to the person being called without question, or else to ask the caller to identify herself. Both are proper and polite. If Jamie herself answers the phone, the interchange would be as follows:

Ring!
Hello?
Hi, is Jamie there?
This is Jamie/This is she.
Hi, it's Susie.

When one calls a business, the person who answers the phone as a representative of the company usually gives the name of the business and may or may not issue a further invitation narrowing the nature of the assistance that the answerer can provide:

Ring!
Bigbucks Enterprises. (May I help you?/How may I direct your call?)

But if you dial the direct line of an employee of the company, he/she is likely to answer the phone either by giving his/her name or by simply saying 'Hello'.

Phone conversations almost always end with the word 'Bye' or one of its variants:

That's fine. I'll see you tomorrow then.
Yeah, seven o'clock at your place.
Right. Take care. Bye.
Bye.
[Hang-up]

The same holds for a business conversation:

All right, I'll expect to get this form from you in a few days, and when I return it to you, you'll set up the account.
That's right. We're all set then.
That's great. Thanks a lot.
Thank you for your business.
My pleasure. Bye.
Goodbye.
[Hang-up]

It is a feature of life in the United States that private citizens are subjected to junk mail and also to junk phone calls. Junk mail – that which solicits monetary contributions to worthy and unworthy organizations or which advertises infinitely numerous unwanted goods and services – can be ignored. Junk phone calls make exactly the same requests, but they arrive when the person being called is sitting down to dinner, enjoying a conversation with family before or during dinner, doing chores after dinner, putting the children in bed, preparing a report due the next day at 8.30 a.m. or engaging in romantic activity. Many people find these phone calls to be extremely disruptive, but there is at least one formula that allows the unwilling recipient to disengage from the conversation while maintaining politeness:

No, thank you, I'm not interested. [Hang-up]

This is one situation in which interrupting the speaker who has the floor is completely defensible; no hesitation is necessary and no apology need be made. As soon as the listener realizes that the call is an unwanted intrusion, it is appropriate to end it. A clear signal that what is to follow is an unsolicited call is exemplified in the following:

> Ring!
> Hello?
> Hello, this is Jeffrey Stone calling from the Policeman's Veterans Association. And how are you today?

This highly personal query into your state of health and state of mind from a total stranger is a red flag, telling you that the caller's sole aim is to be so ingratiating that you will listen to the rest of the message. The rest of the message is invariably a pitch for money in some form, whether it is a request that you buy raffle tickets for the annual fund-raiser that will be held in two weeks, an offer of several magazine subscriptions – at a special low price, of course – or an opportunity to have your windows washed by a contractor that you have never heard of. You are under no obligation to respond to the personal question as to your state of mental and physical well-being. The most appropriate response to such callers is a cold, 'What is this in reference to?' followed by the formula given above, 'No, thank you, I'm not interested' immediately upon confirming that the caller indeed has nothing to offer that is in the listener's best interest.

If a worthy organization is calling to ask for money, one can use the following:

> I'm sorry, but I never agree to give money away over the telephone. If you would like to send me some literature about your organization, then I could consider it at my convenience.

Mail address and telling the time

In the United States, postal addresses are of the following form:

Recipient's name
Name of business, as needed
Street address and apartment or suite number, if any; or any other information that details the location within the town
Town, state abbreviation, ZIP code and, optionally, the 4-digit zip code extension. For example:

> Dr. Joe Brain
> BAN & Associates
> 987 Ellis St., Suite 333
> Rome, GA 30303-8642

Ms. Joan Rathbone
425 S. 4th St., Apt. 3A
Wichita, KS 78622

Prof. Ivy Covered
Dept. of Botany
1506 Greene Hall
University of Southern Wisconsin
Glendale, WI 66851

Some Americans who have travelled overseas – or who would like to appear worldly – use odd variants of the standard form for dates, but the standard remains standard, however much it clashes with the system in other countries. Dates are given as month-day-year, as in 'January 5, 1997'. Written as all numerals, this is '1-5-97' or '1/5/97'. The day of the month is read and pronounced as an ordinal number and the year is read as the century followed by a two-digit number. This produces 'January fifth, nineteen ninety-seven'. This practice continues in the twenty-first century. May 15, 2006 is usually read, 'May fifteenth, twenty-oh-six', although the year could also be given as 'two thousand six'. When the year alone is mentioned, it is typically given as a stand-alone number. Thus one would say, 'The program for the 2006–2007 (two thousand six to two thousand seven) season is ... 'If you add the day of the week, it precedes everything else: 'Monday, January 5, 1997.'

Americans never use the 24-hour clock. It is not used in everyday parlance, nor for theatre or movie times, nor for bus, train or airplane schedules. It is only known in the military and people who are not in the midst of military service are never heard to use it. Instead of the 24-hour clock, Americans use 'a.m.' and 'p.m.' to designate morning (*ante meridiem*, i.e. before noon) and afternoon/evening/night (*post meridiem*, i.e. after noon) respectively, when the part of the day is not obvious from the context. (If I suggest we meet for lunch at 'twelve fifteen', I should not have to specify that this is in the afternoon; I expect you to know that I am not available for lunch shortly after midnight.) In American usage, the hours and minutes are separated by a colon. Thus '1:00 a.m.' or 'one in the morning' is one hour after midnight. Midnight is 12:00 a.m., and noon is 12:00 p.m. The expression 'half four' is unknown in the US. Americans say 'three thirty' (3:30) or 'half past three'.

Privacy, or talking about religion, sex and money

As has been stated and implied many times above, Americans are informal, open and casual. People will talk to total strangers about very intimate matters. However, there are at least two big subjects that should be treated delicately: religion and money.

The United States is a land of cultural diversity. Religious freedom is a highly prized constitutional guarantee and adherents of every religious faith are represented in the population. On the other hand, many communities are fairly homogeneous in terms of ethnicity, national origin, socio-economic status and religion, or at least, the diversity is limited, known and accepted. I grew up in a suburban community that was predominantly Protestant, with many denominations represented. There was a significant minority of Catholics, but there was little conflict between members of Catholic and Protestant congregations. As far as I ever knew, it was limited to a bit of name-calling among children who were too young to know better. Jews were nearly excluded and Muslims were not represented at all. The educational establishment assumed that all children were Christians. While that was not strictly true, it did not make much difference. When Jewish children or teachers missed school for the Jewish High Holidays, it was hardly noticed. The separation of church and state is one of the fundamental tenets of the American way of life and it is cherished as much as the guarantee of freedom of religion. Anti-Semitism and other forms of religious prejudice certainly exist throughout the country, but they are not sanctioned by American culture in any way.

Discussion of religious affiliation is usually limited to situations in which all participants are certain that they can rely on their assumptions about the other participants in the discussion. This means either that they expect the others to belong to some particular religion because they are all of the same background, or else they know that differences in religion are certainly present and will be respected. On one occasion, I had breakfast in a coffee shop in a small town in northern Pennsylvania. The other patrons of the establishment all seemed to be local residents who knew each other. One of them engaged in conversation with me and after learning that I owned some land in the area he asked: 'And what faith are you?' This question demonstrated a huge philosophical and cultural gap between us and it left me speechless. My new acquaintance was asking a friendly question based on the assumption that I was congenial to the local community, no doubt some variety of Protestant. In my permanent home, the vastly more diverse city of Philadelphia, it is understood that a stranger's religious affiliation could be radically different from one's own. The setting always dictates appropriate behaviour. In a city with a diverse population, it is unseemly to ask a comparative stranger about his or her religion. In a small community where relative homogeneity may be assumed, it is acceptable, and even friendly, to ask about religion.

A well known psychiatrist says: 'You can get a good sexual history from anyone in an hour. It takes years to get a good financial history.' Indeed, Americans are not unique: they love to talk about sex. They also love to talk about money, but they are far more discreet about it. You cannot ask a friend or acquaintance about his or her sex life, but with an unmarried friend, if you are reasonably close, you can ask about his or her love life, which is almost the same thing.

However, you can be close friends for many years without having any precise idea what each other earns. You will know what your friends' job titles are, how much responsibility they have, how much vacation they have and perhaps how much some of their expenses are – whether they send their children to private school, for example, or possibly how much they paid for their house, which is a matter of public record – but you must be very intimate friends indeed to hear what someone else's salary is. Asking a direct question about it is absolutely out of the question.

People can talk about their own finances, but it is usually in terms of their limitations: 'We're trying to save up to go to the Grand Canyon next year,' or 'We wanted to redo the dining room at the same time that we renovated the kitchen, but it was a little too much money, so we decided to wait,' or 'Johnny just had to get braces on his teeth, so we're putting off buying a new car.'

A variant on the explanation of what one can't afford is a mitigation of the expense of what one can afford: 'There was an incredible package deal for five days in Paris, so we grabbed it,' or 'It's a beautiful BMW, but it was already eight years old when I bought it,' or 'I'm glad you like this dress. There was a great sale at Talbot's, so I couldn't resist.'

Friendliness

Are Americans friendly? Will they go out of their way to help, inform or befriend a stranger?

This question involves stereotypes and two points should be made before proceeding. First, the United States is diverse, and a generalization that applies reasonably well to one part of the country may not hold true for another. Second, stereotypes may have a grain of truth to them, but they often have so many exceptions that one is forced to question the usefulness of the generalization.

As stereotypes, Midwesterners have a reputation of friendliness, while city people in general and New Yorkers in particular are said to be rude, cold and unfriendly. Southerners are known for' Southern hospitality'. To the extent that these generalizations might be true, they are more likely to correlate with the differences between urban places and small towns or rural communities. In small towns, where most people know each other and it can safely be assumed that other people share the same general views and values as oneself, it is a no-risk proposition to be friendly to strangers. The out-of-towner is exotic, interesting and transient. He will be gone in the morning, so even if he is peculiar or has peculiar ideas, he will not affect one's life in the long run.

In the city, on the other hand, the peculiar stranger with peculiar ideas might be your next-door neighbour. In a chance encounter on the street, she might try to hold you up at gunpoint. She might be dealing drugs at the next corner for her livelihood. City dwellers fear for their physical safety much more than suburbanites do and they in turn are more fearful than small-town folk.

That said, it remains true that there are friendly, honest people everywhere, as well as liars, swindlers and killers. Once I sat in a car that had failed in Philadelphia on a major highway, a commuter route through the heart of the city and continuing out to the western suburbs. The driver of the car had gone to get help; he stood at the side of the road with his thumb out and got a ride almost immediately to a nearby service station. I stayed with the car to make sure nothing untoward happened to it. In the half hour or so that I waited, drivers of three cars stopped to offer assistance. The incident severely contradicts the idea that city people are necessarily unfriendly. Unquestionably, any long-term visitor to the United States will have experiences with people who are unfriendly, unhelpful and downright hostile; at the same time, a visitor who never finds friends, kindness and helping hands among Americans should wonder whether his own behaviour is discouraging friendly overtures.

Stereotypes and misconceptions

Americans don't learn foreign languages

A generalization which might occur to a foreign visitor is that Americans are poor at learning foreign languages. As generalizations go, this one is uncomfortably true, despite the potential for exposure to foreign languages that comes from the United States being a nation of immigrants, with immigration continuing today.

The amount of foreign language instruction in schools has increased in the last decade, but it is still limited, and, more importantly, the effectiveness of that instruction is in considerable doubt. At the elementary school level, counting both public and private schools, 31 per cent offer instruction in at least one foreign language. Private schools are ahead of public schools in this regard, with 53 per cent offering foreign language instruction, compared to 24 per cent of public schools. In secondary schools, there is little difference between public and private schools in the rate at which foreign language instruction is offered; overall, 86 per cent of schools provide instruction in at least one foreign language. In 1997, about 15 per cent of elementary school students were studying a foreign language. At the junior high school level, the rate was about 37 per cent, and in high schools the rate was just over half. The most widely taught language at all levels is Spanish, followed by French, then German, then Latin, and then a number of others, with Japanese, Hebrew, Sign Language, Italian, Russian, Chinese and Greek accounting for most of the market.

Besides the limitation on the number of students receiving foreign language instruction, there is also the matter of the nature of the programmes that are offered. In elementary schools, about 80 per cent merely aspire to introductory exposure to the language, while only 20 per cent aim to achieve overall proficiency. Furthermore, it appears that most of the secondary school programmes do not expect to teach students to be proficient in the target language; language classes are held one hour a day, five days a week.

Concrete data on language learning success comes from the Telephone Survey of North American English and the Phonological Atlas projects at the University of Pennsylvania, sponsored by the National Science Foundation and the National Endowment for the Humanities, respectively. These data paint a sad picture of the prospects of Americans in learning to communicate with speakers of other languages. Out of 181 Americans, only 71 had any experience of a language other than English and *only one* claimed to have learned a foreign language in school well enough to use it for everyday communication with native speakers of the language. It follows that for American learners of foreign languages that have nothing to do with their ancestry, the typical practice is never to attain sufficient competence to use a foreign language to communicate easily with a native speaker of that language. This generalization holds despite the ease and popularity of overseas travel.

Maintenance of ancestral immigrant languages

According to the survey mentioned above, the situation is no better when it comes to the maintenance of ancestral immigrant languages in the second or third generation. Thirty-three of the survey subjects were exposed to a foreign language at home and less than a third of those learned their ancestral language well. A little less than a third had not retained their ancestral language at all. The remainder had acquired miscellaneous words and phrases, but did not have competence in the language as a whole.

This is the typical picture of immigrant languages in the United States. People come to a new land with a strong desire to assimilate, since the promise of America is that one can build a new life and career, with money and material goods to show for it, whatever one's origins. Immigrant languages are most often lost within one or two generations. Time and again, interviewees said that their parents or grandparents spoke Polish, Italian, Czech, Russian or German but they, the younger generation, did not learn it, which they now regret. The parents and grandparents, meanwhile, were keen to have their children learn English, which they knew was essential for their education and economic upward mobility. Moreover, the languages of the lower-status immigrant groups were seen as an embarrassment, so there was actually a disincentive to the immigrant parents to pass the ancestral language on to their children.

The status of English as an official language

Ironically, there is no official language of the United States, not English nor any other. As of 2006, 28 states had passed statutes declaring English as the official language of the state. Nebraska passed such a law in 1920 and Illinois did so in 1923. (The Illinois law was repealed in 1991.) The others date to 1981 and later. Such laws typically have been passed in response to the combination of a perceived threat that English would lose its dominant position and a sentiment of xenophobia directed towards a particular ethnic or national group. The Illinois and Nebraska laws, for example, stemmed from an upsurge in hostility towards the large German-speaking communities in these states in the aftermath of the First World War.

An example of a more recent law declaring English to be the official language of a state was passed in 1988 in Arizona. This law required employees of the state to 'act in English and in no other language'. A bilingual Spanish-English employee of the state brought suit against the state for restricting her right to free speech under the First Amendment to the Constitution. The first court that heard the case, the federal trial court, ruled that the Arizona law was unconstitutional. The state of Arizona declined to appeal, but a group called Arizonans for Official English took the case to the Supreme Court of the United States. The entire action was dismissed by the Supreme Court with no actual resolution, since the woman who had originally brought the suit had since resigned from employment with the state of Arizona. Thus the challenge to the state law, which was accepted by the first court and which the state (the defendant) chose not to appeal, was invalidated by the highest court in the country on technical grounds. The constitutionality of 'English Only' or 'Official English' laws remains uncertain.

At the national level, the English Only movement has been pushing for an amendment to the Constitution since 1981, with the goal of declaring that English is the official language of the United States. Most people do not seem to mind the presence of foreign-language street signs and ballots, but when the economics of accommodation become more serious, strong feelings can be aroused. Bilingual education is one area in which this is a major issue. There are many ways to approach the matter of educating children who do not speak English; what all have in common is that they cost more than education in a monolingual English environment. (Of course, a monolingual education in a language other than English is a theoretical option. It would still inevitably cost more than monolingual English education and it is highly unlikely that parents, eager to promote the assimilation and prospects of their children, would accept it.) Yet, English is clearly the dominant language in the United States and anyone who aspires to economic success, or simply to make contact with the world outside the immediate community, must speak English.

The problems that accompany cultural and linguistic diversity will not disappear readily. Indeed, the foreign-language-speaking population in the US is increasing. Foreign language teaching is on the increase too, but effective foreign language learning has not reached any reasonable level. Besides, it is perfectly true that a person can travel from coast to coast and from the 49th parallel to the Gulf of Mexico without meeting a native speaker of a language other than English. The vast majority of Americans live their lives expecting English to suffice for them, and, most of the time, they are right.

Ethnic stereotypes

The stereotypes that 'Americans' have about 'others' are largely focused on Americans themselves, distinguishing among ethnic groups or other categories. There is a notion of a stereotypical British personality as reserved, always keeping a stiff upper lip, dapper in dress, most likely carrying a cane or an umbrella and wearing a three-piece suit. Attitudes towards a British accent vacillate between admiration and mockery. The fullness of the perception is on a par with the stereotypical view of other European nationalities and all of the stereotypes are probably shared by other Westerners. Canadians, on the other hand, are virtually ignored as far as development of a stereotype is concerned. Canada is so close to the United States, so similar in many ways – the most important being that the dominant language is English in the largest part of the country. Canada is also easily accessible, although a passport is needed for entry. With the US having ten times the population of Canada, Americans are prone to viewing their northern neighbour as a somewhat Anglicized version of themselves.

Australia and New Zealand are too far away and too little known to merit even that much consideration by most Americans. Again, they are thought of as vaguely British.

The stereotypes that Americans hold about groups within the United States, on the other hand, are richly developed. By definition, stereotypes generally have negative connotations and thus they are directed towards the later groups of immigrants, those who came to the United States beginning in the 1880s. At this time, immigration from Northern and Western Europe began to give way increasingly to immigration from Southern and Eastern Europe. Between 1881 and 1890, almost 20 per cent of immigrants were from Southern and Eastern Europe, and between 1901 and 1910 over 70 per cent were from these regions. Immigrants from Italy, Portugal, Spain, Greece, Russia, Poland and other Eastern European countries continued to come to the United States in large numbers until the First World War. Many of these new citizens had little education and few skills and they tended to settle in ethnic communities in large cities, some of which deteriorated into slums. Assimilation to the American mainstream was delayed, while these immigrants worked in hard, low-paying, low-status jobs. Poles and other Eastern Europeans populated the workforce of coal mines, also a hard life of unskilled labour. More recently, there have been major waves of migration of African Americans to northern cities from the rural South since the Second World War, again to the lowest-paying, hardest jobs. Also, the long border with Mexico has seen the migration of huge numbers of people, including many illegal immigrants, typically to labour in seasonal, non-contract, poorly paid jobs as agricultural workers. It is not surprising that these groups have borne the sharpest barbs of ethnic prejudice – and ethnic humour.

The stereotype of a Pole (or Polish American) is of a man who is big, strong and stupid. During the 1960s, there arose a genre of Polish jokes. One of these in turn spawned a whole new genre of lightbulb jokes:

Q: How many Poles does it take to change a lightbulb?
A: Five. One to stand on a table and hold onto the bulb, and four to turn the table around and around.

This has given us a wealth of lightbulb jokes to enjoy, triggered by this small beginning. For example:

Q: How many WASPs does it take to change a lightbulb?
A: Two. One to mix the cocktails and one to call the handyman.

WASP is an acronym for White Anglo-Saxon Protestant; in other words, a member of the most numerous, most dominant and most powerful ethnic and ancestral group in the United States.

Q: How many Californians does it take to change a lightbulb?
A: Six. One to change the bulb and five to share the experience.

Q: How many psychiatrists does it take to change a lightbulb?
A: Only one, but the lightbulb really has to want to change.

The stereotype of an Italian American suggests connections to the Mafia (organized crime). The Irish are not viewed as pejoratively as the Poles or Italians, but they carry a definite image of being hot-tempered, hard-drinking, fast-talking and, often, thick-headed. Jews are another group that is the object of prejudice, resented in the US as throughout the world for being shrewd merchants and purveyors of money: bankers, accountants and so forth. Hispanics, now amounting to 12.5 per cent of the total population, include three significant groups: Mexicans in the Southwest, Cubans in southern Florida; Puerto Ricans in New York. Mexicans are by far the most numerous and the most widespread. The stereotype of a Hispanic encompasses laziness, dishonesty and a lack of cleanliness.

The position of African Americans is a giant step away from that of the ethnic groups mentioned above, however pejorative those may be. Superficially, the lot of African Americans has improved greatly over the last several decades, with the enactment of laws prohibiting discriminatory practices in housing, education, voting, employment and other areas, along with a general public consensus that racism is an attitude that is wholly unacceptable; anyone who is so benighted as to harbour such sentiments at least must know enough to keep them to himself in public. Still, the rift runs deep; the fact that Africans once were stolen from their homes and families, brought to North America against their will and kept as slaves on American soil sets their descendants apart from every other immigrant group in a way that affects virtually all Americans, whether they want to acknowledge it or not. Even the most liberal, consciously right-thinking Euro-American, walking down a sidewalk at night, is likely to be frightened at the approach of a small group of young African American men, but not think twice at the approach of a comparable group of whites.

Regional stereotypes

A few regional stereotypes are as prominent as the ethnic stereotypes of groups of Americans. Most prominent of all, certainly, is the term Yankee. This term is interesting because its definition is relative. There's a saying that in Mexico, a Yankee is anyone from north of the Rio Grande – that is, any American. In the South, a Yankee is anyone from north of the Mason-Dixon Line. North of the Mason-Dixon Line, a Yankee is someone from New England. In New England, a Yankee is someone from Vermont. And in Vermont, a Yankee is someone who has apple pie for breakfast! The point was proved to another Northerner once, when he was travelling in Vermont and stayed overnight at an inn. When he came down for breakfast in the morning, the innkeeper was in the dining room, eating apple pie for breakfast. The characteristics of a Yankee are ingenuity, thrift and shrewdness in business. It is understood that a Yankee is white and, somewhat less decisively, Anglo in ancestry.

The second most salient regional stereotype probably is that of a Southerner. The South is hot, its agricultural produce is bountiful, theoretically making for an easy life (for rich landowners, at least) and its speech is slow and characterized by the famous Southern drawl. Therefore, Southerners are seen as laid-back, slow, never in a hurry and friendly, offering generous hospitality; 'Southern hospitality' is a phrase heard all over the country. A subclass of Southerner is the Southern belle, a beautifully dressed, coy, flirtatious, rich and pretty Southern girl. Scarlett O'Hara, in Margaret Mitchell's *Gone with the Wind,* is the quintessential personification of the Southern belle.

Other regional or semiregional stereotypes are less kind. A redneck is an uneducated, bigoted, reactionary, rural working-class Southern white; he has a red neck because he only works in unskilled jobs and therefore is outside in the sun all day long. A hillbilly is also uneducated, but the term connotes ignorance more than reactionary views. The notion is associated with backwoods or remote areas, especially from the mountain country of the South.

There are many other stereotypes that apply to smaller groups and that are taken rather less seriously. Valley girls are a recent conceptualization, referring to the teenage culture of southern California. The Jewish American Princess, or JAP, is a good-humoured label for a spoiled, affluent – incidentally Jewish – girl who has her father wrapped around her little finger. It comes to life in jokes such as the following:

Q: What does a Jewish American Princess make for dinner?
A: Reservations.

Q: What four words will a Jewish American Princess never hear?
A: 'Attention, K-Mart shoppers!'

K-Mart is a widespread chain discount department store. Every few minutes, patrons are alerted to special sales by announcements over the loudspeaker system and these announcements always prefaced by the cry, 'Attention, K-Mart shoppers!'

The Nine Nations

Joel Garreau, a journalist, published a book titled *The Nine Nations of North America* in 1981. His thesis is that North America consists not of the three nations of the United States, Canada and Mexico, but of nine nations which are distinguished by history, geography, demography, economics and politics. He originally advanced this idea in an article in the *Washington Post* as a radical view, but to his surprise, he found that vast numbers of people agreed with him. A full exposition of his ideas does not concern us here, but his discussion does accurately portray the regional diversity, with its consequent conflicts, that are crucially important features of the United States for anyone who tries to understand what is 'America'. A few words about each of the 'nations' that lie within the boundaries of the United States will suffice here. To a certain degree, his boundaries of the nine nations correspond to the dialect boundaries described above on pp. 241ff. This is to be expected: communities of people with shared linguistic norms consist of communities of people who share other social and demographic features, such as geographic proximity and similar social, economic and geographic concerns; these attributes enable people to be in communication with each other on a full-time basis. Dialect differences arise between communities where there are gaps or weak links in the network of communications, whether imposed by a geographical boundary such as a mountain range or by a meaningful political boundary (state boundaries do not qualify as meaningful political boundaries with respect to the density of communication networks in the United States), by demography, such as the urban-rural opposition, or by economics, as in the difference between an industrialized area and an agricultural region. The match between Garreau's nine regions and the dialect regions presented above is far from perfect, but his nine regions are important realities and they demonstrate the regionalism of the United States just as clearly as do the dialect differences.

Garreau describes an area he calls the Foundry, which roughly corresponds to the linguistic description of the Inland North, though the Foundry extends east to include the cities of New York, Philadelphia and Baltimore. This is a land which, as Garreau puts it, sees itself as the real power centre of the continent, although in fact it is a declining industrial region. It has the ageing factories which produce expensive, durable products such as steel and automobiles. In earlier decades, it was the centre of wealth, the land of opportunity for those seeking jobs from all over the United States, the producer of valuable goods. Today, it is losing population to the South and Southwest, as unemployment, pollution and the lure of new technology elsewhere draw people away.

New England is dedicated to austerity and conservation, in keeping with its compact geography and extremely limited resources. The virtues of Yankee thrift and ingenuity are a necessity in an area where farming was historically a major occupation, but where the soil is made of clay and rocks and the terrain consists of hills and mountains. Still, as one of the primary incubators of American civilization, and with Boston as a renowned centre of culture and higher education, New England regards itself as the only truly civilized region of the United States.

Dixie is the name that Garreau applies to the nation that is the South. Historically it has been poor, with nothing but low-paying agricultural work to offer, except to the tiny class of rich landowners. However, with the advent in the 1960s of ubiquitous air-conditioning, in homes, cars, parking garages, office buildings, shops, malls and covered sports arenas, the South became a viable place to live. Now it is a rapidly developing region, with economic growth taking place throughout its territory, and a concomitant influx of people from other areas. Atlanta is the regional capital, and it draws immigrants from all over the South and from all over the North. A native Atlantan over the age of eighteen is hard to find.

Garreau uses the term the Breadbasket for the vast, irrigated farmland of the Great Plains, the source of grain, beef, pork and dairy products, where commodities futures and grain-trading are giving a voice in national and international affairs to a region that has historically been viewed as a subservient provider of agricultural produce to the rest of the nation.

The Empty Quarter, meaning empty of people, is Garreau's term for the greater part of the West, from the Rocky Mountains up to the narrow temperate strip along the Pacific coast. This land is rich in oil, coal, gas, uranium, copper, molybdenum and snow. Much of the mineral-rich vastness is basically desert, but it promises a rich future in energy production and supplies of raw materials to new technologies. The mountains, with snow and grandeur, are a continuing Mecca for tourists.

The Pacific Northwest, the strip of land along the Pacific coast from Alaska to San Francisco, is called Ecotopia by Garreau. This is the only part of the west that has enough water. It can luxuriate in its temperate climate and it can afford to treasure a wild, untamed river and forest. It is the closest we come to a frontier, where modern history began a mere 150 years ago, with the opening of the land to settlement and the westward migration of more than 300,000 people along the Oregon Trail. Tourism is a major industry and the light industries of the future, in computer technology and related fields, offer blissful ignorance of the pain of unemployment that troubles the ageing industrial base of the Foundry.

Finally, MexAmerica is the term Garreau uses for the arid Southwest, extending down into Mexico. This region, with Los Angeles as its capital, is driven by thirst. The dry, sunny climate has been attracting immigration in vast numbers to terrain that is meant to be a desert. Water and power are imported over distances of hundreds of kilometres to satisfy the insatiable demand of the sun-worshippers.

Garreau's other two nations are Québec and the Caribbean Islands, which do not concern us here. The intention of this tour around the regions of the country is to show that the United States is diverse, with good reasons for having widely different concerns about economic, environmental and social policy in different places. Regional competition is fierce and Garreau declares Americans consider themselves to belong to their region as much as to their country (1981, p. 12).

While the regional diversity and competition within the United States are critically important components of the American scene, at the same time, Americans are united by a clear consciousness of a common history, a shared pride in the origins of the nation, in the breaking away from a monarchy and the founding of a republic on principles of freedom, liberty and justice for all. Americans are also united by a common language, complete with its full complement of regional varieties. Americans are similar to each other in having mixed ancestry: one person is part Scottish, part Norwegian, part Russian Jewish; another is part German, part Irish, part English; yet another is part Polish and part Italian. The resolution of this comparison is 'Well, we're all 100 per cent American.'

The United States is one sovereign state, within which there are subgroups determined by the parameters discussed above: ecology, economics, ethnicity and others. They co-operate at times and they compete at times. Miraculously, it seems plausible that, despite stumbling and lurching, they will move forward into the future together.

Tasks and exercises

Some of the tasks and exercises below will be closely related to the text above, others may require you to look for answers by checking sources like encyclopaedias, and some may require you to do some research. We hope that by doing more than just reading the above general text, students will be able to get more knowledge and will be encouraged to explore American history, institutions and culture in more depth and to draw interesting comparisons with their own native language and culture.

1. St. Augustine, Jamestown and Plymouth Rock are connected with the early history of the United States – explain how. Name three other very well known American cities which were established at the beginnings of settlement.

2. Most democratic countries have some mechanisms safeguarding equal opportunities and basic civil liberties to all their citizens and attempting to reduce racism and prejudice. In the case of the United States these mechanisms can be found in the Declaration of Independence, the Constitution and amendments to the Constitution. Discuss briefly the history of their creation and the role of each of the above documents.

3. What, if any, social mobility (i.e. movement from one social class to another, usually from lower to higher social classes) can be found in your home country and what is the cause of this mobility? How does this compare with the social mobility within the American society?

4. It is often said that Americans are a money-driven society. This may mean a lot of different things. Below you have pairs of adjectives describing various behaviours that may be connected with money. Circle the ones you believe fit the description of Americans in the text above and in other sources available to you:
- stingy
- generous
- closefisted
- lavish
- thrifty
- wasteful.

Now explain your choices giving examples of each.

5. The text describes how some social issues are treated in the United States. Compare the treatment of the following issues in your home culture and in the US:
- homosexuality
- AIDS
- women's rights
- abortion
- gun control
- drugs.

6. Compare the health systems in your home country and in the US.

7. Explain the role of the following people and institutions in the American system of government:
- Senators
- the Founding Fathers

- the Supreme Court
- the President
- members of the House of Representatives.

8. There are many traditional ways of honouring people which are still very much followed in Great Britain and some other English-speaking countries, such as Australia or New Zealand. When the United States declared independence from Britain many of these ways were abandoned and new ones were introduced. Use any resources you can, including the Internet, to find out as much as possible about the ways Americans honour their great or specially deserving citizens and compare it with what is done in your native country and culture.

9. Explain who the following people were and how they have contributed to the American heritage:
- Abraham Lincoln
- Thomas Jefferson
- George Armstrong Custer
- Franklin D. Roosevelt.

10. Are Christian holidays like Christmas or Easter officially acknowledged by the US government, or are they considered occasions to be celebrated privately by individuals?

11. Are religious holidays officially acknowledged and celebrated by the government in your native culture?

12. Name three American lay holidays and explain the origins of each of them.

13. What food and what company would you expect to have in the US on the following occasions?
- Easter Sunday
- New Year's Eve
- Christmas Day
- Thanksgiving
- Halloween.

14. On what days in November would you expect American roads and freeways clogged with traffic and why?

15. What are the two most characteristic features of pronunciation of American English?

16. Name as many American dialect areas as you can before checking with the map in this chapter.

17. Explain the meaning of the following words or phrases originating from African American:
- jive
- banjo
- voodoo
- shades
- jazz
- hip
- hustle
- dig
- chill out
- jerk someone around
- high five
- from the get-go
- lay it on someone.

18. What is the quickest and most effective way to change one's social status in the US?

19. Is modesty considered to be a positive feature in looking for a job in the US? What is the situation in your home culture?

20. Compare your home country and American educational systems.

21. How would you address the following people in the US?
- your husband/wife
- a close friend
- an elderly lady you don't know
- your grandfather
- a dentist
- a colleague from work of the same age as you
- a much older colleague from work
- your boss at work.

22. Someone junior to you at work addresses you very formally and respectfully. How would you invite the person to be less formal in your own culture and how would you do it in the US?

23. What do you say when you pick up a phone in the US?

24. You want to call Basil Cartload at work. How do you ask the receptionist to connect you with him?

25. What are junk calls and how do you respond to them? Do people often get junk calls in your home country? Would the response in that case be similar to the typical American responses or would it have been different? Comment on the similarities and differences between your home and American cultures in this respect.

26. Make a list of popular topics of conversation among Americans. Would these topics be popular in your home culture? And how about 'taboo' topics in your home and American cultures? Are they similar or different?

27. What are the three most popular sports in the US?

28. How does a team win a game of baseball?

29. What is the status of English as an official language in the US?

30. The words and/or phrases below refer to specific groups of people who supposedly have some common features. Explain where these people live and what, according to popular regional stereotypes, their most characteristic features are:
- Yankee
- Southerner
- Redneck
- African Americans.

31. Name all of Garreau's nine nations and describe them briefly.

References

Allen, H. (1973) *The Linguistic Atlas of the Upper Midwest*. Volume 1, University of Minnesota Press.

Feagin, C. (1990) The dynamics of a sound change in Southern States English: From R-less to R-ful in three generations, in: Edmondson, J. A., Feagin, C. and Muehlhaeusler, P. (eds). *Development and Diversity: Linguistic Variation Across Time and Space*. Arlington-Summer Institute of Linguistics and University of Texas, pp. 129–46.

Garreau, J. (1981) *The Nine Nations of North America.* Boston: Houghton Mifflin.

Greene, J. P. (ed.) (1975) *Colonies to Nation, 1763–1780.* New York: W.W. Norton & Co., Inc.

Historical Atlas of the United States. (1988) Washington, D.C.: National Geographic Society.

Kretzschmar, W.A., Jr., McDavid, V.G., Lerud, T.K. and Johnson, E. (eds) (1993) *Handbook of the Linguistic Atlas of the Middle and South Atlantic States.* Chicago: University of Chicago Press.

Kurath, H. (1949) *A Word Geography of the Eastern United States.* Ann Arbor: University of Michigan Press.

Labov, W. (1966) *The Social Stratification of English in New York City.* Washington, D.C.: Center for Applied Linguistics.

Labov, W. (1994) *Principles of Linguistic Change,* Volume 1: *Internal Factors.* Oxford: Blackwell Publishers.

Labov, W., Ash, S. and Boberg, C. (1997) A National Map of the Regional Dialects of American English. http://www.ling.upenn.edu/phono_atlas/home.html

Labov, W., Ash, S. and Boberg, C. (2006) *The Atlas of North American English: Phonetics, Phonology, and Sound Change.* Berlin: Mouton de Gruyter.

Linn, M. (1990) The development of dialect patterns in the Upper Midwest, *Kansas Quarterly* **22** (4): 15–28.

The New Columbia Encyclopedia. (1975) New York: Columbia University Press.

Smitherman, G. (1994) *Black Talk: Words and Phrases from the Hood to the Amen Corner.* Boston: Houghton Mifflin.